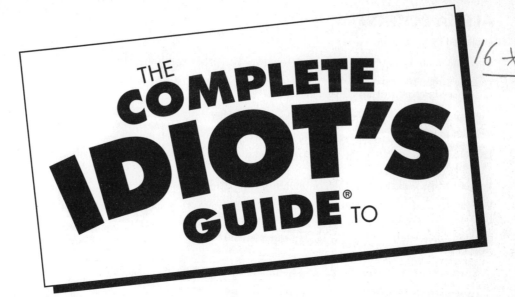

Public Speaking

Second Edition

by Laurie Rozakis, Ph.D.

alpha
books

ALPHA BOOKS

Published by the Penguin Group

Penguin Group (USA) Inc., 375 Hudson Street, New York, New York 10014, USA

Penguin Group (Canada), 90 Eglinton Avenue East, Suite 700, Toronto, Ontario M4P 2Y3, Canada (a division of Pearson Penguin Canada Inc.)

Penguin Books Ltd., 80 Strand, London WC2R 0RL, England

Penguin Ireland, 25 St. Stephen's Green, Dublin 2, Ireland (a division of Penguin Books Ltd.)

Penguin Group (Australia), 250 Camberwell Road, Camberwell, Victoria 3124, Australia (a division of Pearson Australia Group Pty. Ltd.)

Penguin Books India Pvt. Ltd., 11 Community Centre, Panchsheel Park, New Delhi—110 017, India

Penguin Group (NZ), 67 Apollo Drive, Rosedale, North Shore, Auckland 1311, New Zealand (a division of Pearson New Zealand Ltd.)

Penguin Books (South Africa) (Pty.) Ltd., 24 Sturdee Avenue, Rosebank, Johannesburg 2196, South Africa

Penguin Books Ltd., Registered Offices: 80 Strand, London WC2R 0RL, England

International Standard Book Number: 978-0-02-863383-1
Library of Congress Catalog Card Number: 99-62368

09   08   07   12   11   10   9

Interpretation of the printing code: the rightmost number of the first series of numbers is the year of the book's printing; the rightmost number of the second series of numbers is the number of the book's printing. For example, a printing code of 99-1 shows that the first printing occurred in 1999.

Printed in the United States of America

Most Alpha books are available at special quantity discounts for bulk purchases for sales promotions, premiums, fund-raising, or educational use. Special books, or book excerpts, can also be created to fit specific needs.

For details, write: Special Markets, Alpha Books, 375 Hudson Street, New York, NY 10014.

Alpha Development Team

Publisher
Kathy Nebenhaus

Editorial Director
Gary M. Krebs

Managing Editor
Bob Shuman

Marketing Brand Manager
Felice Primeau

Acquisitions Editor
Jessica Faust

Development Editors
Phil Kitchel
Amy Zavatto

Assistant Editor
Georgette Blau

Production Team

Development Editor
Amy Bryant

Production Editor
Suzanne Snyder

Copy Editor
Krista Hansing

Cover Designer
Mike Freeland

Photo Editor
Richard H. Fox

Illustrator
Brian Mac Moyer

Book Designer
Scott Cook and Amy Adams of DesignLab

Indexer
Tim Wright

Layout/Proofreading
John Bitter
Pete Lippincott
Marie Kristine Parial-Leonardo

Contents at a Glance

Part I: Clearing Your Throat   **1**

1 What Fresh Hell Is This?   3
Discover how people feel about public speaking and how public speaking affects your career and personal life.

2 Stage Fright   11
Learn how to fight your fears.

3 All the World's a Stage   21
Discover the importance of listening and what makes public speakers really effective.

4 Do You Hear What I Hear?   31
Find out what we mean when we talk about the communication process, focusing on the five types of communication.

5 Common Communication Problems   39
Explore popular misconceptions about communication.

Part 2: It's All in the Planning   **47**

6 Fun with SPAM   49
Learn the SPAM model of public speaking: situation, purpose, audience, and method.

7 Getting to Know You: Audience Analysis   57
Analyze your audience's interests, desires, and level of knowledge so you can match your speech to their needs.

8 Types of Speeches   67
Explore the three main kinds of public speaking, along with an A-to-Z guide to speeches.

9 Hear Ye, Hear Ye: Speaking to Inform   77
Choose and narrow a topic, decide on an organizational pattern, and research information.

10 My Way or the Highway: Speaking to Persuade   87
Use accurate logic, powerful appeals to emotion, and trust to overcome the listener's objections and move the audience to belief or action.

11 The Life of the Party: Speaking to Entertain   99
Learn the skills you'll need to speak at ceremonial occasions that build goodwill.

Part 3: Writing Your Speech 107

12 Whose Speech Is It, Anyway?: Speech Style 109
Select your personal speaking style, and suit the audience and occasion.

13 Getting Organized 121
Learn how to arrange your speech and allocate time.

14 Time to Outline 131
Take your ideas and arrange them in an outline. You'll be glad you did!

15 Start at the Very Beginning, A Very Good Place to Start 141
Explore the many different ways to get your speeches off to a great start.

16 Body Building 153
Select a framework and flesh it out with details, examples, and support.

17 Are We There Yet?: Conclusions, Revisions, and Titles 165
End a speech with power and assurance, correct errors, and select a title.

18 Ever Hear the One About...?: Using Humor 173
Learn how, when, and why you should use humor in your speeches.

19 Taking the Show on the Road: Multicultural Concerns and International Speeches 181
Write and deliver speeches that meet the needs of multicultural and international audiences at home and abroad.

Part 4: Take It On Home: Tackling Specific Kinds of Speeches 193

20 Informational Speeches 195
Craft speeches that clarify a concept or process, define terms and relationships, or expand your audience's knowledge.

21 Persuasive Speeches 203
Construct the most useful types of persuasive speeches that address a wide variety of audiences.

22 Entertaining Speeches 215
Write speeches that build goodwill, create social cohesion, and delight audiences.

23 Speaking Off-the-Cuff 229
Master the skill of thinking and speaking on your feet.

24 Debate and Parliamentary Procedure   239
    Learn the rules of debate and parliamentary procedure.

Part 5: Master of Your Domain   **253**

25 A Thousand Words: Visual Aids   255
    *Discover the importance of visual aids—posters, flip
    charts, videotapes, slides, and more.*

26 Preparing and Using Visual Aids   263
    *Create and use visual aids to add a fuller dimension to
    your speeches.*

27 Byte Me: Using PowerPoint   275
    *See how Microsoft's PowerPoint can make it easy to create
    professional presentations that include audio, video, slides,
    text, and handouts.*

28 Smashing the Sound Barrier   281
    Pay attention to the subtle importance of voice.

29 An Ounce of Prevention: Rehearsing   291
    *Find out why rehearsal is crucial to a smooth, successful
    public speaking event—and learn how to rehearse.*

30 Let Me Hear Your Body Talk: Body Language   299
    *Learn the importance of nonverbal communication to your
    speeches.*

31 Dress and Grooming   309
    Maximize your presentability.

Part 6: The Moment of Truth   **317**

32 Delivery   319
    *Make sure your speech is polished (but not too polished),
    and deal with potential problems.*

33 Last Licks   327
    *Learn about speaker's bureaus, and review the speech
    process.*

Appendices

A Word Power Glossary   333

B Sample Speeches   337

C Further Readings   347

Index   **349**

Contents

Part 1: Clearing Your Throat   **1**

1 What Fresh Hell Is This?   **3**

You Mean I Have to Get Up and Say Something? 4
Fright Night 4
Top Ten Excuses People Use to Avoid Public Speaking 6
Why We Feel Nervous About Public Speaking 9

2 Stage Fright   **11**

Armchair Diagnosis: Symptoms of Stage Fright 12
    The Downside 12
    The Upside 12
Why You're Afraid 13
    Fear of the Audience 13
    Fear of Failure 14
    Fear That Your Speech Stinks 15
Conquer Your Fear 16
Physical and Mental Exercises for Releasing Stress 16
    The "No Pain, No Gain" Route 17
    The "Less Pain, Still Gain" Approach 17
Symptoms and Solutions 18
Take a Test Run 19
Use It! 19

3 All the World's a Stage   **21**

Reach Out and Touch Someone 22
    Top Ten Reasons Why Speeches Make
    Good Marketing Sense 22
So Why Do This to Yourself? 23
    Making the Cut 23
    Test Time 24
    Public Speaking Inventory 24
The Leader of the Pack 25
Why You're Reading This 30

4 Do You Hear What I Hear?   **31**

First Contact 32
You're Only Human 32
  Meaning Matters 32
  The Medium Is the Message 33
  Sign and Symbol 33
Types of Communication 34
Special Delivery 35

5 Common Communication Problems   **39**

Say What? 40
Check Mate 41
Communication Isn't Always Valuable 42
Communication Can't Solve Everything 42
More Communication Isn't Always Better 43
Say What You Mean 44
Communication Can Be Complex 45

Part 2: It's All in the Planning   **47**

6 Fun with SPAM   **49**

Situation 49
  X Marks the Spot 50
  Walk This Way 50
Purpose 51
  Ulterior Motives 52
  A Case in Point 52
Audience 53
Method 54
  We Can Work It Out 54
    Method to Your Madness 54
  Hammer It Home 55

7 Getting to Know You: Audience Analysis   **57**

Why Me? 58
People Who Need People 58
Let Me Entertain You 60
  Country Mouse and City Mouse 60
  Stranger in a Strange Land 60

Why Are They Here? 61
   Size Matters 61
   Age Before Beauty 61
Appearance Doesn't Matter—Or Does It? 62
Gender Bender 62
Dumb as Toast? 63
   Audience Knowledge and Opinions 63
Spin Doctor 64
Your Place in the Sun 64
Location, Location, Location 65
Pull It Together 65

8 Types of Speeches 67

The Three Main Kinds of Public Speaking 68
   Speeches That Inform 68
   Speeches That Persuade 68
   Speeches That Entertain 69
A-to-Z Speeches 69
   Addresses of Welcome 69
   Appeal for Funds 69
   Appreciation and Awards 70
   Closing Remarks 70
   Court Testimony 70
   Dedications of Buildings, Ships, Vehicles, and So On 70
   Election Campaigns 71
   Eulogies 71
   Incident Reports 71
   Installation Ceremonies 71
   Introductions 72
   Job Interviews 73
   Job Training Sessions 73
   Nominations 73
   Presentations 73
   Process Analysis 74
   Retirement Speeches 74
   Sales Presentations 74
   Toasts and Roasts 75

9 Hear Ye, Hear Ye: Speaking to Inform 77

Dream Theme 78
 This Porridge Is Just Right! 78
 Joined at the Hip 79
 Be True to Yourself 79
What If You Have Nothing to Say? 79
Basic Patterns 80
 Alphabetical Order 81
 Cause and Effect: What Happened and Why? 81
 Chronological Order 81
 Numerical Order 81
 Problem-Solution: Q & A 82
 Spatial: The Order of Space 82
 Topical: The Order of Subjects 82
Hit the Books 82
 Five Ws and an H 83
 Press the Flesh 84
 Types of Support 84
Leaving it Unsaid 84

10 My Way or the Highway: Speaking to Persuade 87

I've Looked at Life from Both Sides Now 88
Surfing the Net 89
Buyer Beware 89
 Quality 90
 Bias 91
 Appropriateness 91
Taking a Side 92
Appealing to Logic 92
 Inductive Reasoning 92
 Deductive Reasoning 92
Appealing to Emotion 93
Would You Buy a Used Speech from This Person? 94
Truth or Consequences 95
 Begging the Question 95
 Bogus Claims 95
 False Analogies 96
 Loaded Terms 96
 Misrepresentation 96
 Oversimplifying the Issue 97

A Little Latin *97*
Reasoning Backward *97*

11 The Life of the Party: Speaking to Entertain   99

Playing the Crowd 100
Developing a Clear, Central Theme 100
Doing the Heavy Lifting 101
   Method 1: Point and Proof *102*
   Method 2: Spoof Point and Proof *102*
Get the Facts! 102
Share and Share Alike 104
Making Happy Talk 104
   The You-Attitude *105*
   Tug the Heart Strings *105*

Part 3: Writing Your Speech   107

12 Whose Speech Is It, Anyway?: Speech Style   109

Words and More Words 110
   Easy on the Ears *111*
   To the Point *111*
Hone the Tone 112
   Avoid Clichés Like the Plague *113*
   Avoid Euphemisms *113*
   Avoid Jargon *114*
Avoid Sexist Language, Baby 115
Go Figure 116
   Illustrate with Images *116*
   Dare to Compare with Similes and Metaphors ... *117*
   Hyperbole (or Overstatement) and Personification ... *117*
Throw Out the Rule Book: A Look at Grammar 118
A Final Word: Be True to Yourself 118

13 Getting Organized   121

Time Marches On 122
   Less is More *122*
   Hello, I Came to Say I Cannot Stay *122*
   The "20-Minute" Rule *123*
Be Sincere, Be Brief, Be Seated 123

Another Look at Methods of Organization 124
Time Flies When You're Having Fun: Chronological Order 124
I Feel Your Pain: Problem-Solution Order 125
The Order of Subjects: Topical 125
Be Supportive 126
Laying the Foundation 127
Follow the Leader 128

14   Time to Outline   131

What, Me Outline? 132
How to Know a Good Outline When You See One 132
Full-Text Outline 132
Key Word Outline 133
Note Card Outline 133
Outline Rules 133
No Mix and Match: Use Uniform Letters and Numbers 134
Go Solo: Include Only One Idea Per Line 135
Get Down: Subordinate Ideas Properly 136
Indent Lines to Show the Relationship of Items 137
On the Straight and Narrow: Use Parallel Structure 138
Recipe for a Great Outline 138
The All-Purpose Outline 139

**15   Start at the Very Beginning, A Very Good
      Place to Start   141**

Hand-in-Glove: Intro and Speech 141
Story Time 142
(Not So) Trivial Pursuit 143
Danger, Will Robinson 143
Clip-n-Save 144
Asked and Answered 144
Who Done It? 144
Personal Touch 145
Greetings from the Home Team 145
You Could Look It Up 146
Quote with Class 146
Words to Live By 147
Looking for Quotes in All the Right Places 147

The Numbers Game 148
   Stats It! 149
   Date Night 150
Sex, Lies, and Videotapes 150
Laugh In 150

16 Body Building   153

Write Away 154
   You Got the Time, I Got the Place 154
   Write On 155
Tailored to Fit 155
   It's as Simple as A, B, C 156
   Cause-Effect 156
   Time Travel 157
   You Can Count on It 157
   Problem-Solution 157
   Gas, Food, Lodging 158
   Map It Out 158
Cast and Crew 158
   Once Upon a Time 158
   Comparisons and Contrasts 159
   Examples 159
   Facts 160
   Figure It Out 160
   Order in the Court! 161
Go with the Flow: Transitions 161
Getting It on Paper 162

17 Are We There Yet?: Conclusions, Revisions, and Titles   165

End Game 166
   Help Me, Rhonda: Using Appeal 167
   Picture Perfect: Using Illustration 168
   Might Makes Right: Using Inducement 168
   What's the Good Word? Using Quotations 169
   The Grand Finale: Using Summary 170
Body Shop: Matching the Conclusion to the Speech 170
Reading and Revising 171
Crafting a Title 171

18 Ever Hear the One About...?: Using Humor   **173**

Laugh In 174
   Humor 101 174
   So The Joke's Not On You... 175
What Makes a Good Joke? 175
Be of Good Cheer 176
   Borrow Good Jokes 176
   But First, a Little About Me 177
   Live at Five 177
   Play with Words 178
Making Humor Work for You 178
Jokes That Never Work 179

19 Taking the Show on the Road: Multicultural Concerns and International Speeches   **181**

Vive la Difference 182
   John/Jean/Juan Q. Public 183
   Do You Have Anything to Declare? 183
Ways to Get Your Message Across in Any Language 183
Stroll Through the Cultural Minefield 185
   *You Can Check Out Anytime You Like, But You Can
   Never Leave* 186
   Our Neighbors Across the Pond 187
   Shop 'Til You Drop? 187
   When in Rome (or America Today) 188
   Eat, Drink, and Be Merry 189
Lingua Franca 189

Part 4: Take It On Home: Tackling Specific Kinds of Speeches   **193**

20 Informational Speeches   **195**

Insert Tab A into Slot B: Explaining a Process 196
Working Nine to Five: Job-Training and
Teaching Sessions 197
The Corner Office: Interviews 198
   Interview Preparation Checklist 198
   Power to the People 198
   Whack 'Em and Stack 'Em 199
In the Hot Seat: Giving Testimony 199

Let's Get Critical 200
Listen Up: Describe an Object, Person, or Place 201
Define a Concept 201

21 Persuasive Speeches   203

True to Type 203
Three on a Match.. 204
Strategic Air Strikes 204
Sales Presentations... 205
Up Close and Personal: The Direct Approach 206
Through the Side Door: The Indirect Approach 207
Checkpoint Charlie 207
Styles Presentation Checklist 207
Dead, But Not Forgotten: Eulogies 208
Proactive Problem-Solvers 211
Vote Early and Often 211
Nominating a Candidate 212

22 Entertaining Speeches   215

The Host with the Most: Introducing a Speaker 216
Coming Attractions... 216
Speaker Introduction Checklist............................... 217
Always-Fail Clichés 217
Making the Grade: Giving a Graduation Speech 218
Voyage of Discovery 219
Put Your Hands Together For… 220
Toasts 221
And Roasts 221
The Envelope, Please: Presenting an Award 221
In Grateful Appreciation...................................... 222
Award Presentation Checklist................................... 222
Take the Money and Run: Receiving an Award 222
Speaking at Conventions 222
Happy Birthday to You! 223
Going to the Chapel: Speaking at Weddings 224
The Best Man 224
Father of the Bride 224
The Groom 224
*How to Make Sure That Rice Is the Only Thing That
Gets Thrown* 225
Cutting the Ribbon: Dedicating an Imposing Edifice 227

23 Speaking Off-the-Cuff   229

Been There, Done That 230
Know Your Stuff 230
   A Method to This Madness 231
   On-the-Spot Organization 231
Lost in Space 232
Uh, Like, Wow: Speak in Complete Sentences 233
Nowhere to Hide: Question-and-Answer Sessions 234
When the Well Runs Dry 235
   Prime the Pump 235
   A Deer in the Headlights 235
Practice Makes Perfect 236
    Impromptu Speaking Checklist 237

24 Debate and Parliamentary Procedure   239

Point/Counterpoint 240
   Let Me Proposition You 240
   Evaluate the Proposition 240
Assume the Position 240
Doing Hard Time 241
   In Brief 242
   Are Three Enough? Are Six Too Many? 244
Me and My Shadow 244
Debate Format 245
   Standard Format 246
   Cross-Examination Format 246
   Lincoln-Douglas Format 247
The Rules 247
Parliamentary Procedure 248
   Peace in Our Time 249
   Take A Walk on the Mild Side 249

Part 5: Master of Your Domain   253

25 A Thousand Words: Visual Aids   255

The Short History of Medicine 255
Show and Tell Time 256
   Do… 257
   Don't… 258

A Dollar Late and a Day Short 259
   Dot the I's and Cross the T's 259
   Plan B 260
Use and Abuse 260

26   Preparing and Using Visual Aids   263

Audiotapes 264
Blackboards 264
Charts and Graphs 264
Computers 266
Diagrams 267
Films 267
   Flip Charts and Posters 267
Handouts 269
Maps 269
Models 270
Overhead Projectors 271
Photographs 272
Slides 272
Videotapes 272

27   Byte Me: Using PowerPoint   275

Power to the People 275
   Run, PowerPoint, Run 276
   Lock and Load 276
Tool Time 276
Views 277
Wizards of Ahhs 277
Somewhere Over the Rainbow: Colors 278
What's the Object? 279
   Picture This 279
   Charts 279
   Movies and Sound Clips 279
Text Time 279

28   Smashing the Sound Barrier   281

Read My Lips: Voice 282
   Voice Quality 282
   Clarity and Articulation 283
   Rate of Speech 283

Pitch and Inflection 284
Pace and Rhythm 285
Ditch the Fillers 286
Loud, Louder, Loudest: Volume 286
In and Out 286
Coming Up for Air 287
Cord Care 288
Pump Up the Volume: Using a Microphone 288
Listen Up 289

29 An Ounce of Prevention: Rehearsing   291

Why Rehearse? 292
How to Rehearse 292
Rehearsing with Others 294
Preparing Index Cards or a Speech Manuscript 295
Note Cards 295
Full Text 296

30 Let Me Hear Your Body Talk: Body Language   299

The Hidden Persuaders 300
It's Later Than You Think 300
The Eyes Have It 301
Finger Play 302
Gestures 303
Break the Code 304
Platform Movement 305
Know When to Fold Them 305
Point the Way 306
Groove to the Beat 307
Culture Clash 307

31 Dress and Grooming   309

Dress for Success 310
A Clean Machine 312
Night Moves 313

Part 6: The Moment of Truth   317

32 Delivery   319

See and Say 320
    To Memorize or Not to Memorize? 320
    Put on a Happy Face 320
I Should Have Stayed in Bed 321
    You Think You Have Problems? 321
    Live and Learn 324
I'm Glad You Asked Me That... 324
    I'm Not Glad You Asked Me That... 325
    Humor 325
Making a Graceful Exit 326

33 Last Licks   327

Speaker's Bureaus 327
End Game 331
    Before... 331
    During... 332
    After... 332

Appendices

A Word Power Glossary   333

B Sample Speeches   337

Sample Informative Speech 337
    The History of Comic Books 337
Entertaining Speech 340
    Mark Twain Reveals Stage Fright 340
Persuasive Speech 341
    "Be Ye Men of Valour" 341
Seven Speeches to Study and Remember
(or: Only Crib from the Best) 344

C Further Readings   347

Index   349

Foreword

The Complete Idiot's Guide to Speaking in Public with Confidence well deserves a second edition. Why? Because unlike so many texts, which make up the endless seas of public-speaking tomes, manuals, and guides, Laurie Rozakis's work lucidly displays the function, guidance, and satisfaction that have maintained public speaking for over 2,000 years. Keeping the style that has made *The Complete Idiot's Guide* series so popular, Dr. Rozakis casually makes public speaking a delight to study, rather than a burden to bear.

It has been said that 90 percent of people "would rather be in the coffin than behind the lectern!" Yet, for the sake of these would-be morgue dwellers, there is a reprieve from the rhetorical abyss: *The Complete Idiot's Guide to Public Speaking, Second Edition*. The Table of Contents details every strategy needed to traverse the mazes inherent in speech making: from eliminating stage fright, to understanding research, to delivering vocal panache. The book is comprehensive, readable, entertaining, and instructive. In critiquing public-speaking texts, I have found none that merge the last three adjectives so productively. In textbook writing such a combination is highly coveted, but hardly achieved.

As a teacher, author, and professional in the delightful albeit maddening realm of public speaking, I know the frustration and attractiveness of the discipline. When Thomas Mann wrote, "Speech is civilization itself. The word, even the most contradictory word, preserves contact. It is silence that isolates," rhetoric (refined, persuasive communication) discovered yet another mantra to advocate, and Dr. Rozakis ably keeps that pledge.

I have found that the beginning student in public speaking needs not only training in putting an address together, but, above all, that same student requires assurance in presenting the speech before an audience. It may be that this aura called confidence is the most demanding of all. Like any subject that requires practice, success comes from the teacher's responsibility to instill resolution and the pupil's determination to exhibit that resolve. In public speaking, with each member of the audience an individual critic, the speaker must possess that sureness in both personal demeanor and schooled ability, if the speech is to be worthwhile. The speaking arena has only the speaker, the message, and the listener. However, first and foremost, the lone speaker becomes a catalyst for fusing the message to the audience. And that ability comes from proper instruction through teacher and book. Both entities must be clear in purpose, especially with public-speaking skills being demanded of most people in the work force today.

It has been my experience, in teaching both students and business professionals, that a text is of utmost importance, inasmuch as the pupil spends more time with it, than with the teacher. In a stimulating way, *The Complete Idiot's Guide to Public Speaking,*

Second Edition represents the spirit of all texts in *The Complete Idiot's Guide* series, which is an enjoyable combination of humor and training. With this book the novice public speaker may talk about a coffin long before ever wanting to be in one!

Larry Stephen Clifton, Ph.D.

Larry Stephen Clifton, Ph.D., member of the International Speaker's Network, is author of several books, including *Public Speaking: An Academic and Professional Source, Your Platform is the World: Interpersonal Communication Through Vocation, Education, Inspiration, and Recreation*, and *The Terrible Fitzball: Melodramatist of the Macabre*. In addition to his work as a public speaker and radio talk show host, he has taught and lectured at a variety of colleges and universities, including Tennessee State University, Michigan State University, and Dalton State College. Mr. Clifton, who holds his Ph.D. in Speech Communications from Southern Illinois University, currently teaches speech and rhetoric at Carson Newman College in Jefferson City, TN.

Introduction

What's as reliable as losing your quarter in a public telephone, as constant as dandruff, and as invariable as middle-aged spread? It's the scores of students who stream into my speech class every semester looking like they're ready to face a tax audit or a root canal.

Gender's not a factor: The men and women seem equally wretched. It's not age, either: I've had 18-year-old freshmen and 75-year-old retirees with equally long faces and hunched shoulders. Size, shape, style—they all look like someone has killed their puppy.

Every semester, I remind these woebegone men and women that they signed up for this class. (I didn't drag anyone out of their warm bed to break rocks on the chain gang.) I tell them that public speaking is not a flat tire on the expressway, a missed train, or a burned casserole. I tell them that they'll enjoy learning the fundamentals of public speaking and sharing their skills with the class. And yet they all look morose—tragic, even.

By the end of the semester, the class has undergone a wondrous transformation. They're happy, really happy. Why? They've learned that they can write and deliver a good speech. And in nearly all cases, they've actually gotten to enjoy speaking in public. And you will, too—I promise.

First, you'll discover that speaking in public is not a difficult skill, if you have the proper training. (That's why you bought this book.) Second, you'll acquire the tangible economic, social, and political benefits that come with mastery of public speaking. You'll see that these rewards are well worth the time it takes to learn to speak in public. And you'll discover that the intangible benefits—the pride and self-esteem that come with learning to stand up and express yourself with poise and eloquence—are even more important.

Note to the second edition:

The Complete Idiot's Guide to Public Speaking was one of the groundbreaking books in the *Complete Idiot's Guide* series. It's with great pride, then, that I embrace the task of revising the book as it goes into its second printing. Now you get even more for your money!

The second edition of *The Complete Idiot's Guide to Public Speaking* contains brand-new chapters on the communication process, debate, parliamentary procedure, nonverbal communication, and evaluation. There's even an entire chapter on using Microsoft PowerPoint to create effective and impressive presentations. I was able to add many more speeches for you to use as models, too. Many of these are now included in the chapters for ease of use.

I'm thrilled that the first edition of *The Complete Idiot's Guide to Public Speaking* was received so well. I know you'll find this edition even more useful.

What You'll Learn in This Book

This book is divided into six sections that take you through the process of writing and delivering a speech. You'll come to learn that giving a speech involves much more than just standing at a podium and talking—in fact, that's the easy part!

You'll discover that before the speaking event comes detailed planning, analysis, research, writing, revising, and rehearsing; and that after the speaking event comes gathering your notes, walking to your seat, and soliciting feedback. And you'll find out that *how* you say it can be every bit as important as *what* you say. Here's what the six parts of this book cover:

Part 1: Clearing Your Throat first explores how people feel about public speaking. This part discuss the importance of public speaking in both your personal and public lives. It's here that we take care of everyone's No. 1 worry about speaking in public: stage fright. Last, you'll learn about common communication problems.

Part 2: It's All in the Planning gets into the nitty-gritty of speech preparation: audience analysis, speaking to inform, speaking to persuade, and speaking to entertain. In this part, you'll learn how all speeches are the same—and different.

Part 3: Writing Your Speech explores speech style as well as techniques for clearly communicating your meaning, suiting your personal speaking style to audience and purpose, and fitting the audience and occasion. Here's where you'll find out all about organization, with a special focus on the backbone of complete speech preparation: outlining. I'll take you through the process of writing a speech from the beginning (the opening), through the middle (the body), to the close (the conclusion). Then you'll learn all about using humor in your speeches and meeting the needs of multicultural and international audiences.

Part 4: Take It On Home: Tackling Specific Kinds of Speeches provides a detailed description of informational, persuasive, and entertaining speeches. Here you learn to master impromptu and extemporaneous speaking, the skill of thinking and speaking on your feet. This section also covers the rules of debate and parliamentary procedure.

Part 5: Master of Your Domain helps you prepare visual aids, audiovisual aids, and props to add a fuller dimension to your speeches. Here's where you'll learn all about using PowerPoint, too. This section also tells you in detail why and how you should rehearse your speech. Finally, Part 5 describes how to use your voice, body language, and appearance to maximize your chances for success.

Part 6: The Moment of Truth describes how to actually deliver the speech. Then come ways to evaluate your performance. The last section explores how speaker's bureaus may suit your professional speech needs.

Finally, there's a glossary of key words and definitions and an appendix containing sample speeches, both new and classic examples.

More for Your Money!

In addition to all the explanations and teaching, this book has sidebars to make it even easier for you to learn how to speak in public with confidence. Here's how you can recognize these features:

Encores and Exits

These contain interesting, useful background information that can streamline the learning process. They're the facts that you can skip, but they're so interesting that you won't want to!

Class Act

Use these hints to make public speaking easier and more enjoyable.

Talk Soup

As with every other skill worth knowing, public speaking has its own jargon. Here's where I explain these terms so that you can talk the talk with your fellow pros in the speech biz.

Speech of the Devil

These warnings keep you on track. They help you avoid the little pitfalls—and the big craters.

Acknowledgments

To my brilliant, patient, thoughtful husband: gratitude for your unflagging belief in me, the vacuuming, and the two loads of laundry you do every day. I also thank you for the comic book speech that appears in the appendix. (While I'm here, my car needs windshield wiper fluid and the oil could stand a change....)

And, to my children, whose voices will ring out gloriously through the ages.

Special Thanks to the Technical Reviewer...

The Complete Idiot's Guide to Public Speaking was reviewed by experts in the field who not only checked the technical accuracy of what you'll learn here, but who also provided insight and guidance to help ensure that this book gives you everything you need to know to begin speaking like a pro. Our special thanks are extended to:

Professional speaker, author, and entrepreneur Sam Silverstein has a solid track record of building million-dollar dreams. The numbers speak for themselves—he has sold over 100 million dollars of products and services and successfully sold one business to a Fortune 500 company.

Through his books and personal appearances, Sam teaches personal and professional empowerment and helps organizations internationally become more effective in managing change, learning leadership skills, creative marketing, and solution-based selling techniques.

Sam is the author of the highly acclaimed books, *The Success Model* and *The Power Of Choice*. Sam is also a featured author in *Only the Best on Leadership*.

As a professional speaker, Sam takes his message internationally to audiences who learn and grow from his experiences. Through the use of humorous anecdotes and moving stories, Sam paints a vibrant picture of what it takes to be a success. Sam is an active member of The National Speakers Association. He can be reached at www.samsilverstein.com or 1-888-MOTIVATE (1 888-668-4828).

Part 1
Clearing Your Throat

It's like this: You've listened to scores of public speakers and said to yourself, "Hey, I can do this." You can, *but the thing is, you never actually have. That's where your collar gets tight and your hands begin to shake.*

Or, it's like this: You have a chance to make a speech that could make a significant difference to your career, reputation, and public profile. You don't really have to make the speech, but it would be a shame to pass up the once-in-a-lifetime opportunity.

Or, even this: One bright Monday morning, your boss says, "By the way, Bob, I've slated you to deliver the presentation at the sales conference next week in Glassy Point, Idaho. Remember, this is our key market, so we're really counting on you." The last time you gave a speech was in 10th grade English, in 19… oh, we're not going to get into that.

So what's your problem? Weren't you supposed to learn all about public speaking in high school and college? Sure you were, but you had your bad days and your good days. So did your teachers. The upshot is that you missed it. That's what this first part is all about.

Chapter 1

What Fresh Hell Is This?

In This Chapter

➤ How we feel about speaking in public

➤ Public speaking and your career

➤ Public speaking and your personal life

➤ Excuses, excuses, excuses

➤ Qualities of an accomplished public speaker

The Roman emperor Nero went to the arena to see the lions do lunch with the Christians. The determined animals were munching away with their usual gusto—until one Christian spoke to his lion, who listened attentively and then trotted away with its tail tucked between its legs. The same fellow continued to speak to lion after lion. Each one hurried away, as meek as it had been ferocious a few moments before. Finally, Nero could take the suspense no longer and had the Christian brought to him. Nero said to him, "If you tell me what you said to the lions, I'll set you free."

The Christian replied, "I told them, 'The lion who wins this contest has to get up and say a few words to the audience.'"

Anyone who has ever had to deliver a speech can identify with these lions. For many people, being at the podium is not unlike being dangled over the fiery pit of hell.

In this chapter, you'll learn how people feel about speaking in public. You'll discover that it's natural to approach a podium with some trepidation—and why. You'll also learn some of the excuses people give to deal with their fear about speaking in public.

The information in this chapter will help empower you to take positive steps to overcome any fears you may have about public speaking. This chapter helps give you the tools you need to realize that you can be an effective, powerful public speaker and that you can speak to large and small groups with confidence and skill.

You Mean I Have to Get Up and Say Something?

According to conservative estimates, about 5 million speeches are delivered in the United States every year. Out of all these speeches, about 1 million are delivered by and for business people.

"Ah ha!" you shout. "I'm not in a business where I have to do a lot of talking. After all, I'm not a disk jockey, talk show host, teacher, or professional gossip." You should know, however, that if you're in the general work force, you're going to be doing some serious time as a public speaker. Following is a list of some of the careers for which oral communication skills are especially important:

➤ Auctioneer
➤ Director
➤ Audiologist
➤ Reporter
➤ Librarian
➤ Radio commentator
➤ Manager
➤ Teacher
➤ Clergy person
➤ Human resources associate
➤ Physician
➤ Receptionist
➤ Commentator
➤ Sales associate
➤ Social worker
➤ Sales manager
➤ Fund raiser
➤ Travel guide
➤ Clerk
➤ Training representative
➤ Interpreter
➤ Engineer

And we haven't even discussed all the public speaking that occurs *outside* a business setting! About 4 million speeches a year are given at social occasions. This means that there's a good chance that at some point you're going to address a group of colleagues, friends, or relatives—or perhaps a service organization, religious group, or civic association. Like death and taxes, public speaking is an inescapable part of your life. You can run from public speaking, but you can't hide.

Fright Night

Speakers know that the audience is evaluating them not only for their ability to speak, but also for their ability to think. They also know that there are scores of things that can—and probably *will*—go wrong while they deliver their speech. Nonetheless, you're no idiot. I know that you can learn to speak in public with confidence. And if you know what you're doing, public speaking can also be enjoyable. I'm even going to make it easy and fun for you—I promise.

As Franklin Delano Roosevelt said, "We have nothing to fear but fear itself." However, a team of professional market researchers found that a lot of other things terrify us even more than fear; these include flying, deep water, and insects. I also have surveyed my students over the years, asking each person to rank 10 common things or situations that can cause fear.

Encores and Exits

When the founders of the United States added the Bill of Rights to the Constitution in 1791, they put the right of free speech first in the aptly named First Amendment: "Congress shall make no law respecting an establishment of religion, or prohibiting the free exercise thereof; or abridging the freedom of speech, or of the press; or the right of the people peaceably to assemble, and to petition the Government for a redress of grievances." Even if you're afraid of speaking in public, it's your right to do so.

The greatest fear of all? Speaking before a group! Nearly half the people I surveyed were more terrified of speaking before a group than of anything else. This fear was followed by a fear of heights, insects, financial problems, deep water, illness, death, flying, loneliness, and dogs.

The same research team found that only 20 percent of Americans admit that they have never suffered from "stage fright" at any point in their lives. (They probably lied!)

Some enterprising folks have developed a list of excuses to get out of speaking in public; they're all listed in the next section. By the time you finish this book, however, you won't need any of these excuses—you'll be too busy delivering entertaining, persuasive, and informative speeches. You'll be a master of *public speaking,* the art of addressing a group of people.

Speak of the Devil

"The brain starts working the moment you are born and never stops until you stand up and speak in public."　—Anonymous

Top Ten Excuses People Use to Avoid Public Speaking

What follows are the top excuses people use to try to avoid speaking in public. See which excuses you think are most valid. Then I'll tell you how reasonable they really are.

Talk Soup

Public speaking is the art of delivering a speech to a group of people.

1. I don't have anything to say.
2. I'll make a fool of myself in front of (a) friends, (b) family, (c) community members, or (d)business associates.
3. I have laryngitis.
4. I didn't have time to write a speech.
5. I'm embarrassed about how I might look to others.
6. I just moved here from Bora-Bora (or Tibet, Mars, New York City), and no one can understand my accent.
7. I'm too nervous—I'll drop dead from fear.
8. I just had a root canal, and my lips are numb.
9. I will forget what I have to say.
10. My cat ate my speech.

Now let's take a closer look at these excuses.

Excuse #1: *I don't have anything to say.* You don't have *anything* to say? Sorry, that excuse won't work. Everyone has *something* to say. In fact, everyone has *a lot* to say. If you don't believe me, try this experiment.

For one day, carry around a notepad and pencil. Every hour, take out the pad and list the people you spoke with during that hour. Next to their names, write down the things you discussed. And don't forget telephone calls! Your list might look something like this:

Speech Log

7:00–8:00 AM

➤ Reminded spouse about late afternoon meeting
➤ Told kids to stop arguing over the cereal
➤ Talked to people in the deli when I got my coffee about the merits of cream versus milk
➤ Spoke with fellow commuters on the bus about my father's hernia operation

8:00–9:00 AM

- ➤ Asked assistant for reports
- ➤ Spoke with co-workers at the coffee machine about the strange smell coming from the office refrigerator
- ➤ Logged on e-mail and answered the boss's query about where to find a good acupuncturist
- ➤ Attended the 8:30 meeting and spoke with everyone about hiring the copy machine repairman full-time

9:00–10:00 AM

- ➤ Visited another division and spoke to the employees about being considerate in the ladies' room
- ➤ Met with the legal department about copyrights
- ➤ Called Mom to say hello
- ➤ Called a restaurant to make lunch reservations

Did I make my point? Every day, you end up speaking to dozens of people about dozens of things, whether you're shy or not.

Excuse #2: *I'll make a fool of myself in front of (a) friends, (b) family, (c) community members, or (d) business associates.* Actually, the opposite response is much more likely: People will respect you for having the courage to speak in public. This goes back to what you discovered earlier in this chapter: People would rather die, drown, or be bitten by a rabid pooch than give a speech. Cross this excuse off, too. (See Chapter 4, "Do You Hear What I Hear?" and Chapter 5, "Common Communication Problems" for additional information.)

Excuse #3: *I have laryngitis.* No matter how careful you are to avoid people with colds, you can get sick before a speech. Ever notice that you seem to get ill most often when you're under pressure? Often it's because you're not eating right or getting enough sleep. If you're like me, you get a little run down, and then—bang! You've got a whopper of a cold!

Unfortunately, you often can't reschedule a speech—especially if it's a crucial business presentation, awards ceremony, sales talk, or eulogy. What can you do? If you must speak while ill, or if you are simply worried about catching a bug, follow these steps:

- ➤ First, recognize that preparing for and giving speeches is a pressure situation that can force you to neglect your health.
- ➤ If you know that you must give an important speech on a specific day, take special care to eat properly and get sufficient sleep the week before. It's very important to rest up for the big day.

➤ If possible, avoid people with colds and the flu. Wash your hands frequently; avoid touching your nose, eyes, and mouth; and take vitamin C.

➤ Try to rest your voice as much as possible before the actual speech. This is one time I suggest that you don't rehearse your speech.

➤ Try to reschedule the speech. If you can't, cut your speech back to the bare bones.

➤ Be honest with your audience. Explain that you have laryngitis. People will understand, especially because most of them have plenty of personal experience being sick!

➤ If possible, try to use a microphone when you are speaking, even if you ordinarily wouldn't need one. This will help you put the least amount of strain on your voice. See Part 5, "Master of Your Domain," for more information about using a microphone and other audio-visual aids.

➤ Use your normal speaking voice. Don't whisper—it actually puts more stress on your voice than speaking in normal tones.

➤ Above all else, don't try to be a hero. You can do permanent damage to your voice by straining your vocal chords. If your throat is sore and your voice is gone, see a doctor. If the doctor advises you not to speak, do yourself a favor and comply with your doctor's wishes: Take a well-deserved rest!

Excuse #4: *I didn't have time to write a speech.* Part 3, "Writing Your Speech," takes you step by step through the process of writing a speech. The writing part does take time, but it's time well spent.

Excuse #5: *I'm embarrassed about how I might look to others.* While your appearance does have an impact on how the audience receives your message, remember that the audience is primarily there to hear you speak, not to judge your personal appearance. You'll find that when your speech is good, everything else falls into place. But just for a little extra insurance, Part 5 explains how to groom and dress for success in speech-making.

Excuse #6: *I just moved here from Bora-Bora (or Tibet, Mars, New York City), and no one can understand my accent.* It's true that having a foreign accent or regional dialect can make you uneasy about speaking in public. But in most cases, people will understand you just fine and will respect you even more for making the attempt. This topic is covered further in Part 5.

Excuse #7: *I'm too nervous—I'll drop dead from fear.* If you weren't a little nervous about public speaking, you probably wouldn't be human. But after an exhaustive search of speech records, I've determined that no one has ever dropped dead from fear of speaking in public. (It was probably the rubber chicken that did it!) Chapter 2, "Stage Fright," covers ways to deal with jitters before a speech. You'll even learn how to make your fear work for you instead of against you. So relax.

Excuse #8: *I just had a root canal, and my lips are numb.* See Excuse #3. This is lame, ladies and gentlemen. Who schedules a root canal before an important public speaking engagement?

Excuse #9: *I will forget what I have to say.* This is an easy one to fix. To help you remember what you want to say, just write out your speech. This is covered in Part 3.

Excuse #10: *My cat ate my speech.* It's doubtful *that* would happen, but speeches do get lost more often than you would guess. Sometimes pets—or kids— eat them (or hide them). Speeches can vanish into the depths of briefcases, desk drawers, and car seats. I've even accidentally thrown out a speech! Part 5 covers steps you can take to make sure that you always have a copy of your speech on hand.

Class Act

Stage fright is not altogether a bad thing: You can learn to use the jitters to your advantage. For example, nervousness can make you more animated, alert, and vibrant. Find out more in Chapter 2.

Why We Feel Nervous About Public Speaking

Obsessing about your performance comes with the territory. It haunts beginning and experienced speakers alike: Even the most skilled public speakers battle their nerves before a big presentation. In Japan, for example, to relieve the speaker's nervous anticipation and to limit the length of the speeches, the traditional "after-dinner" speeches come before the meal. In Chapter 2, you'll find out more about stage fright.

What actually causes this sense of nervousness is a sudden rush of the hormone adrenaline, or the so-called "fight or flight" syndrome. When we are confronted with a threatening situation, such as an automobile swerving toward us, this adrenaline stimulates our physiological reactions so that we have a better chance of defending ourselves or escaping. The adrenaline rush is nature's ingenious way of helping us save our skins.

As speakers, you can use adrenaline to your advantage. Start by recognizing that the nervous tension you feel as you are addressing a group is a form of positive energy. Being nervous is also healthy because it shows that you really care about getting your message across. You value sounding and looking good, which is a good thing!

The Least You Need to Know

➤ A majority of people rank public speaking as their No. 1 fear—before dying, diving, and dogs.

➤ Public speaking is one of the most important skills for professional and personal success.

➤ People make a lot of excuses to avoid speaking in public.

➤ You can follow a few simple tips to make sure that you won't need excuses to avoid public speaking.

➤ Fear of public speaking creates an adrenaline rush, which helps prepare us for a "fight or flight" response. When properly harnessed, adrenaline can actually help you.

Chapter 2

Stage Fright

In This Chapter

➤ Down and dirty with stage fright

➤ The audience and stage fright

➤ Overcoming performance anxiety

➤ Why fear is your friend

➤ Quick and easy anti-stage fright exercises

➤ Symptoms and solutions

A recent poll found that the No. 1 fear among Americans is public speaking—and the No. 6 fear is death. Perhaps police should consider threatening violent criminals with the lecture circuit!

Actually, *stage fright* is the wrong name for this condition: For most people, the fear of performing begins long before they get to the stage. For many public speakers, stage fright actually starts when they receive the invitation to speak. Fortunately, it usually recedes during the actual performance, which shows the effect of anticipation on the actual event. Of course, this is scant consolation if you're the one with a herd of elephants thundering through your stomach!

This chapter teaches you sure-fire ways to master stage fright. You'll discover that fear is a normal and natural emotion when it comes to public speaking. And, believe it or not, fear can even be an asset to public speaking.

Armchair Diagnosis: Symptoms of Stage Fright

Take the Stage Fright Quiz here to see how badly you suffer from stage fright.

Stage Fright Quiz

When you have to speak in public...

➤ Your stomach churns.	___yes	___no
➤ Your palms sweat.	___yes	___no
➤ Your forehead perspires.	___yes	___no
➤ Your heart pounds.	___yes	___no
➤ Your mouth gets dry.	___yes	___no
➤ You start to twitch.	___yes	___no
➤ Your armpits get really, really, *really* damp.	___yes	___no
➤ Your hands shake.	___yes	___no
➤ Your legs feel wobbly.	___yes	___no
➤ Your knees give way.	___yes	___no
➤ You feel nauseous.	___yes	___no
➤ You wish you were dead.	___yes	___no

How bad is your case of stage fright? Let's find out.

If you said "yes" to...	
10–12 answers	You need me, you really need me.
8–9 answers	Have some chocolate while you read this chapter.
5–7 answers	This isn't going to hurt a bit.
1–4 answers	Start booking those speaking engagements!

The Downside

The bad news? Nervousness affects almost every speaker or performer—even the most experienced. The list is endless: Actress Helen Hayes never lost her fear of performing. Comedian Red Skelton was always a complete wreck before he went on stage. Dean Martin was famous for his stage fright. Barbra Streisand is, too.

The Upside

The good news? You can learn to control your nervousness so that it actually helps you improve your performance. Your reflexes are sharpened by the nerve impulses generated by stage fright, which means some degree of fear actually works for you. Check out this next section to find out how to channel the adrenaline pouring into your blood in a positive direction.

Why You're Afraid

Betcha didn't know...

When opossums play 'possum, they are not actually "playing." They pass out from sheer terror.

See what having to appear in public can do?

We've already established that all public speakers are nervous. But why? Take a look at some of the reasons people have stage fright—and some of the best ways to overcome these fears.

Talk Soup

Stage fright is the physical and psychological terror some people feel when speaking in public. The symptoms include shaking, nausea, sweating, and dry mouth.

Fear of the Audience

I've actually had speakers tell me, "I know the audience hates me. They're out to get me!" My response? "Your audience *wants* you to do well. In fact, these people are delighted that you're up there instead of them. It means that they can merely sit in the audience and enjoy the speech."

Audiences are usually very sympathetic to the problem of stage fright. To the extent that listeners may notice symptoms of stage fright, they will usually react in a friendly and encouraging manner.

How we perceive the audience affects our degree of apprehension and nervousness. The more you fear the audience, the more nervous you become. Try these strategies for overcoming this source of stage fright:

➤ **Pick your own subject matter.** The more you like your subject, the more apt you are to see your audience as friendly. You'll assume your audience shares your passion and thus will transfer your enthusiasm for the speech to the listeners.

➤ **Concentrate on your subject.** Many speakers lack confidence because they think too much about themselves. They obsess: "Will I do as well as the last guy when my turn comes? I hope I don't have to follow so-and-so. Now, *there's* a hot speaker." Instead of working yourself into a lather, work on developing an

Class Act

Avoid drinking or eating anything with high caffeine content the day before your speech and the day of the speech. People who are prone to nervousness can be overstimulated by caffeine.

enthusiasm for your topic. Say to yourself, "I have a topic that I want to talk about with these kind people sitting on those hard chairs. I want to make sure they are (well-informed, entertained, and so on). I'll do everything in my power to make sure that they are." Once you begin thinking about your subject rather than yourself, your stage fright is likely to recede.

➤ **Put on a happy face.** If you're upbeat, your audience will be, too. Likewise, if you're depressed, they'll pick up on that. You set the tone, so set the tone you want. Be enthusiastic.

➤ **Remember that you're the boss.** Here's your mantra: "I know what I'm talking about. That's why they asked *me* to be the speaker. I'm in charge." Trust in your own ability. If you trust yourself, the audience will, too. It's amazing how well the power of positive thinking works.

➤ **Think of silly situations.** Imagine your audience in an absurd scenario. When Carol Burnett faces an audience, she often imagines them in the bathroom. Winston Churchill liked to imagine that everyone was completely undressed. (Okay, so that can be frightening rather than absurd. But you get the idea.) The situation should be absurd enough to relax you, but not so ridiculous that you dissolve into helpless laughter.

➤ **See the audience as non-threatening.** Forge a link between the audience and yourself. The more complete your audience analysis, the more likely you are to see them as friendly—or at least not actively hostile. More on this comes in Chapter 7, "Getting to Know You: Audience Analysis."

➤ **Give speeches as often as you can.** "Right, Rozakis," you mutter. "Like I'm going to ask for this again and again? Is this *The Complete Masochist's Guide to Public Speaking*? It's bad enough I have to do it once."

As with anything else, practice makes perfect. Confidence in public speaking is built by experience. When I wrote this book, I had been teaching for more than 20 years. I'd done many, many live speeches in front of both large and small groups, but I'd never been on television. When my *Complete Idiot's Guides* started selling, I got lots of calls from television shows. Suddenly, I had to do the media thing. The first few shows were terrifying, but by the time I appeared on the fifth or sixth one, I started to relax. Now I really enjoy the experience, from the bagels and juice in the "Green Room" to the on-air chat with the host. In some cases, I've even asked to go back on the same show again (with a new book) because I had such a pleasant time with the host! (Maury Povich, Donna Hanover, and the crew from *20/20* were all especially gracious.)

Fear of Failure

Stage fright arises in part from a fear of doing poorly. You think, "I'll make a fool of myself in front of my friends!" Even worse, you may be afraid of making a jerk of yourself in front of someone specific, such as your spouse or your boss. Try these two ways to overcome this kind of stage fright:

➤ **Fight it.** Yes, you're scared out of your wits, but unless you show it, no one will know it. After all, you're under no obligation to reveal your feelings. Don't say, "I just want to tell you how nervous I am," or "You wouldn't *believe* how upset I am about speaking in front of you." You may think that your fear is written all over your face. In nearly all cases, it isn't—unless you deliberately reveal it.

Class Act

How often should you speak in public to raise your confidence level? Aim for at least one major speech a month.

➤ **Visualize success.** Ever hear about self-fulfilling prophecies? They take place when you talk yourself into something. For example, if you assume that you are going to do a bad job behind the podium, you'll very likely undermine your speaking performance.

Instead of talking yourself into something that will create more fear and less confidence, talk yourself into something that will create less fear and more confidence. Imagine yourself making the perfect speech.

Control your mental image of yourself; tap all your confidence. Realize that even though you may not bewitch the crowd with your silver-tongued orations, there is still a reason they asked *you* rather than the schleps in the audience.

Fear That Your Speech Stinks

"My speech isn't good enough. My material is terrible." This is the easiest fear to overcome because you are in total control of the speech. You wrote it; you know it cold. Nonetheless, here are some methods you can use to overcome this kind of thinking:

➤ **Write well.** The better your speech, the more confident you'll be. The more confident you are, the less stage fright you'll feel. Take the time to write and rewrite your speech—it's time well spent. And once you *know* that you have a well-written speech, you'll stop worrying about stinking up the place.

➤ **Get feedback.** Have people in your field read your speech and offer suggestions. Invite trusted colleagues, friends, and relatives to offer their comments. Then revise as needed.

➤ **Rehearse.** As you'll learn in Chapter 29, "An Ounce of Prevention: Rehearsing," you've got to practice, practice, practice. I recommend that you practice one hour for every minute of your speech; the more you practice, the more relaxed you'll be. Naturally, the best kind of practice is actual public speaking—which means that the more speeches you do, the better you'll get.

Class Act

Here's a bonus: The more you practice, the less time you'll have to be nervous.

Speech of the Devil

It's perfectly natural to put off doing something you find unpleasant. As a result, many speakers delay practicing. Don't fall into this trap.

Conquer Your Fear

Believe it or not, stage fright has its good points. Because people imagine public speaking as terribly difficult, you'll automatically be perceived as a powerful person. This means that as the speaker, you don't have to actually do anything: Just standing at the podium automatically confers a certain amount of fear in your audience.

Recognize this: Once you believe that you can become a self-assured speaker, you *can* be. The best way to overcome stage fright? Believe in yourself.

Have the following steps in mind to keep fear in its proper place:

➤ Admit that you have some stage fright. (After all, admitting that you have a problem is half the battle.)

➤ Understand that all public speakers are nervous during most performances.

➤ Draw from the energy that fear produces.

➤ Understand that no one has to see your fear. In many situations, appearance is the reality.

➤ Imagine yourself as a successful speaker.

➤ Analyze your audience.

➤ Be fully prepared.

➤ Be confident; believing in yourself will help others believe in you.

Physical and Mental Exercises for Releasing Stress

Some speakers physically shake when they're under stress. If you're a trembler, take heart: it doesn't show half as much as you think. Try these tips anyway to help you deal with the shake-and-bake syndrome:

➤ Instead of holding a hand microphone, leave the mike on its stand.

➤ Draw attention away from your hands. For example, avoid holding a glass of water so that the audience won't be distracted by the tidal waves in the glass.

➤ Leave your notes on the lectern so that people can't see them shake in your hand.

➤ If your legs are trembling, shift your weight between them. Lean forward and grasp the lectern with both hands. If you're sitting down, keep your hands gripped on your knees. This does double-duty: It stops both your hands and your legs from trembling.

Stage fright may not be something to look forward to, but you should recognize that it's normal. The next sections address some other techniques for mastering performance anxiety.

The "No Pain, No Gain" Route

Below are some suggestions you can use to help you deal with stage fright. They're all easy and even pleasant, to help you relieve tension *and* enjoy yourself.

Speech of the Devil

Alcohol and public speaking don't mix. Some speakers think a drink or two will help them relax before a performance—and they're right. Alcohol will indeed help you relax. However, even the smallest amount of alcohol can result in slurred words, fluffed timing, and fumbled notes.

➤ A few days before your performance, burn off some of your nervousness by doing some exercise. Physical activity is an easy and beneficial way to release tension.

➤ Just before you speak, go off by yourself to an empty room and do a few jumping jacks or run in place. Don't get all sweaty and worn out; just do enough to release that extra bit of nervous energy.

➤ Before you speak, sit in a slumped position in a chair as if you are a rag doll. Let your arms dangle beside the chair, your head slump to your chest, and your mouth hang open. Then tighten all the muscles in your body one at a time, starting with your toes and working up to your neck. Then gradually relax each set of muscles, starting at your neck and working back down to your toes. Repeat this process several times.

➤ Slowly yawn a few times. This will loosen and help clear your throat.

➤ Focus on the part of your body that feels the most nervous, such as your stomach, hands, or knees. Working slowly and carefully, tighten the muscles in this part of your body. Hold them a second, and then release. Do this two or three times, and you'll feel the area relax.

➤ Right before you enter the room where you'll be giving your speech, swing your arms a few times, alternating each side.

The "Less Pain, Still Gain" Approach

Here are even a few more suggestions you can try. As always, select the ones that work best for *you*. But first, why not try them all on for size?

➤ Conjure up a pleasant daydream, such as a Caribbean vacation, a camping trip, or a monster-sized income tax refund. Try to make your daydream as vivid as possible; thinking about something pleasant will help you release tension.

➤ Psyche yourself up. Tell yourself, "I am completely prepared. I wrote a good speech, and I know it thoroughly. I will go out there and do a wonderful job."

Symptoms and Solutions

Use these ideas to help you overcome some of the most common (and upsetting) symptoms of stage fright.

Symptoms	Solutions
1. Trembling hands	Use 3-by-5-inch cards. Don't hold them, though: Instead, place them on the lectern and slide each card to one side after it has been used.
2. Tongue-twisted speech	Slow down! Pause between words and sentences. No one has a train to catch.
3. Shortness of breath	Breath from your diaphragm (your stomach) and through your nose. Don't breath through your mouth.
4. Fear of the audience	Look right above their heads. Later, find a friendly face to focus on. If need be, bring some friends you can use as focal points.
5. Serious sweating	Ignore it. No one will know unless a pool forms on the floor beside you. And that won't happen.
6. Cold hands	Rub your hands together under the lectern.
7. Squeaky voice	Before the speech, tape-record your voice and concentrate on eliminating the squeaks. If you squeak during a speech, just press on.
8. Dry mouth	Speak slowly. Wear a *light* coating of petroleum jelly on your lips. If you must, put a glass of water on the lectern, pause, and sip from it. Keep this to a minimum. No guzzling, please.
9. Tense muscles	Use some appropriate body language. More on this comes in Chapter 30, "Let Me Hear Your Body Talk: Body Language."
10. Upset stomach	Try to ignore it.
11. A desire to bolt	Resist it. The best defense is a great offense: Have a super speech and be sure to practice a lot.
12. Foolish feeling	Dress well. If you look your best, you'll feel your best.

Take a Test Run

Your test run can be imaginary or real. Let's take a look at how to have an imaginary test run—sort of a "virtual" speech.

Visualize yourself giving the speech and doing a fantastic job. Close your eyes and take yourself through the process, step by step. Imagine yourself walking onto the stage, standing at the lectern, delivering the speech, using your visual aids, accepting applause, answering questions, and calmly walking back to your seat. Imagine as many of the details as you can. Seeing yourself successful during this test run in your mind will help you give a better speech.

Your test run can be more real than this, too. Deliver the speech by yourself in front of a mirror. As you speak, make eye contact with the "audience" by looking into the mirror. See which facial expressions and gestures work best.

You can also take a test run in front of a real audience. Gather some friends or relatives who didn't run fast enough to elude your entreaties. Deliver the speech for them and then solicit their opinions. Ask them to be honest (but not brutally so) and weigh their comments.

Be sure to practice the entire speech all the way through—don't just practice the beginning or ending. If you make a mistake while practicing, don't go back and start all over again. Just keep on going, because that's what you'd have to do during the real speech.

Use It!

Still scared? Realize that a certain degree of nervousness can actually make you a better speaker by sharpening your edge.

The Least You Need to Know

➤ Virtually every public speaker suffers from stage fright; it's a normal reaction to a stressful situation.

➤ Recognize that the audience is on your side.

➤ You can learn specific techniques to make stage fright work for you instead of against you.

➤ Practice makes perfect.

Chapter 3

All the World's a Stage

In This Chapter

➤ Public speaking and spinach: good, and good for you

➤ The importance of listening

➤ What makes public speakers really effective

➤ How public speaking can help you

➤ Join the rubber chicken circuit

A fool with two red ears went to her doctor. The doctor asked her what had happened to her ears and she answered, "I was ironing a shirt and the phone rang—but instead of picking up the phone, I accidentally picked up the iron and put it to my ear."

"Oh dear!" the doctor exclaimed in disbelief. "But what happened to your other ear?"

"The creep called back," she replied.

You're no fool—so why did you agree to speak in public? Because you know that public speaking is one of the single most important tools in professional and private advancement.

In this chapter, you'll learn how important it is to speak with confidence in both personal and public aspects of your life. You will also discover what makes a good public speaker. After you fill out the Public Speaking Inventory included in this chapter, you'll have a fuller understanding of your own personal strengths and weaknesses as a speaker. This, in turn, will enable you to concentrate your time and efforts on areas where you need the most help.

Reach Out and Touch Someone

The way we interact with other people in both our personal and public lives has very little to do with the written word: It's almost totally based on speaking. Yet, very few people actually stop to consider how important the way they speak is to every aspect of their lives.

When I realized the importance of improving my ability to speak in public, I turned to formal education and training. The fact that you're reading this book shows that you've reached the same conclusion I have: Powerful public speakers are made, not born.

Public speaking can be powerful in promoting your organization or building your practice. As a marketing tool, public speaking is one of the best ways to attract new clients and customers, and to build a reputation with people who can make referrals to you. Take a look at my top 10 reasons why:

Top Ten Reasons Why Speeches Make Good Marketing Sense

10. When you set up speeches and seminars the right way, your audience will want to hear what you have to say.

9. Your audience will get to talk with you directly.

8. You will be talking to a group of prospective customers and referral sources.

7. Your audience will not automatically resist what you say because you won't be specifically "selling."

6. You will be educating and helping your audience with a problem.

5. Your audience will see you as an expert.

4. You will be able to follow up immediately with people who seem especially interested.

3. Your audience may include people of influence whom you would find difficult to meet otherwise.

2. Public speaking can enhance your exposure and your standing in your field, community, or profession.

And the No. 1 way public speaking can help your professional life is:

1. Your audience will appreciate your willingness to speak to their organization. You'll build valuable goodwill.

So Why Do This to Yourself?

Okay, I know that the idea of speaking in public still doesn't thrill you. You're probably even muttering in despair, "I'll never be able to do this." But you're starting off with much more on your side than you might realize.

Speech plays an all-pervasive role in our lives. Without words and the power to voice them, it is very difficult to complete our daily routines effectively. Speaking well affects our ability to apply for a job, plan or take a trip, elect public officials, argue for a raise, or even argue in general. Knowing how to speak with power helps us tell our doctor where it hurts, dine with a friend or business associate, and choose a career.

No matter what your occupation, your success depends in part on your ability to speak well. For example, people select doctors, dentists, real estate brokers, financial advisors, and lawyers not only on the basis of their professional competence, but also on the basis of how well they "click" or relate to each other. Anyone who has to deal with the public, from salespeople to stockbrokers, and from servers to supervisors, has to establish rapport with the people they deal with in their jobs. This rapport is established through speech.

Making the Cut

The difference between success and failure is often the ability to communicate clearly and effectively. Never has this been more true than in today's competitive business climate. One of the most outstanding examples of a contemporary person who has achieved success because of his speaking skills is Lee Iacocca.

Mr. Iacocca saved the Chrysler Corporation by using his considerable talent as a speaker to win

Speech of the Devil

If at all possible, don't cancel a planned presentation—and never at the last minute. You'll create far more ill will than goodwill.

Class Act

You know more than you think you do. Follow your instincts—and my advice—and the odds are that you'll do a great job. Use your common sense and do what you feel is most comfortable.

the backing of the President, Congress, and the American public in the largest corporate bailout in America's history. Even Iacocca credits his professional success to his skills as a speaker. In his autobiography, Iacocca writes: "I've seen a lot of guys who are smarter than I am and a lot who know more about cars. And yet I've left most them in the smoke. Why? Because I'm tough? No…. You've got to know how to talk to them, plain and simple."

Public speaking affects every area of communication. Yet many people insist on separating "public speaking" from "one-on-one" speaking. They think the former is stilted and ceremonial, while the latter is casual and relaxed. In some circumstances, this may be the case, but truly effective speakers put the power of speech to work for them whenever they communicate verbally. Remember, all the great speakers were once bad speakers.

Test Time

The ability to express ideas is as essential as the capacity to have ideas. Take a closer look at your strengths and weaknesses as a public speaker by filling out this Public Speaking Inventory worksheet.

If necessary, use blank paper to provide more space.

Public Speaking Inventory

1. List the qualities you think an effective public speaker should have.

   _____

2. List which of these qualities you now have.

   _____

3. What are your strengths as a public speaker?

   _____

4. What are your weaknesses as a public speaker?

   _____

5. When do you have to speak in public?

   _____

6. What public speaking situations do you find the most difficult?

   _____

Save your Public Speaking Inventory. When you finish the book, fill out another copy of the inventory and compare the two versions to see how much you have learned about public speaking and how your feelings about it have changed.

The Leader of the Pack

Being a good public speaker makes you visible to the high achievers in business, money, resources, and power. Speaking in public with confidence gives you the edge. And there's really no mystery about what makes someone an effective public speaker.

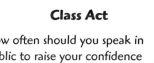
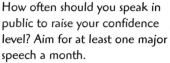

Class Act

How often should you speak in public to raise your confidence level? Aim for at least one major speech a month.

Here's my list of the qualities you need to be a good public speaker. I've included the 10 characteristics most likely to make you a success at the podium or the head of the table.

1. **Knowledge.** The famous American writer and humorist Mark Twain said, "It takes three weeks to prepare a good ad-lib speech." If that's the case, imagine how much time it takes to prepare a good *written* speech.

   Twain was exaggerating to make his point, but not by much. Reading widely will help you gather the information to make your speeches successful. However, you don't have to wait a long time to give a speech. One of the skills you'll learn in this book is how to get the facts you need to make your point. Various research techniques are covered in depth in Part 2, "It's All in the Planning."

2. **Preparation.** There's no substitute for doing your homework. The more background work you do, the more you'll be convinced that your speech is good—and it *will* be. Work and rework your speech until it is entertaining, important, and meaningful. All good speech writers will tell you that there's no such thing as good writing—only good rewriting.

3. **Language.** Powerful speakers use language skillfully. A speaker's choice of words can make the difference between a good speech and a great one—or even between failure and success. Unfortunately, learning to choose the best words to suit the occasion and the audience is one of the most difficult tasks a speaker faces (and you thought it was actually getting up to speak!).

Speech of the Devil

Beware! In most instances, oral channels of communication are better than written channels for group decision making because they allow misunderstandings to be rectified much more quickly. Oral communication also seems more personal, which offers another big advantage in business.

4. **Message.** Your audience may be potential supporters at a political debate, friends at a retirement dinner, students at a graduation, or executives at a corporate meeting. But whoever they are, you will either win or lose them with the speech you write and deliver. This list details just a few of the most important things that a good speech can do:

Encores and Exits

You might become famous (make that *infamous!*) if you don't select the proper words. Mrs. Malaprop, a character in Richard Brinsley Sheridan's *The Rivals,* used many "high sounding" words out of her ignorance and vanity. Her name soon became a synonym for the misuse of words, especially by speakers who are trying to sound important. Here are a few of her famous examples: "She's as headstrong as an *allegory* [alligator] on the banks of the Nile," "I would by no means want a daughter of mine to be a *progeny* [prodigy] of learning," and "He is the very *pineapple* [pinnacle] of politeness."

➤ Launch a successful campaign
➤ Build credibility
➤ Clarify issues
➤ Persuade voters
➤ Correct misconceptions
➤ Forge bonds
➤ Help a worthy cause
➤ Motivate employees
➤ Generate publicity
➤ Rev up a sales team
➤ Position yourself
➤ Calm upset people
➤ Garner support
➤ Spark interest in a new service
➤ Help you earn income
➤ Make you well-known

Also think about these points as you evaluate your message:

➤ Can I teach people something they didn't know?

➤ Can I impart some knowledge that will help people?

➤ Can I entertain the audience?

➤ Can I move people to thought or action?

➤ Can I persuade people to do something for the good of the community?

➤ Can I pay tribute to a person?

5. **Self-confidence.** I've already mentioned that the impression you convey can say as much about you as your words. Many factors determine how nervous you may feel: the people in the audience, how much sleep you got the night before, or what the speech means to your career.

Exhibit poise about what you have to say and your ability to say it well. Don't leave the door open for your audience to doubt you; for instance, if you cite a surprising fact, acknowledge it and say that you doubled-checked and verified it.

Don't apologize about what you have to say. Under no circumstances should you begin your speech with, "I'm not much of a public speaker, so you'll have to give me a little latitude," or "Unaccustomed as I am to public speaking...." Chapter 2, "Stage Fright," explores different ways to conquer initial jitters and harness your natural self-confidence.

6. **Enthusiasm.** A close friend of mine once gave a speech at a bridge banquet. As a nationally ranked bridge player, she knew the game inside out and is passionate about it. Yet her speech was lifeless, dull, and tedious. I was astonished, because she is normally animated on the subject of bridge. Of course, I wasn't planning to say anything if she didn't ask for an assessment, but ask she did. "Well," I said cautiously, "this speech lacked your usual enthusiasm." She replied, "That's because I'm not a morning person. It takes me until noon to really wake up." Her speech had reflected that sluggishness.

Effective speakers have an intensity or involvement that helps them reach out and make contact with their audience. They possess an enthusiasm about their subject that excites the audience. Even if they're tired, powerful speakers summon the energy to inspire their audience. They convey their vitality about the subject with their words, gestures, and body language.

7. **Listening skills.** Speaking is a two-way process that involves not only making contact with the audience, but also receiving feedback from them. It's not enough to be a good speaker; you must be a good listener as well. The broad topic of listening actually falls into three main categories. These skills will be most useful during question-and-answer sessions or in small group discussions after the speech. They will help you listen and really *hear.*

Class Act

How can you glean what the "corporate culture" is in order to establish compatibility with the audience? Ask around to find out the unwritten rules. Listen to stories to find out who the company heroes are and what they did to earn that respect.

➤ **Empathetic listening.** The purpose of this type of listening is to provide the person speaking with emotional support to help him or her come to a decision, solve a problem, or resolve a situation. As a result, this type of listening focuses more on emotions than on reason or ethics. As an empathetic listener, you can ask questions and critically analyze the issues. Your intention here is not to make a decision for the person speaking. Rather, it is to support the person speaking in his or her own independent decision-making process. You do this by providing the person speaking with the chance to express all of his or her ideas and feelings. For example, if prospective clients ask about a problem they had with your product, you might want to ask questions to bring certain facts to light. By supplying these facts, you are giving your version of events as you also allow the clients to express their fears about future problems with the product. You can allay those fears as you provide emotional support.

➤ **Comprehension listening.** In this case, the listener gathers as many facts as possible to craft an accurate perception. This is the type of listening you do when members of an audience offer comments. It's the type of listening you need when you're first asked to speak so that you make sure you understand the task and the audience. Comprehension listening demands that you focus on specific details, distinguish between different pieces of information, and organize the information into a meaningful whole.

➤ **Critical listening.** Here's where you weigh what has been said to see whether you agree with it. Start the process with informational listening to make sure that you have all the facts. When you are fairly sure that you understand the issues, you can then evaluate them and make decisions based on the facts, evidence, and speaker's credibility. This type of listening is most helpful for public speakers in decision-making and confrontational positions.

8. **Sense of self.** This refers to the way that you look at yourself. It's a relatively unchanging set of labels that describe how you perceive yourself.

What is the source of self-concept? How does it develop? Some social scientists believe that it comes from within; others believe that it develops from what others think of us. In other words, we use feedback from others to forge our own identity, matching our interpretation of ourselves with how we perceive others view us. These people weigh the feedback from different sources, accepting the appraisals from the people they consider most important—parents, bosses, lovers, husbands, wives—as most meaningful.

Even before they put pen to paper, effective speakers have a clear sense of who they are. They have judged communication from various sources, sifted through facts and data, and formed their own self-images. This firm sense of self is communicated to audiences as confidence, power, and self-assurance—and it makes their message all the more meaningful.

9. **Integrity.** In *The Rhetoric*, Aristotle wrote that public speakers need more than an ample vocabulary and the good taste to pick the right words for the right occasion. They also need more than intelligence, self-control, and balance. They even need more than being up-to-date on the issues, although all these accomplishments and traits are useful. Above all else, Aristotle claimed, good public speakers must be good people. If you want a group of people to accept your ideas, you must be respected and trusted.

People never just listen to a speech; they focus also on the person who is speaking. This fits with what you just read about forming a strong sense of self. Of course, effective speaking calls for a mastery of basic skills and techniques. Foremost, however, it requires you to be respected by others and by yourself. You probably already have integrity; this book will help you master knowledge, self-confidence, and preparation as well.

Encores and Exits

Being able to listen well is an invaluable skill for effective speakers. We all have bad listening habits that can be overcome with training and practice. This list covers three of the most common bad–listening habits:

➤ *Pseudo listening* occurs when you only go through the motions of listening. You *look* like you're listening, but your mind is miles away. Correct this by really focusing on what the speaker is saying.

➤ *Self-centered listening* occurs when you mentally rehearse your answer while the person is still speaking. This focuses on your own response rather than on the speaker's words. Correct this fault by letting the other person finish speaking before you begin to frame your answer.

➤ *Selective listening* happens when you listen to only those parts of a message that directly concern you. For instance, during a business meeting you may let your mind drift away until you hear some specific information that is directly relevant to your concerns. You'll be a more effective communicator if you listen to the entire message.

10. **Sincerity.** Effective public speakers believe in what they are saying. They're genuine, not gold-plated. They make it easy for their audience to believe their message, too.

Why You're Reading This

Having the ability to speak clearly and effectively pays off in every walk of life, from acing job interviews to working as the president of a successful corporation. The ability to write and deliver a speech also is of enormous value, partly because there aren't a whole lot of people who can do it with any skill or grace.

There's no doubt that you've seen it over and over yourself: Good speeches with a dash of humor, a touch of class, and an entertaining approach can be the difference between winning or losing a business deal; between raising a little money or a lot for your favorite worthy cause; between having your listeners on their feet applauding with enthusiasm or skulking for the door; and between an audience nodding in understanding or nodding off.

The Least You Need to Know

➤ Everyone feels nervous about speaking in public; it's an inborn physiological reaction. It's what you *do* with the fear that counts.

➤ Good public speakers have knowledge, self-confidence, a strong self-image, and integrity. They convey an important message and prepare thoroughly.

➤ Effective speakers listen closely to what others are saying. They process what they have heard and avoid common listening faults.

➤ The ability to speak clearly, cogently, and competently in public pays off.

➤ Any idiot can learn to speak in public with confidence (and it will be even easier for you because you're no idiot).

Chapter 4

Do You Hear What I Hear?

In This Chapter

➤ The definition of *communication*

➤ The communication process

➤ Communication and context

➤ Communication and symbolism

➤ The five types of communication

➤ Feedback loops and public speaking

A little girl ran out to the backyard where her father was gardening and asked him, "Daddy, what's sex?"

Her father sat her down and told her all about the birds and the bees—the works. By the time he was finished, the little girl was awestruck with the sudden influx of bizarre new knowledge. Her father finally asked, "So why did you want to know about sex?"

"Oh, Mommy said to tell you lunch would be ready in a couple of secs...."

And you thought communication was easy! As this story illustrates, communication can be hindered because our listeners don't always hear what we're saying—or what we *think* we're saying.

What do people mean by "*communication*," anyway? The first thing we'll tackle in this chapter is the definition of communication. Then we'll cover the process of communicating. You'll discover how to make your meaning clearer at the lectern or in the board room, in the classroom, at the civic center, or even in your backyard.

First Contact

Let's jump right in, shall we? *Communication* is the process people use to achieve understanding. When you want others to grasp your thoughts, you choose *words* to form your message and then *say* the message. Your receiver must *read* the message if he or she is to get your point. Often, the whole process takes only a few minute, but a great deal can happen within that time.

One of the best ways to understand communication is to visualize it. Here's how communication works on the basic level:

Sender   Message ———————————————————→ Receiver

Kick it up a notch and we get this:

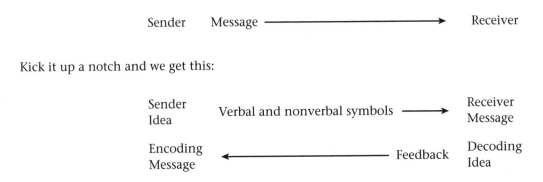

Sender   Verbal and nonverbal symbols ———→   Receiver
Idea   Message

Encoding   ←——————————————— Feedback   Decoding
Message   Idea

Let's look at the process a little more closely.

Talk Soup

Communication is a human, social process whereby people in a specific situation create meaning by using symbolic behavior. Communication occurs when a sender encodes a message using symbols that a receiver then decodes to achieve understanding. The receiver reacts by using feedback to let the sender know how the message has been received.

You're Only Human

Communication is a human process. Although scientists have shown that some animals—notably apes and dolphins—communicate in a highly complex way, it's safe to say that most people don't do a lot of public speaking before apes and dolphins.

Humans make their needs known through verbal and nonverbal communication. Painting, sculpture, music, dance, and other art forms also communicate our feelings. More than half our communication, however, takes place through speaking and writing. Here we'll focus on the most common type of communication (and the kind most relevant to this book): *speech*.

Meaning Matters

Communication is the process of creating meaning. Sometimes people think of communication as a series of isolated actions. Person A says one thing; person B says another. But that's not how communication works. Communication involves four parts: sender, message, receiver, and response. The way we interpret speech and communicate in specific situations depends on a wide variety of variables. Some of these include our personal experiences, our mood at that moment, and our overall values. Communication is an ongoing process with variable conditions and outcomes.

The Medium Is the Message

Communication arises from context. *Context* is the time and place of the communication experience. *Meaning* is constructed as a social process and is embedded in the context of the interchange. Context influences what we say, how we say it, and the way others understand what we say. For example, the meaning you take from a friend's praise of your new outfit depends in part on when the praise is offered. If it comes at the beginning of the day, it has one meaning. "What a nice way to start the day," you might think. But if your friend asks to borrow your car right after she compliments your outfit, you're likely to construct a different meaning. "She said something nice just to get a favor," you might think. The communication changed because of the time and the circumstance.

Encores and Exits

Movie magnate Sam Goldwyn (1882–1974) was a real life mangler of language. After Goldwyn Pictures became part of Metro-Goldwyn-Mayer in 1924, he struck out on his own and produced over 80 motion pictures. He received the Medal of Freedom in 1971 for "proving that clear movies could be good box office." Goldwyn's genius at the box office didn't stop him from doing some awful things to English. No doubt many of the word manglings attributed to Goldwyn were created by savvy press agents, but they nonetheless became part of his legend. Some of the most famous examples include "An oral contract isn't worth the paper it's written on," "Our comedies are not to be laughed at," and "Modern dance is so old-fashioned."

Sign and Symbol

Communication is a symbolic process. Words and actions carry symbolic overtones, or meanings greater than what they appear to be. First, think about words. For example, to a person who speaks English, *pain* refers to aches, discomfort, and suffering. To a French speaker, however, the word carries no such meaning. Instead, it means "bread."

Every language has *grammar*, or a system of rules that tells us how to use these symbols to communicate with each other. Understanding and following these rules enables us to communicate with each other.

The word is not the only thing to consider when we communicate, though; actions also have symbolic meanings. For example, making a circle by placing your thumb and forefinger together means "A-OK." It's generally accepted as a symbol for agreement in the North American culture. In the Latin American culture, however, this is an obscene gesture. On the other hand, some actions are universally accepted. Scientists have discovered that people in all cultures smile to convey happiness. But few actions cross cultures, which can create embarrassing and even dangerous communication problems. You can find out more about communication as a symbolic process in Chapter 30, "Let Me Hear Your Body Talk: Body Language."

Communication skills are vital to our professional and personal lives because communication allows us to constantly analyze what we see, feel, and hear. From this sensory input, we form convictions, opinions, needs, likes, and strengths—the sum and substance of our personalities.

Types of Communication

Communication can be divided into five categories: intrapersonal communication, interpersonal communication, small group communication, public communication, and mass communication. Let's take a look at each one.

1. *Intrapersonal communication* addresses how you communicate with yourself. Here's what you do:
   - ➤ Evaluate feedback
   - ➤ Construct meaning

2. *Interpersonal communication* handles communicating with people. When you engage in interpersonal communication, you do this:
   - ➤ Talk with one or more people
   - ➤ Work as equals

3. *Small group communication* addresses communicating with three or more people. With small group communication, you do this:
   - ➤ Work together to reach consensus
   - ➤ State beliefs as a group
   - ➤ Work with others to solve problems

4. *Public communication* handles large group communication. This is the type of communication people fear most. When you're a part of public communication, you engage in these actions:

   ➤ Share as audience and speakers

   ➤ Receive less feedback

5. *Mass communication* involves communicating through mass media. This type of communication involves people who do this:

Class Act

Don't confuse intrapersonal communication with crystals, pyramids, and past lives. We're dealing with inner voices here, not inner children.

   ➤ Communicate through TV, radio, films, and so on

   ➤ Separate the audience and the speaker and thus limit feedback

Special Delivery

Q: What do you call a boomerang that doesn't work?

A: A stick.

Successful communication is like a boomerang—it comes right back at you. This is true because the *feedback process* is crucial to successful public speaking. In essence, the feedback process involves three stages: prespeech, presentation, and postspeech. These stages are referred to as the *feedback loops*. All three steps reinforce the idea that successful communication has no distinct beginning or end, which means that the process is continuous.

Here's how the feedback loops work:

1. **Prespeech.** In this stage, the speaker anticipates the audience's response and creates a speech that will be clear, effective, and powerful. The following diagram illustrates this process:

Loop 1

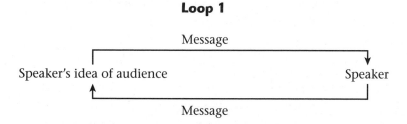

This loop uses intrapersonal communication and relies a great deal on the speaker's perceptions of the audience.

2. **Presentation.** Here, the speaker delivers the speech. As the audience responds, the speaker adjusts his or her words to make the speech more effective. Here's how it works:

Loop 2

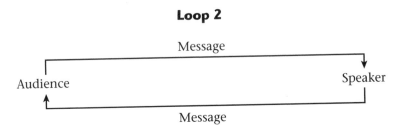

The *presentation loop* involves both intrapersonal communication and public speaking skills. The speaker and the audience send feedback to each other.

3. **Postspeech.** During the postspeech stage, the speaker evaluates the effectiveness of the speech by observing the audience's reactions. This includes the audience's comments as well as their body language. The speaker then uses these observations to help construct future speeches. Study this illustration to see the process in action:

Loop 3

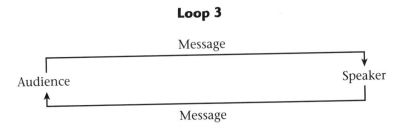

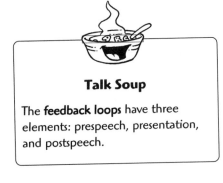

Talk Soup

The **feedback loops** have three elements: prespeech, presentation, and postspeech.

In the postspeech loop, the speaker deals with interpersonal communication, intrapersonal communication, and group feedback. That's because members of the audience think about the speech and talk to their friends and associates about it. To analyze the success of the speech, the speaker considers the message as well as feedback. Because of the circular nature of the communication process, postspeech feedback analysis often becomes a jumping-off point for future speeches.

The Least You Need to Know

➤ *Communication* is the complex, ongoing process people use to achieve understanding. It involves sending and receiving messages.

➤ Communication is a human process.

➤ Within the process of creating meaning, communication arises from context.

➤ Communication is a symbolic process with five categories: intrapersonal communication, interpersonal communication, small group communication, public communication, and mass communication.

➤ Feedback loops show how the audience affects the preparation, presentation, and evaluation of a speech.

Chapter 5

Common Communication Problems

In This Chapter

➤ Communication and the gender war

➤ Common communication fallacies

➤ Words and meaning

➤ Perception and reality in the communication process

➤ How to communicate more effectively

Ever hear this classic story?

Two women approached Calvin Coolidge. One said to the closed-mouthed president, "Mr. Coolidge, I just bet my friend that I could get you to say three words."

Said Coolidge: "You lose."

In this chapter, you'll find out why communicating can be so hard—especially when it comes to speaking confidently in public. Next, you'll find out how good you are at communicating by taking a simple communications quiz. Then you'll learn some of the most common communication fallacies so that you can avoid the faux pas that novice public speakers can make.

By the end of the chapter, you'll know the basics of being a responsible communicator so you can deal with people confidently, calmly, and competently.

Say What?

Communication can be complicated. Just look at these examples:

Top 10 Rejection Lines Given by Women (and What They Actually Mean)

Kiss-off Line	Meaning
10. I think of you as a brother.	You remind me of that inbred banjo-playing geek in *Deliverance*.
9. There's a slight difference in our ages.	I don't want to date my dad.
8. I'm not attracted to you in that way.	You are the ugliest dork I've ever laid eyes on.
7. My life is too complicated right now.	I don't want you spending the whole night, or else you may hear phone calls from all the other guys I'm seeing.
6. I've got a boyfriend.	My cat and a half gallon of Ben and Jerry's are better company than you.
5. I don't date men where I work.	I wouldn't date you if you were in the same solar system, much less the same building.
4. I'm concentrating on my career.	Even something as boring and unfulfilling as my job beats dating you.
3. I'm celibate.	I've sworn off only men like you.
2. Let's be friends.	I want you to stay around so I can tell you in excruciating detail about all the other men I like. It's that male perspective thing.
1. It's not you, it's me.	It's you.

Encores and Exits

Gaps in communication are often bridged with fillers, words like *Uh-huh* and *um*. All these expressions have been traced back to the 1830s. Stuart Berg Flexner in *I Hear America Talking* has described *huh?, uh-uh*, and *um* as "among the most common 'words' heard in America...truly native earmarks of an American." Others are not quite so charitable toward these conversation fillers, calling them "Neanderthalese." One of the newest entries is *y'know*.

Check Mate

How good are you at communicating? Take this assessment to find out. (Put a check next to each answer that you think is correct.)

❏   1. Communication is always meaningful.

❏   2. Communication is not always valuable.

❏   3. If people could only communicate openly with each other, the world would be a better place.

❏   4. Unfortunately, some problems can't be solved through communication.

❏   5. Miscommunication is the source of much of the world's misery.

❏   6. You are usually better off speaking more, because then you can get your meaning across more fully.

❏   7. It's the quality of communication that matters, not the quantity.

❏   8. Many communication problems stem from the idea that meaning comes entirely from words.

❏   9. Meaning is derived from nonverbal as well as verbal communication.

❏   10. Communication is like breathing—you do it naturally.

Now the moment of truth: Check your responses against our answers. What does your score reveal about your CQ (Communications Quotient)?

❏   1. No. Spoken language is not necessarily a good thing in itself. Communication can be cruel, unethical, or misleading.

❏   2. Yes. See #1.

❏   3. No. Communication can't cure all the world's evils.

❏   4. Yes. Communication can help people understand each other better, but it cannot always resolve strife or bring people together.

❏   5. Yes. Better communication can prevent misunderstandings, which can lead to much upheaval.

❏   6. No. Communication is more elusive than that. At times more is better, but sometimes keeping quiet conveys the most effective message of all.

❏   7. Yes. See #6.

❏   8. Yes. Meaning comes from the emotional associations that words carry, nonverbal communication, and context—not just from words.

❏   9. Yes. See #8.

❏   10. No. If only that were so! Communication is neither easy nor especially natural. As you'll soon find out, speech is not the same as communication.

Score Yourself	
8–10 correct	You're almost ready for tabloid TV!
6–9 correct	Not bad for a beginner!
4–8 correct	What's the frequency, Kenneth?
0–3 correct	How's that again?

Communication is such a complex process that it's no wonder a number of myths have sprung up about it. What's astonishing is the stubbornness of these myths. Some have become so enshrined that they now appear to be fact. Let's take a closer look at the most common communication myths and discover why they're not valid.

Communication Isn't Always Valuable

As you learned earlier, our founding fathers believed so strongly in freedom of speech that they placed it first among our rights, along with the freedom of religion, press, and the right to petition. Unfortunately, some misguided souls have interpreted this to mean that communication is always important and helpful. Well, it's not. Here's why.

Spoken language can be used to express important ideas, to bring people together, and to share feelings. On the other hand, some words spoken carelessly or deliberately can distort issues, shatter relationships, and suppress emotions. Does that sound like solving everything to you?

Even if communication is not unkind or unethical, it's neither always appropriate or prudent. For instance, sometimes an impulse to share feelings creates anger rather than trust, or resentment rather than security. You shouldn't try to make communication artificially valuable. In the same way, you shouldn't try to make an important social impact when you're merely introducing a speaker at a seminar.

Speech of the Devil

"I had a linguistics professor who said that it's man's ability to use language that makes him the dominant species on the planet. That may be. But I think there's one other thing that separates us from animals. We aren't afraid of vacuum cleaners."
—Jeff Stilson

Communication Can't Solve Everything

Ever hear these time-honored sayings?

➤ "If only people could talk openly with each other, there wouldn't be so many problems."

➤ "If only countries understood each other, we could all live in peace and harmony."

These clichés make it appear that all the world's ills could be solved if everyone could just sit down and really communicate with each other. That's pretty simplistic.

Now, there's no doubt that better communication is a step in the right direction. But it's also undeniable that there are many problems that even the best communication can't solve. Some countries, cultures, groups, and people have values so far apart that no amount of communication would bring them together. The conflicts would remain long after the communication was completed. You have probably realized in your own life that at times, it's better to abandon a conflict, even if it's just to wait for things to cool down.

Better communication can help people *understand* each other's problems, but it won't automatically *solve* those problems. There's no guarantee that better communication can make people love—or even like—each other any more than they already do.

Speech of the Devil

Occasionally, gestures can work alone to communicate meaning. This is especially true when traffic is stalled during rush hour, at ball games presided over by hard-of-hearing umpires, and when the ATM line stretches into the horizon. However, words and actions often work in tandem to enable us to communicate. As a result, don't communicate by word or gesture alone unless you know that your meaning will be absolutely clear.

More Communication Isn't Always Better

Old story: The poet Wordsworth visited the poet Coleridge at his cottage. Wordsworth walked in, sat down, and did not utter a word for three hours. Neither did Coleridge. Wordsworth then rose and left, after sincerely thanking his friend for a perfect evening.

Some people believe that if a brief conversation doesn't make others see things your way, a longer discussion will. Sometimes, of course, your opponent will simply capitulate from exhaustion and give in to anything you say. In most cases, however, a great deal of talk has the opposite effect as intended.

Now, I'm not suggesting that the world institute a universal gag rule (though at times this seems like a splendid idea). Rather, I'm suggesting that communication is more subtle than better. At times reinforcing a point can be useful. At other times, though, running off at the mouth just worsens a situation. There are even times when it's best not to say anything at all: Keeping quiet can prevent you from saying things that you might later regret.

Class Act

Better communication can perhaps help people and groups more fully understand each other's position, but there's no saying that communication will soften or shift long-held opinions.

The most effective communication occurs when you know both when to speak and when not to. These guidelines can help:

➤ Extending communication cannot always help people resolve their problems.

➤ Less talk is often more productive than a great deal of talk.

➤ With communication, the content is important, not the amount.

➤ Some problems can actually be made worse by too much talking.

➤ Sometimes, it's best to just keep quiet.

Say What You Mean

Communication is a social process of making meaning. Communication is not made up of separate, isolated acts, such as the encounter in the supermarket parking lot.

Communication would be easy if people asked and answered questions in predictable ways. It would be even easier if every exchange was scripted in advance and we just read from the pages.

But such is not the case. Our interpretation of words in a specific situation and the way we respond to them depends on our experiences, values, and emotions. Sometimes people even use different words to describe the same thing. For example, some people call artificially flavored carbonated water "soda," while others call it "pop."

Class Act

There are some excellent specialized dictionaries and word books available that explain a word's denotations. If you're shaky on word use, why not check out some of these volumes?

Many words carry loaded overtones, or *connotations*, that differ from their dictionary meanings, or *denotations*. Study the following chart to see some examples.

Word	Denotation	Connotation
Stubborn	Persistent	Pigheaded
Resolute	Persistent	Determined
Famous	Well-known	Celebrated
Notorious	Well-known	Disreputable
Cheap	Inexpensive	Tight-fisted
Thrifty	Inexpensive	Frugal
Home	Residence	Warmth, welcome

Communication Can Be Complex

Fellas, imagine that a woman asks you if she looks fat. The correct response to this question is a confident, emphatic "Of course not!" (Then quickly leave the room.)

Wrong answers include these:

    A. I wouldn't call you fat, but I wouldn't use the word *thin* either.

    B. Compared to what?

    C. A little extra weight looks good on you.

    D. I've seen fatter.

    E. I didn't hear you, I was thinking about your insurance policy.

Many people believe that you're born knowing how to communicate well. It's not a skill you have to learn, some argue. Of course, these same people think that models don't have to work to stay thin and that Santa is busy making toys all year.

It's true that speaking itself isn't hard, but you've learned in the opening chapters of this book that *communication* is not exactly the same as *speaking*. Training and practice can make an enormous difference in our ability to make our meaning understood and our ability to understand what others are saying.

Communication is also influenced by what we subconsciously choose to perceive. In many cases, we assume that other people feel the same way that we do. As you've probably discovered (the hard way), this is not always the case. We also tend to tune out messages that are unpleasant, threatening, or disturbing. Instead, we absorb messages that reinforce our sense of well-being or that tell us what we want to hear.

Take the "Are You a Responsible Communicator?" test to see how sensitive a communicator you are.

Are You a Responsible Communicator?

Put a check next to each answer that you think is true.

    ❑   1. It is important to treat others as unique individuals.

    ❑   2. It's a good idea to avoid thinking of people as typical or stereotypes.

    ❑   3. You shouldn't attempt to convince people that you're right unless you are well informed on the subject.

    ❑   4. You don't reject what other people say out of hand.

    ❑   5. It's wrong to use information about yourself to manipulate others.

    ❑   6. It's important to accepting responsibility for the words that pass through your lips.

❏   7. It's important to be careful when you talk about other people.

❏   8. It's important to avoid using private facts as a weapon.

❏   9. You anticipate the effects of your speech.

❏   10. You should be aware of the limits of your knowledge.

If you got...	
8–10 checks	I'll talk to you any day!
5–7 checks	You're on your way to becoming a responsible communicator.
1–4 checks	Dish that dirt, baby (but not about me, please).

Because the process of communication is multi-faceted, it's often easier to misunderstand people than it is to communicate with them. Even the most skilled communicators can benefit from training and practice—especially when it comes to giving a speech.

The Least You Need to Know

➤ Good communication can correct misunderstandings, but communication alone cannot change deep-seated feelings and long-held values.

➤ More communication is not always better.

➤ Our interpretation of words in a specific situation and the way we respond to them depend on our experiences, values, and emotions.

➤ Silence can sometimes be the most effective form of communication.ience affects the preparation, presentation, and evaluation of a speech.

Part 2
It's All in the Planning

In a recent interview, John H. Johnson, the owner and publisher of Ebony *magazine said this:*

"I developed my communication skills as a technique of survival. I was born in poverty and spent two years on the welfare rolls, and I learned early that I had to communicate or die. And so I talked my way out of poverty—I communicated my way to the top." (source: John H. Johnson, owner and publisher of Ebony *magazine, quoted in Gloria Gordon, "ECEL Award Winner John H. Johnson Communicates Success." IABC* Communication World *6, no. 6 [May 1989]: 18–19.)*

As Johnson's experience shows, learning how to speak in public with confidence can have a tremendous positive impact on your life. Let's find out how you can plan speeches that will communicate your message effectively and powerfully.

Chapter 6

Fun with SPAM

In This Chapter

➤ Situation

➤ Purpose

➤ Audience

➤ Method

It's a luncheon meat, a furniture polish, a junk e-mail—and now, it's a speech model! Yes, it's SPAM! Actually, SPAM is an acronym for the standard public speaking model: *situation, purpose, audience*, and *method*. In this chapter, we'll explore each of these elements.

Situation

Remember that all communication—especially public speaking—happens at a certain place and time. This is called the *situation*. It's the physical, social, psychological, and time elements in which communication takes place.

For example, Abraham Lincoln delivered his "Gettysburg Address" during the Civil War at the dedication of the Gettysburg National Cemetery. Even though everyone in attendance knew the situation, Lincoln opened his speech by reminding them of it:

"Now we are engaged in a great civil war...."

Talk Soup

Situation is the time and place where you deliver your speech. Situation can be simply *where* and *when*, but it often embraces the historical circumstances as well.

X Marks the Spot

Lincoln further noted the situation when he said, "We are met on a great battle field of that war." This statement reveals that the audience was actually standing on the site of the conflict. So far, so good—but there's even more to the situation.

1. Lincoln realized that the entire history of the United States formed the backdrop for his speech. He summarized this history when he noted that America had been "conceived in liberty and dedicated to the proposition that all men are created equal."

2. Further, he knew that the Battle of Gettysburg had strained the ties that held the Union together.

3. Last, he had taken a great deal of heat for the war and his role as commander-in-chief.

Lincoln brought all this knowledge of the situation to his speech. This reveals that Lincoln was concerned with far more about his speaking situation than simply *where* and *when*. In the same way, you must carefully analyze each of your public speaking situations.

What happens if you don't have a handle on the situation? You'll miss the chance to make valuable connections between the situation and your speech. As a result, your speech will lose impact, no matter how effective your delivery.

Walk This Way

While we're here, why not read the entire Gettysburg Address? It's a classic model of memorable prose:

> Four-score and seven years ago, our fathers brought forth on this continent a new nation, conceived in liberty and dedicated to the proposition that all men are created equal. Now we are engaged in a great civil war, testing whether that nation or any nation so conceived and so dedicated can long endure. We are met on a great battle field of that war. We have come to dedicate a portion of that field, as a final resting place for those who here gave their lives that this nation might live. It is altogether fitting and proper that we should do this. But, in a larger sense, we can not dedicate, we can not consecrate, we can not hallow this ground. The brave men, living and dead, who struggled here have consecrated it far above our poor power to add or detract. The world will little note nor long remember what we say here, but it can never forget what they did here. It is for us the living,

rather, to be here dedicated to the unfinished work which they who fought here have thus far so nobly advanced. It is rather for us to be here dedicated to the great task remaining before us, that from these honored dead we take increased devotion to that cause for which they gave the last full measure of devotion; that we here highly resolve that these dead shall not have died in vain; that this nation, under God, shall have a new birth of freedom; and that government of the people, by the people, for the people, shall not perish from the earth.

Encores and Exits

Today, "The Gettysburg Address" is one of the best known speeches in American history. After his delivery, however, Lincoln thought the speech had been a failure. It made little apparent impact on the crowd, and newspapers printed it with few comments. However, Edward Everett, the main speaker for the day (he had blathered on for more than two hours), thought more of the President's speech. He wrote to Lincoln, "I should be glad, if I could flatter myself that I came as near to the central idea of the occasion, in two hours, as you did in two minutes."

Purpose

The second variable in every public speaking situation is *purpose*—the goals the speaker hopes to achieve with his or her speech. Your ability to determine the purpose of your speech comes from your understanding of the situation. (That's why *situation* comes before *purpose*).

Lincoln wasn't the only speaker that day at Gettysburg, but he *was* the only one with a clear sense of purpose. All of the other speakers simply wanted to dedicate a portion of land for a war memorial. Lincoln pushed his speech further; his larger purpose was to rededicate America to the belief that "a government of the people, by the people, for the people, shall not perish from the earth."

Class Act

One of the best ways to learn to write an airtight speech is by studying the masterpieces. You'll find some great speeches in the back of this book.

Ulterior Motives

What happens if a speech is missing a purpose? As you listen to the purposeless speech, you're likely to ask yourself, "What is this speaker's point? Why am I listening to this? It's not going anywhere."

A Case in Point

After months of silence about charges of infidelity and perjury, President Bill Clinton finally addressed the American people about the charges. He delivered his speech live from the White House during prime time on August 17, 1998. What purpose do you think Clinton had for delivering the speech? The text of this speech follows.

Good evening. This afternoon in this room, from this chair, I testified before the Office of Independent Counsel and the grand jury. I answered their questions truthfully, including questions about my private life—questions no American citizen would ever want to answer.

Still, I must take complete responsibility for all my actions, both public and private. And that is why I am speaking to you tonight.

As you know, in a deposition in January, I was asked questions about my relationship with Monica Lewinsky. While my answers were legally accurate, I did not volunteer information. Indeed, I did have a relationship with Ms. Lewinsky that was not appropriate. In fact, it was wrong. It constituted a critical lapse in judgment and a personal failure on my part for which I am solely and completely responsible.

But I told the grand jury today, and I say to you now, that at no time did I ask anyone to lie, to hide or destroy evidence, or to take any other unlawful action.

I know that my public comments and my silence about this matter gave a false impression. I misled people, including even my wife. I deeply regret that. I can only tell you I was motivated by many factors: first, by a desire to protect myself from the embarrassment of my own conduct. I was also very concerned about protecting my family. The fact that these questions were being asked in a politically inspired lawsuit which has since been dismissed was a consideration, too.

In addition, I had real and serious concerns about an independent counsel investigation that began with private business dealings 20 years ago—dealings, I might add, about which an independent federal agency found no evidence of any wrongdoing by me or my wife over two years ago.

The independent counsel investigation moved on to my staff and friends, then into my private life, and now the investigation itself is under investigation. This has gone on too long, cost too much, and hurt too many innocent people.

Now this matter is between me, the two people I love most—my wife and our daughter—and our God. I must put it right, and I am prepared to do whatever it takes to do so. Nothing is more important to me personally. But it is private. And I intend to reclaim my family life for my family. It's nobody's business but ours. Even Presidents have private lives.

And so, tonight, I ask you to turn away from the spectacle of the past seven months, to repair the fabric of our national discourse and to return our attention to all the challenges and all the promise of the next American century.

Thank you for watching, and good night.

Clinton's speech was clearly aimed at clearing his name and convincing the American people that he sincerely repented his transgression. Had Clinton not made his purpose as plain, the speech would very likely have accomplished just the opposite purpose and convinced listeners that Clinton didn't take the situation seriously enough.

Audience

Audience is the easiest of the four public speaking variables to understand. As a result, it's the one public speakers most often overlook. Why? Because they're too busy obsessing about what to say, how to say it, how to fill the allotted time (or how not to run over the allotted time), and so on. What novice speakers don't realize is that all these concerns—and many more—depend on their audience.

Talk Soup

Audience refers to the people to whom the speech is directed.

Audience is so important, in fact, that we've devoted an entire chapter to it. Chapter 7, "Getting to Know You: Audience Analysis," covers every aspect of audience analysis.

Because the audience is comprised of the people to whom the speech is directed, audience is part of the situation as well. Remember that the speaker's purpose is to affect the audience in a planned, deliberate way. The audience's response determines whether the speech has flown or flopped. Situation, purpose, and audience are therefore very closely linked.

Talk Soup

Method is the speaker's means of adapting the message to the audience. Method includes the speaker's tools and strategies, such as organization, language, and mood.

Method

Once you have determined your public speaking situation, purpose, and audience, it's time to consider the method. *Method* is any means of adapting the message to the audience. As the speaker, you select the method or methods that you think will work best.

Don't worry: Different methods you can use are presented throughout this book. Consider these preliminary elements:

➤ How to organize the speech

➤ What language to use

➤ What mood to convey

➤ How to begin and end the speech

We Can Work It Out

Use the following worksheet to help you weigh the different method options for each speech. For example, if you were delivering an award acceptance speech in front of a community group, you would use language that creates a gracious yet happy mood. You would show your gratitude, acknowledge the contributions of others, and celebrate the occasion. A funeral eulogy, in contrast, would use far more somber language to create the appropriate mood. Also consider how visual aids can enhance your speech.

Class Act

Although situation, purpose, audience, and method were presented in a specific sequence, you don't have to analyze each element in this order. For example, in some public speaking situations, you might first analyze your audience and then the purpose and situation. Or, if you're assigned a set topic with a specific purpose (a sales speech, for example), you're best starting with purpose.

Method to Your Madness

1. Which methods best fit my situation?

   _____

2. Which methods best fit my purpose?

   _____

3. Which methods best fit my audience?

   _____

4. Which methods could be combined for a better effect?

   _____

5. Which public speaking methods am I most comfortable with? Why?

   _____

Hammer It Home

Carrie Chapman Catt delivered the following speech in 1915 to sway legislators to grant women the right to vote. In the following excerpt, notice how she uses repetition to get her point firmly across. (Hint: Watch the phrases that are capitalized.)

DO YOU KNOW that the question of votes for women is one which is commanding the attention of the whole civilized world?

DO YOU KNOW that the women of New Zealand and the women of Australia possess all the political rights accorded to men?

DO YOU KNOW that the women of Finland vote in all elections upon the same terms as men, and that since their enfranchisement in 1906, from 16 to 25 have been elected to the different Parliaments?

DO YOU KNOW that in Norway all women have the full Parliamentary vote, and that in 1910 one woman sat in the Norwegian Parliament, and that numbers of women are serving as members and alternates to city councils?

DO YOU KNOW that the women of Iceland have the full Parliamentary franchise and that since 1902 one-fourth of the members of the council of the capital city have been women?

DO YOU KNOW that in Sweden women have had some measure of suffrage since the eighteenth century?

DO YOU KNOW that in Denmark all women who pay taxes and the wives of men who pay taxes were given the municipal franchise in 1908?

DO YOU KNOW that in England, Ireland, Scotland, and Wales women vote in all elections except for members of Parliament; that they are eligible and have been elected to office as mayors and members of city and county councils; and that on the Isle of Man women who pay rent or taxes can vote for members of the Manx Parliament?

DO YOU KNOW that in eight of the provinces of Canada—Ontario, New Brunswick, Manitoba, Prince Edward Island, Quebec, British Columbia, Alberta, and Saskatchewan—tax-paying widows and spinsters have the municipal vote, while in Nova Scotia married women whose husbands are not voters are included also?

DO YOU KNOW that women have the municipal vote in Rangoon, the capital of Burma; in Belize, the capital of British Honduras; and in the cities of Baroda and Bombay in British India; and that in certain provinces of Austria, Hungary, and Russia they have limited communal franchise rights?

The Least You Need to Know

➤ *Situation* is the time and place where you deliver your speech. It includes the physical, social, psychological, and time element in which communication takes place.

➤ *Purpose* is the goal the speaker hopes to achieve with his or her speech.

➤ *Audience* refers to the people to whom the speech is directed.

➤ *Method* is the speaker's means of adapting the message to the audience. Method includes the speaker's tools and strategies, such as organization, language, and mood.

➤ Consider all four factors when planning your speech.

Chapter 7

Getting to Know You: Audience Analysis

In This Chapter

➤ "Read" your audience

➤ Audience size, age, appearance, and gender

➤ Audience knowledge and opinions

➤ Topic choice

➤ Your place on the agenda and the location of the speech

➤ Meeting your audience's unique needs

➤ Final concerns

Striking up a conversation with the attractive woman seated beside him on a coast to coast flight, a would-be Romeo asked, "What kind of man attracts you?"

"I've always been drawn to Native American men," she replied. "They're in harmony with nature."

"I see," said the man, nodding.

"But, then, I really go for Jewish men who put women on a pedestal, and I can rarely resist the way Southern gentlemen always treat their ladies with respect."

"Please allow me to introduce myself," said the man. "My name is Tecumseh Goldstein, but all my friends call me Bubba."

To be an effective public speaker, you need to understand how your audience is likely to react to what you say and how you say it. That doesn't mean you have to be all things to all people, however. You can meet your audience's needs in a superlative way, without becoming Tecumseh "Bubba" Goldstein.

Audience analysis helps speakers decide how best to grab their audience from the very beginning and hold them throughout. Successful speakers take into account the audience's interests, level of knowledge, and specific requirements. This chapter will help you analyze your audience and match your speech to their needs.

Why Me?

Let's start at the very beginning—the reason why you were asked to speak in the first place. In some cases, you received an invitation requesting that you speak for a specific occasion. This invitation no doubt explains why you were invited, but still, consider what you have to offer the audience. Here are some possibilities:

Class Act

Don't worry about looking foolish by asking why you were selected to speak in public. They're the fools for not having told you!

➤ You're well-known and will draw people to the event. (This is common with a fund-raising or charity event.)

➤ You're an expert in a field and have knowledge to share.

➤ You're entertaining.

➤ You have something to sell.

The reason why you were selected will obviously affect the content of your speech. As a result, it's always a good idea to find out specifically why you made the cut.

People Who Need People

It's important to figure out who your audience is. Members of the local Chamber of Commerce? Representatives from a manufacturing industry? Guests from financial companies? Knowing who is in the audience directly impacts what you decide to say.

Use this list to help you evaluate the composition of your audience:

➤ **Retail workers (shopkeepers and salespeople).** If you are called upon to speak before retail audiences, you should remember that these people are likely concerned about real estate costs, theft rates, and popular trends.

➤ **Insurance brokers.** Examples of what insurance brokers are interested in include sales techniques, advertising methods, and the concerns of small-business owners.

➤ **Medical workers (doctors and nurses).** Kicking off your speech with the same old medical jokes will likely fall flat. Odds are, the audience has heard every classic, including the one about the doctor who left in the sponge, and the doctor who played golf with the rabbi (or priest, or minister). And no jokes about cutting off the wrong leg, either!

➤ **Lawyers.** Unless you know your audience well, steer clear of lawyer jokes; they are often in questionable taste.

➤ **Librarians.** No quips about eagle-eyed matrons with buns, steel-rimmed glasses, and orthopedic shoes, please. Today's "information specialists" (as librarians are now called) are much more likely to be interested in hearing about computerized catalogues and retrieval methods.

➤ **Educators (teachers and principals).** Today's educational hot spots include homogeneous vs. heterogeneous class grouping, budgets, and tenure.

➤ **Industry regulators.** Know that an audience comprised of industry regulators is likely to take offense at a speech about radical environmental ideas.

➤ **Accountants.** Don't assume that accountants are dull; that stereotype is as stale as yesterday's bagel. Consider how the latest software and recent changes in the tax code have transformed the industry.

Talk Soup

Yesterday's "librarians" are now "information specialists" to reflect their changed role in the Internet Age.

➤ **Computer specialists and systems analysts.** Be sure you know what you're talking about when you take on computer specialists and systems analysts. Don't throw around computer jargon without a real understanding of its meaning.

➤ **Marketing personnel.** Discuss what's in and what's out. Share ideas about vendors and trends.

➤ **Engineers.** Stick with the basics: solid information that's professionally delivered. This kind of audience tends to appreciate visual displays such as relevant, well-prepared charts and graphs.

➤ **Stock and bond brokers.** The market's volatile, so there's lots of room for discussion here. You can discuss trends, foreign markets, and creating a balanced portfolio, for example.

➤ **The self-employed (such as writers).** Increasingly, self-employed professionals are concerned with issues such as medical coverage, retirement plans, child-care, computer needs, and networking.

Let Me Entertain You

Stacey was invited to a new friend's home for the first time. When she arrived, Stacey's new friend excused herself to fetch her mom. As Stacey was standing in the living room next to the fireplace, she picked up the attractive vase on the mantle.

When Stacey's new friend returned with her mother, Stacey was still staring curiously into the vase. "Oh, those are my father's ashes," her friend said. This startled Stacey so badly that she dropped the vase and scattered the ashes.

"Oh, no…I'm, oh! I, can't…didn't mean to…" she stammered.

"It's okay, dear," the mother said. "The vase was from Wal-Mart."

Stacey caught her breath enough to say, "But…but your husband's ashes…."

> **Class Act**
>
> To find out about the group to which you'll be speaking, check the invitation you received, the corporate year-end report, members of the organization, friends who know about the group, and the public relations department. Don't be shy about getting as much information as you can about your audience and the reason for the speech. Remember: More research means a better speech.

"Well," the mother said, "looks like he'll just have to get off his lazy butt and get the ashtray from the kitchen from now on."

As this story shows, you should never assume. For example, if the audience is one you're familiar with, they're apt to think they can anticipate the content of your speech. That's because they know you and think of you as one of their own. Suppose, for example, that you have the reputation for having a great sense of humor. If you decide to deliver a serious speech, your audience is likely to be startled and unsure of your intent. Take this into consideration when you plan the content of your speech.

Country Mouse and City Mouse

If members of your audience come from a variety of places, you can draw on your common experiences as visitors to the city. People will take your speech more seriously if they feel you're trying to meet their specialized needs.

Stranger in a Strange Land

If you're speaking to a group of total strangers, however, you have to be that much more careful about making a good first impression. The way you come across in your speech is the way that these people will remember you; there's no room for second tries with strangers.

Why Are They Here?

Why are all those well-dressed people sitting around the conference table, on those hard chairs, or on the pews? (Well, that one should be sort of obvious.) Is the audience present because they want to hear your speech, or did someone force them to attend? There's a huge difference as far as the speaker (that's you) is concerned. Let's compare the difference:

Captive Audience	Want to Attend
Less tolerant	More tolerant
"Prove it" attitude	"Accepting" attitude

Size Matters

The size of the audience is another key element to consider when planning your speech. People in smaller groups tend to pay closer attention. They hesitate to show their restlessness or to zone off because it's much noticeable in a small group.

The inverse is equally true. Individuals in larger groups tend to daydream more. They might shift in their seats or even whisper to the person sitting next to them. After all, it's easier to be anonymous in a crowd.

Adjust your speech to the size of the audience. For example, if 15 or fewer people are in attendance, you can strengthen your points with personal references to audience members. Here's how one speaker personalized her speech: "It's important to order at least 10 extra books to account for late registration, as Dr. Brown discovered with her British Literature 101 course last semester." Personalization also works well with large audiences. It builds connections.

Age Before Beauty

Age is another audience consideration. Find out if you will be speaking to people who are younger than you are, who are your age, or who are older than you. Then select material that's right for the people in your particular audience. Consider what effect the age of your audience might have on these elements of your speech:

➤ Topic

➤ Purpose

➤ Main points

➤ Language

➤ Visual aids

Speech of the Devil

With speeches, one size does not fit all. It's rarely a good idea to give the same speech to different audiences. No two audiences are alike; the closer you tailor your speech to your audience, the better your speech will be.

> **Encores and Exits**
>
> Who is the "average" American today? According to the most recent census, America boasts about 264.6 million citizens. Nearly a third of us chose to identify ourselves as minorities. Here's how we describe ourselves:
>
> ➤ 33.5 million (13 percent) of us are black;
>
> ➤ 27.7 million (11 percent) of us are Hispanic;
>
> ➤ 9.5 million (4 percent) of us are Asians and Pacific Islanders.
>
> ➤ 2.3 million (1 percent) of us are Native American/Inuit;
>
> All told, 23 million of us are foreign-born, the highest level since before World War II. Expect delightfully diverse audiences at your speaking engagements.

Appearance Doesn't Matter—Or Does It?

It's important to consider appearance as well. How is your audience likely to be dressed? How do they expect you to look? If there is a great difference in appearance and style between you and your audience, you might feel either intimidated or superior. The same is true of your audience. For example, if your audience is dressed casually in shorts and T-shirts and you deliver your speech dressed in a suit, they are apt to feel anxious or even hostile. This makes it harder for you to win their trust.

What to do? Check with your host before the speech. Make sure that you are dressed appropriately for the occasion. There's lots more on this in Chapter 31, "Dress and Grooming."

Gender Bender

If possible, it's helpful to find out what percentage of audience members will be female and what percentage will be male. Why? A number of researchers believe that the gender differences in conversational styles result in the miscommunication that often occurs in male-female conversations.

For example, researchers have learned that women are much more likely to indicate understanding by nodding and giving affirmative verbal cues than are men. Men, in contrast, interpret these signs as meaning "I agree," rather than "I understand." A male speaker who sees female audience members nodding may feel that they are inconsistent in action if they later question what he has said. A female speaker who does not receive any feedback from male audience members may feel that she is being ignored.

Also consider whether male and female audience members might view your topic differently. Different members might very likely have different interests, experiences, and knowledge about the topic you are discussing. This clearly affects your choice of topic and method of development.

Dumb as Toast?

It's easy to overestimate the knowledge that your audience has. People outside your own area of expertise may not really know what it is you do. Even people who have once worked in your field may have forgotten specific details now that their work has changed. When you are presenting new information, try to open your speech with familiar facts. Make a special effort to be clear, to link new information to familiar information, and to use visuals to illustrate difficult concepts.

Class Act

Make photocopies of this worksheet and use them for each speech that you give. (For that matter, go ahead and make copies of all the handy worksheets found in this book.)

In addition, before each speech, analyze your audience's level of knowledge. Use the following worksheet to evaluate your audience's level of expertise on your topic.

Audience Knowledge and Opinions

1. How much does my audience know about my topic?

   _____

   _____

2. How does my audience feel about my topic?

   _____

   _____

3. Will my audience be against me, or will I be preaching to the converted?

   _____

   _____

4. Does my organization have a history of conflict or cooperation with this group?

   _____

   _____

5. Is my audience neutral?

_____

_____

6. Why was I asked to speak?

_____

_____

Spin Doctor

Sometimes you'll be given free reign on topic choice; other times, you'll be given a topic. What happens if you've been assigned a topic that's a real stinker?

By all means, address the topic you've been assigned. However, you can slant your topic to appeal most to your audience and also meet your strengths. Next to elementary school orchestra concerts, few things are as unendurable as listening to a series of speakers parroting the same weary platitudes. You want to speak to the audience's concerns.

If you think your audience is opposed to what you have to say, start your message on common ground. As you speak, be as clear as you can be. Never assume that your audience is getting your point: Messages that might be clear to receptive audiences can easily be misread by negative ones.

This is not the time to go out on a limb, because hostile audiences can be the verbal equivalent of a chain saw. Also, avoid flaming the fire; don't say anything that will rile up your audience. Spin doctor techniques are discussed in detail in Part 3: "Writing Your Speech."

Class Act

The most important tools in audience analysis are common sense and empathy, which is the ability to put yourself in someone else's place. Most likely, your audience is not just like you. Use what you already know about people in addition to what you find out about the organization to predict likely responses to your speech.

Your Place in the Sun

Your place on the agenda can determine the tone of your speech, as well as its content. Sometimes, your speech may be the single most important event at a gathering. In these cases, you'll often be the opening speaker. This means that your speech will set the tone for the event—you will essentially affect how the audience receives the entire program.

Or you may be speaking in the middle of the program. In these instances, you are carrying the entire weight of the event, since the bulk of the program will be under your control.

If you're part of a panel, you want your speech to blend in with those of your peers. At the same time, you also want your speech to stand out in a positive way. Listen to what your peers have to say. Match their time limit, or speak for a little less time. Talk to panel members ahead of time to find out what they are going to say so you'll present fresh material.

Find out where your speech falls on the agenda. And don't be afraid to change your spot if you think it can lead to a better speech and better use of your time.

Location, Location, Location

The three most important rules for real estate—"location, location, location"—also work for successful public speaking. Where you will be speaking can be as important as when and why. Research the place where the speech will take place so that you can tap topics of local interest, such as famous local people, inventions, and athletic teams.

On the flip side, something may be going on in the town where you're speaking that you would like *not* to mention in your speech. For example, jokes about California earthquakes won't work if the place where you're speaking has just been hit with a series of tremors.

Even the room where you deliver your speech can impact your speech. Use the following guidelines.

In a small meeting room...

> ➤ There's probably no microphone, so remember to project your voice.

> ➤ Make sure visuals are large enough.

In a large auditorium...

> ➤ Use a microphone.

> ➤ Use video or an overhead projector.

> ➤ Encourage people to sit up front. Invite them to come and join you. Explain the benefits of having a court-side seat!

Class Act

For the directionally impaired (like yours truly), never forget to map out your route well before the speech. And get good directions—you don't want to end up driving around a strange town instead of giving your speech.

On an outdoor platform...

> ➤ Take background noise into consideration.

> ➤ Take weather into account.

> ➤ Try to avoid speaking outdoors. There are too many distractions.

Pull It Together

Before each speech, review and make notes about these questions to help you begin your evaluation of your audience:

Encores and Exits

Sophisticated audience analysis is commonplace in the advertising business. The Volvo campaign is a good example of this. Its ads emphasize different benefits for different audiences: economy and durability in America, leisure and status in France, performance in Germany, and safety in Switzerland.

➤ Who is going to be in the audience?

➤ How can I find out more about the audience?

➤ What is the political situation?

➤ How much do my listeners know about the topic?

➤ Are they on my side?

➤ If not, how can I spin the topic to be more appealing to the audience?

➤ When on the agenda will my speech be given?

➤ How does the location of the speech affect its content?

➤ Are there any special circumstances I must take into account?

The Least You Need to Know

➤ Analyze your audience before you write your speech.

➤ Find out why you were asked to speak, who will be in the audience, and where your audience is from.

➤ Learn the size of the audience, their reason for attending, and their level of expertise.

➤ Consider your audience's age span, appearance, and gender.

➤ Make sure you know your place on the agenda and the location of the speech.

➤ If possible, *talk with* audience members ahead of time, before you write your speech. This can be a big plus.

Chapter 8

Types of Speeches

In This Chapter

➤ Speeches that inform, persuade, and entertain

➤ Addresses of welcome, appreciation, and awards

➤ Appeal for funds, closing remarks, and dedications

➤ Eulogies, process analyses, testimonies, and installation ceremonies

➤ Introductions, job interviews, nominations, and presentations

➤ Incident reports, retirement speeches, election campaigns, and toasts and roasts

➤ Sales presentations

While giving a speech on honesty, Mark Twain told this story:

"When I was a boy, I was walking along a street and happened to spy a cart full of watermelons. I was fond of watermelons and snitched one. Then I ran to a nearby alley and sank my teeth into the melon. No sooner had I done so, however, when a strange feeling came over me. Without a moment's hesitation, I made my decision. I walked back to the cart, replaced the melon—and took a ripe one."

When was the last time you were called upon to "say a few words"? Perhaps you had to give a toast at a birthday party, wedding, retirement dinner, or installation ceremony. Or, as part of your job, you might have been required to run a training session, sell a product, or interview a job applicant. Perhaps you ran for election or nominated a candidate.

Whatever the task, few of us have made it this far in life without giving a formal or informal speech—and snitching a watermelon or two while we were at it.

In the previous chapters, you learned about the communication process, along with some widespread communication difficulties. In this chapter, you'll explore different kinds of public speaking tasks. The following sections give you a list arranged in alphabetical order for quick, easy reference. But first, let's take an overview of the three different kinds of public speaking.

The Three Main Kinds of Public Speaking

Some people seem to be able to stand up in front of a group and talk about anything at any time. In large part, their social ease is due to a complete understanding of the different speaking tasks. These speakers are familiar with each type of speech, inside and out. They know how different speeches are organized and delivered. And they know how to be true to themselves and to their audience. So will you.

All speeches fall into one or more of these three categories: speeches that *inform*, speeches that *persuade*, or speeches that *entertain*. We'll examine each of these in greater detail.

Class Act

Because people absorb information much more readily when it is interesting, it is especially important to fill informative speeches with details. Visual aids such as graphs, charts, and video clips are a great way to make information clear and palatable. See Chapter 25, "A Thousand Words: Visual Aids," for step-by-step instructions for using audio-visual aids.

Speeches That Inform

Speeches that inform fulfill the following actions:

➤   Explain

➤   Report

➤   Describe

➤   Clarify

➤   Define

➤   Demonstrate

Even though sometimes these speeches may move your audience to action or belief, their primary purpose is to present facts, details, and examples. (That's why they're classified as *informative speeches*. Speeches that inform are discussed in depth in Chapter 20, "Informational Speeches.")

Speeches That Persuade

Speeches that persuade are designed to convince. When your goal is to influence your audience's beliefs or attitudes, you're speaking to persuade. You can approach the persuasive speech from a number of angles: You can use your own credibility to strengthen your argument. You can appeal to your audience's emotions, reasons, or sense of right and wrong. But whatever you do, your speech must include information that supports the logic of your position. These types of speeches are covered in depth in Chapter 21, "Persuasive Speeches."

Speeches That Entertain

Speeches that entertain fulfill a social need by promoting a feeling of social unity that draws people together. To accomplish this aim, you will most likely have to include elements of informative speeches: statistics, illustrations, and examples.

For instance, a speech honoring community member Bob Schlob could discuss how he has taught a free writing program for 10 years, led the Boy Scout troop for 3 years, and donated 55 pints of blood in the past 10 years.

Class Act

Many people think that entertaining speeches must be funny, and indeed many of them are. But they don't *have* to be funny—nearly anything that is interesting can be the basis of an entertaining speech.

Because these three different types of speeches often overlap, it's important for you to isolate and understand the primary purpose of your speech before you start writing it. For example, if your supervisor asks you to deliver the opening speech at the annual sales convention and you read the sales report to your audience, you haven't fulfilled the primary purpose of your speech (to persuade). Check out Part 3, "Writing Your Speech," for guidelines.

A-to-Z Speeches

Okay, so I lied about that A-to-Z part, but just a little (it's not often that public speakers are called on to talk about zebras, zippers, or zeppelins). This section covers some of the most common types of speeches. These are arranged in alphabetical order.

Addresses of Welcome

As the presiding officer or designee, your task is to give a brief but gracious speech that welcomes guests and members. See Chapter 22, "Entertaining Speeches," for specific guidelines.

Appeal for Funds

If you are active in community or public activities, you'll likely have many occasions to "pass the hat" for funds or action. Follow two steps when organizing a speech that appeals for financial support:

➤ Explain your reason for speaking. State the cause, purpose, or urgency of your appeal.

➤ Request the actual contribution to the cause. Chapter 21 covers this speech task in depth.

Appreciation and Awards

It's an honor to present an award—and even more fun to receive one! When you're the recipient of an award, follow these four steps when accepting it:

➤ Offer your thanks to the giver and the organization he or she represents.

➤ Praise the donor.

➤ Say something appreciative about the gift or the honor. Recognize the assistance others gave you in this achievement.

➤ Explain what benefit or pleasure you expect to reap as a result of receiving the gift.

You can find more information about this type of speech in Chapter 22.

Speech of the Devil

It's especially important to keep your remarks brief when closing a meeting. People are ready to leave, so you don't want to hold them up any longer than necessary.

Closing Remarks

As the head weenie at any roast, your job isn't over until you have adjourned the meeting. In so doing, your speech should express thanks for the audience's interest and cooperation, and then bid them a cordial good-bye. This is explained in detail in Chapter 22.

Court Testimony

Giving testimony in court is a type of informative speaking. As a witness, your job is to give facts and evidence from which judges, juries, or committee members will draw conclusions. See Chapter 20 for a list of rules that a witness should follow when giving testimony in court.

Dedications of Buildings, Ships, Vehicles, and So On

This type of speech cements a group, community, or organization by creating a feeling of goodwill. As such, this is a speech that entertains and builds social cohesion. You want to go for emotional appeals and personal identification rather than appeals to reason, logic, or ethics. To craft and deliver a winning speech, you have to appeal to the interests and values you share with the audience. You learn how to do this by following the step-by-step directions in Part 4, "Take It On Home: Tackling Specific Kinds of Speeches."

Election Campaigns

This is a classic persuasive speech—actually, a whole series of persuasive speeches, each tailored to the needs of your particular audience, time, and place. You can use a direct appeal: Tell the audience what you want, give them the facts they need, and tell them again. Or, you can appeal to their emotions as well as their reason. When combined with direct requests, emotional appeals make surprisingly strong election campaigns. Specific techniques to use for election speeches are described in Chapter 21.

Eulogies

A *eulogy* is a speech given in praise of a person. Most often, eulogies are given at funerals and memorial services, but they can be delivered any time someone is being honored. The most effective eulogies focus on one or two of the subject's positive qualities. The speaker lists the quality and offers specific anecdotes from the person's life to illustrate their point. If the eulogy is offered at funerals and memorial services, it is appropriate to offer an expression of sorrow or shock at the person's passing and sympathy for the family of the deceased. Chapter 21 offers detailed instructions on delivering eulogies.

Incident Reports

Ever witness a traffic accident? A robbery? A natural disaster? If so, you know how important reliable eyewitnesses can be when it comes to settling the matter quickly and fairly. If you are an eyewitness to an incident that must be reported to the authorities, present the facts as you saw them, without embellishment or commentary.

Another aspect of reporting an incident is to understand cause-and-effect relationships.

➤ The *cause* is why something happens.
➤ The *effect* is what happens, the result.

When you are called upon to report an incident to an authority, it's important to analyze the causes and effects. First, understand that causes come before effects. Second, realize that not all the events that came before the incident helped cause it. It's also important to remember that more than one cause can contribute to an effect—and if there are several causes, they may not contribute equally to an effect.

Installation Ceremonies

These speeches formally install people in offices such as president, vice president, secretary, and treasurer. They're also important for inducting people in union offices and other types of positions.

If you are the installee, express your appreciation for the honor and pledge to faithfully perform the duties of the office.

If you are the installer, pay tribute to the person who is being honored. Such tributes are comprised of two elements: praise and good wishes for the task ahead. Call the person by name and offer specific reasons why he or she will be a fine officer.

Introductions

Follow these three steps when you introduce a speaker:

➤ First, present a brief statement about the speaker's background, emphasizing what qualifies the speaker to give this specific speech.

➤ Praise the speaker.

➤ Give the speaker's name and the title of his or her speech.

Keep your introduction short: no more than 2–3 minutes long. Remember, the focus is on the speaker, not you.

Encores and Exits

It's crucial to use the correct title when introducing the speaker. Here's a list of general titles that should come in handy, should you be making an introduction:

Speaker	Title
Governor	The Governor, or The Governor of (state)
Mayor	Mayor (last name)
Senator	Senator (last name)
Member of Congress	Mr. or Ms. (last name), Representative from (name of state)
Cardinal	His Eminence, Cardinal (last name)
Archbishop	The Most Reverend, The Archbishop of (name of the state)
Bishop	Bishop (last name)
Priest	The Reverend Father (last name)
Monsignor	Monsignor (last name)
Protestant clergy	Mr. (last name), Ms. (last name)
Doctor of Divinity	Dr. (last name)
Doctor of law	Dr. (last name)
Lutheran clergy	Pastor (last name)
Rabbi	Rabbi (last name)

Job Interviews

Interviewing candidates for a job is one of the touchiest areas of informative speech because what an interviewer should—and should not say—at an employment interview is subject to strict federal guidelines. Chapter 20 explains the guidelines for this speaking situation.

Job Training Sessions

As a type of informative speaking, job training sessions are unusual because they involve much more audience participation than most informative speech situations. As a result, you'll want to urge audience members to participate actively. Often, the speaker functions more as a moderator. Try these suggestions:

➤ Limit the information you will cover.

➤ Organize the information in an easy-to-follow manner.

➤ Include ample visual aids, such as handouts, videos, charts, and graphs to clarify difficult concepts.

➤ Think about dividing the audience into small groups to discuss the presentation.

See Chapter 20 for more detailed instructions on preparing to speak at job training sessions.

Nominations

A speech that nominates a candidate can be a simple statement: "I nominate Hector Ruiz for the office of president." Or, it can be more elaborate, giving the audience an explanation of your candidate's qualifications and attempting to generate excitement about your candidate. The first type of nomination is an informative speech; the second type is a persuasive one. See Chapter 21 for a detailed explanation of the second type of nomination.

Presentations

You've been selected to give the plaque, certificate, bond, or pat on the back to the deserving honoree. These speeches include two main steps: (1) praise the recipient; (2) hand over the gift. Your praise should be simple and sincere. Do research to find a relevant but special aspect of the recipient's background to praise. Keep your speech factual and straightforward.

Presentation speeches can be thorny because they often pop up without much notice. Find out more about these speeches in Chapter 22.

Process Analysis

Process analysis speeches tell and audience how to do something, such as how to change a tire, prepare the perfect rice-and-beans casserole, assemble a widget, and—that most difficult of all processes—program a VCR. These speeches often use transition words such as *first, second, next,* and *finally,* and they use numbered steps to make the process clearer.

To explain a process, start by telling the audience why the procedure is important. Give an overview of the process by stating the steps you will be describing. Next, explain each step, one at a time. If possible, demonstrate (or illustrate) each step. And look carefully at your audience to make sure that they understand what you're saying. Finish by summarizing the steps again. This topic is covered in depth in Part 4.

Retirement Speeches

If you are in this position, begin your speech by expressing your appreciation for the honor of serving and by thanking your associates and friends for the support you have received.

Speakers offering their good wishes to the retiree isolate specific examples of the person's tenure in office and end with heartfelt wishes for their happiness and continued success in the future.

Sales Presentations

Sales presentations can be *direct* or *indirect.*

Direct sales presentations have three basic aspects:

➤ A hook that grabs the audience's attention

➤ A list that provides your audience with the facts

➤ A handle that gives your audience a reason for supporting your idea

Indirect sales presentations have eight basic steps:

➤ Analyze the audience.

➤ Establish common ground.

➤ Define the problem.

➤ Explain how your proposal will solve the problem.

➤ Show how the advantages outweigh the disadvantages.

➤ Acknowledge and deal with changing needs.

➤ Summarize benefits.

➤ Give the audience directions for action.

See Chapter 21 for a detailed description of direct and indirect sales presentation techniques.

Toasts and Roasts

When toasting or roasting a person, open with an overview of the meeting's purpose. Follow this by introducing the members of the head table. Next, make a toast to the guest of honor and invite the guests to join in. Then introduce the speakers. At the end of the roast, thank the guests and add one final sally. Hosting toasts and roasts is covered in Chapter 22.

The Least You Need to Know

➤ Three main kinds of speeches exist: speeches that inform, speeches that persuade, and speeches that entertain.

➤ Different types of speeches demand different approaches.

➤ Successful speakers are familiar with the different types of public-speaking tasks and what each one entails. Now you are, too.

75

Chapter 9

Hear Ye, Hear Ye: Speaking to Inform

In This Chapter

➤ The speech's theme

➤ Methods of organization: alphabetical, cause and effect, chronological, numerical, problem-solution, spatial, and topical

➤ Research

➤ Interviews

➤ What *not* to say in an informative speech

Late one night a mugger wearing a ski mask jumped into the path of a well-dressed man and stuck a gun in his ribs. "Give me your money," the mugger demanded.

Indignant, the affluent man replied, "You can't do this—I'm a U.S. Congressman!"

"In that case," replied the robber, "give me *my* money."

It's time to show them the money. How? By writing an informative speech, one of the most common speaking tasks you'll face.

As you will recall from the discussion in Chapter 8, "Types of Speeches," the main purpose of an informative speech is to convey information to the audience. These speeches explain, teach, and clarify. To give the audience the information they've come for, you need to learn how to focus on a topic, decide on a clear method of organization, and get the facts.

In this chapter, you first learn how to choose and narrow a topic. Next, you'll learn how to decide on an organizational pattern specifically suited to your informative speech. Finally, I'll provide step-by-step guidelines to researching the information that you need to make your informative speech fulfill its goal. You'll even learn what *not* to include. What more could you ask?

Dream Theme

Said the after-dinner speaker: "I feel like Roseanne's fourth husband. I know what I'm supposed to do, but I'm at a loss as to how to make it different."

You won't feel like Roseanne's fourth husband if you plan all your informative speeches by picking a central theme, the speech's one main idea.

Talk Soup

A speech's **theme** is its central idea, its one main idea. The specific purpose of your speech is called your **thesis**.

When planning your speech, ask yourself, "What is the *one* thing I want my audience to get from my speech?" That's your theme. A speech without a theme is like a swimming pool without water, a car without an engine, Roseanne's fourth husband without a clue—well, you get the idea.

This Porridge Is Just Right!

Your theme must be general enough to fill the allotted time, but specific enough to respond to the topic, fit with any overall conference theme, and hold the audience's attention. Study this chart for an illustration:

Topic Wide Enough to Tow a Battleship Through	Topic Narrow Enough to Fit in a Coach Seat
College	Paying for a college education in the 90s.
Work	Jobs for the 21st century.
Athletics	Should amateur athletes be paid?
Television	Should "infomercials" be banned?
Computers	Jumping on the Information Superhighway.

Take the following quiz to see which topics have been sufficiently narrowed for a 20-minute speech. Circle the number for each topic that you think is specific enough for our mythical speaker. (Ignore the ones that would have the poor sucker speaking long after the audience has gone home.)

1. Child care
2. Ways to find caring, reliable, and inexpensive childcare
3. Divorce in the United States

4. How counseling and mediation can help reduce the divorce rate

5. Sexual harassment

6. The problems of sexual harassment in the workplace

7. Exercise classes/aerobic exercise

8. How to pick the exercise class that's right for you

9. Stocks and bonds

10. How to invest wisely in the bond market

You're on to me, aren't you? In each case, the even-numbered choice is better because it has been narrowed enough to make a good base for a 20-minute speech. The odd-numbered topics are wide enough to be used as suspension bridges.

Joined at the Hip

Once you have your theme, you're ready to locate the second and third most important points to make. However, everything in the speech must directly link to the theme. Make secondary points only if they do not detract from the impact of your primary theme. Also keep your audience in mind as you develop your main ideas. Remember, your speech must be carefully tailored to meet your audience's needs and interests. Refer to Chapter 7, "Getting to Know You: Audience Analysis," for guidelines.

Class Act

Many people find that writing down their specific purpose—to convey information—helps them focus their thinking and stay on the topic. Why not try it yourself?

Be True to Yourself

There's an implied contract between the audience and the speaker: The audience must sit still and listen politely. The speaker must have something to say.

This works only if you believe in what you have to say; if you don't buy your own message, the audience won't either. As Shakespeare said, "To thine own self be true." That advice may be trite, but it's true. Pick a theme that interests you as well as your audience, and develop a theme that you feel comfortable speaking about. You want your theme to suit your values, interests, and personality.

What If You Have Nothing to Say?

But what happens if you follow all this great advice and you *still* find that you have absolutely nothing to say? Start over by asking yourself some basic questions about yourself and your interests (including your fraternal organizations, your political affiliations and ambitions, your hobbies, your community work, your company, your business, or your career). Ask yourself these questions:

Speech of the Devil

Don't select a theme that embarrasses you—or anyone else. Remember, you're under no obligation to speak about anything that makes you uncomfortable.

➤ Why did I join this particular civic group?

➤ What have we accomplished during my tenure?

➤ Why do I enjoy my hobbies?

➤ Have I been able to turn any hobbies into jobs?

➤ What community work gives me the greatest pleasure?

➤ What makes my company different or special?

➤ How has our organization helped the community?

➤ What was our company's most recent success?

Don't get too hung-up on setting aside time for thinking about themes. We're not advocating procrastination as a lifestyle, but spending hours hunched over your desk while pulling out your hair isn't a great solution, either. You can plan a speech while you're doing the dishes. Sometimes your best ideas will come when you least expect them—and the dishes will get done, too!

Need more assistance? Here's a list of useful sources.

➤ Academic journals

➤ Trade magazines

➤ Newspapers

➤ Training films

➤ Foreign publications

➤ Television

➤ Painting and sculpture

➤ Talks with coworkers

➤ Almanacs

➤ Encyclopedias

➤ Radio talk shows

Basic Patterns

The purpose of an informative speech is to get the audience to understand your ideas. It's not a race: The winner is not the person who covers the most information in the shortest length of time. Instead, focus on helping others to grasp and remember the essential ideas you present.

To be sure that your informative speech is clearly organized, don't include too many main points—usually no more than three or four. Then group the remaining facts under these main points. Be sure to link these main points logically and clearly—don't jump back and forth among ideas.

The more clearly your speech is organized, the more easily your audience will grasp your ideas. The following sections review seven basic patterns for organizing informational speeches.

Class Act

Pick a theme you like. If you're interested in what you're talking about, your enthusiasm will rub off on your audience.

Alphabetical Order

For this type of organization, simply arrange items in the order of the alphabet. Alphabetical ordering works best with discrete topics that lend themselves to easy division, such as the names of products, places, and companies.

Cause and Effect: What Happened and Why?

If you read a daily newspaper or watch the news on television, you are being exposed to cause and effect. Remember, the *cause* is why something happens; the *effect* is the result. Cause and effect is an especially suitable way to organize your speech because it's easy to follow. In most cases, start with the causes and lead into the results.

Chronological Order

Chronological order presents your ideas in terms of time. As a result, it's an especially good method of organization for an informative speech. For example, you might explain how to hook up a modem by taking the audience through the steps in order from first to last. See Chapter 13, "Getting Organized," for more information on chronological order organization.

Numerical Order

As with alphabetical order, numerical order provides audiences with easy benchmarks. Sometimes speechmakers include the actual numbers in their speech. Or, a speaker can use transitions that indicate order. Here are some of the most common transitional words:

➤ First

➤ Second

➤ Third (and so on)

➤ Then

➤ Next

➤ Following

➤ After

➤ Later

➤ Finally

➤ Subsequently

Speech of the Devil

Don't forget to use transitions to link ideas and help listeners follow your speech's organization.

Problem-Solution: Q & A

This method of organization begins with questions and follows with answers. This method can be used for persuasive and entertaining speeches as well as for informative ones. See Chapter 13 for more information on the problem-solution method of development.

Spatial: The Order of Space

Here, information is arranged in the order of direction: up to down, down to up, north to south, east to west, inside to outside, right to left, and so on. A building can be discussed floor by floor, for example, or the layout of a plaza can be described from the fountain in the center to the parking fields on the outskirts.

Topical: The Order of Subjects

Some themes lend themselves to topical arrangements through long use: For example, financial reports are usually divided into assets and liabilities; and the federal government is broken down into the executive, legislative, and judiciary branches. You don't want your method of organization to be shopworn, but remember that audiences are listening, not reading. Dividing your theme into familiar subtopics makes it easier for an audience to follow your logic. Because this method of organization can be used with all three kinds of speeches, it is covered in greater depth in Chapter 10, "My Way or the Highway: Speaking to Persuade."

Class Act

People learn new things by associating them with what they already know. Connect new facts with familiar ones to help your audience grasp your ideas.

Hit the Books

While their primary purpose is to teach, effective informative speeches need not be dull or dry. People absorb information much more easily when it's interesting, so pepper your speeches with juicy facts, tantalizing details, and delectable examples.

Specific facts are the backbone of the informative speech. Read as much as you can about your topic. If you're plugged into the Internet, you can download piles of information from any of the online services to which you subscribe. However, keep in mind that not all sources are reputable.

Five Ws and an H

One of the best ways to research is to ask yourself the standard reporter's questions: *who, what, when, where, why,* and *how.* As you prepare an informative speech, think of yourself as a journalist. Here's what I mean:

Who?

➤ Whom should I ask for facts and advice?

➤ Whom should my speech discuss?

➤ To whom should I give thanks in my speech?

What?

➤ What do I already know about this topic?

➤ What other information can I discover (fast)?

➤ What should I include? What should I cut?

When?

➤ When can I get this material?

➤ When will people be able to help me?

➤ When on the agenda do I have to speak?

Where?

➤ Where can I find information?

➤ Where can I find people to help me?

➤ Where am I going to deliver the speech?

Why?

➤ Why do I need this information?

➤ Why am I delivering this speech?

➤ Why will people like my speech?

Speech of the Devil

Speakers who do research with the 5Ws and an H in mind often feel an urge to structure their speech like a news story, with a lead that contains all the facts. You're under no obligation to do so, however: Structure your speech to suit your audience and purpose.

How?

➤ How can I make use of what I already know?

➤ How will facts help my speech?

➤ How can I make my informative speech even better?

Class Act

To achieve their goals, informative speakers must follow these guidelines:

➤ Give the speech a clear structure

➤ Present specific details, facts, and examples

➤ Relate ideas to the listeners' existing knowledge

➤ Use precise language

Press the Flesh

If you want the right information, you have to ask the right people. Here are some tried-and-true ways to conduct an effective interview:

1. Always make an appointment for an interview. Because you are asking the favor, let the interviewee select the time and place.

2. Write your questions down before the interview; keep them short.

3. Bring paper and a pen to the interview. Take detailed, legible notes.

4. Never tape-record an interview without getting the person's prior permission, preferably in writing.

5. Be sure to clarify confusing points. Double-check important information.

6. End the interview on time. You don't want to overstay your welcome. And say thank you!

Types of Support

As you know, it's the details that convey your theme. Effective support includes quotations, illustrations, analogies, and statistics. Each of these methods of support is covered in depth in Part 3, "Writing Your Speech."

Leaving it Unsaid

As the speech-writer and the speaker, you're in charge. You get to decide what goes into your speech, and what's out. What you don't decide to include can be just as important as what you do include. Use this checklist to help you decide what to leave out:

❏ Did I cut material that I can't verify?

❏ Did I cut out all extraneous details?

❏ Did I cut anything that I don't want the neighbors gossiping about or that might embarrass my friends and family?

❏ Did I cut anything that might embarrass me in the future?

❏ Did I cut anything that's boring?

The Least You Need to Know

➤ Select an interesting theme (main idea) that appeals to both you and your audience.

➤ Narrow your theme to fit into your allocated time slot.

➤ Select an organizational pattern that properly matches the theme and information in your speech.

➤ Include specific facts, details, and examples.

Chapter 10

My Way or the Highway: Speaking to Persuade

In This Chapter

➤ The importance of facts

➤ Research: text and electronic media

➤ Quality, bias, and appropriateness

➤ Inductive and deductive reasoning

➤ Appeal to emotion

➤ Logical fallacies: begging the question, bogus claims, false analogies, loaded terms, misrepresentation, oversimplifying the issue, *Post hoc ergo propter hoc*, and reasoning backward

---

Getting right to the heart of persuasive speaking, a harried executive once said, "We're not paying you to make us look like a bunch of idiots. We're paying you so others won't find out we're a bunch of idiots."

Effective persuasion is based on accurate logic, powerful appeals to emotion, and trust. Persuasive speeches have several purposes:

➤ They provide information.

➤ They overcome the listener's objections.

➤ They move the listener to belief or action.

In this chapter, you'll learn how to speak to persuade. First, you'll learn the importance of facts and how to research text and electronic media. Then you'll learn how to evaluate your sources by assessing their quality, bias, and appropriateness. Next comes inductive and deductive reasoning, and appeals to emotion. The chapter concludes with a discussion of logical fallacies: begging the question, bogus claims, false analogies, loaded terms, misrepresentation, oversimplifying the issue, *Post hoc ergo propter hoc*, and reasoning backward. By the end of this chapter, you'll know the basics of constructing a powerful persuasive speech.

I've Looked at Life from Both Sides Now

Q: Why are there so many Smiths in the phone book?

A: They all have phones.

There's one sure way to stop an argument: Drop a hard fact on it. The strength of your argument depends on three aspects of persuasion: logic, emotion, and credibility. That's why you must research opposing arguments as well as the argument you wish to support.

Start with logic—the facts.

Bank robber Willie Sutton explained that he robbed banks because "That's where the money is." Well, the library is where the facts are: There are more than 100,000 in the United States, with more than 2 billion books in them.

Class Act

After you do your own research, go for the heavy artillery: the reference librarian. A good reference librarian is a priceless source. It pays to become friendly with these wonderful people—they can save you hours of toil. A cooperative reference librarian might even answer questions on the telephone, saving you a trip to the library.

You can easily find a great deal of information at your local library. First, check basic reference sources such as dictionaries, encyclopedias, newspapers, magazines, almanacs, and Facts on File. Some additional reference sources also are chock-full of facts:

➤ Akey, Denise. *Encyclopedia of Associations*.

➤ American Society of Composers, Authors & Publishers. *Hit Songs*. (ASCAP).

➤ Asimov, Isaac. *Isaac Asimov's Book of Facts*.

➤ Hatch, Jane, ed. *The American Book of Days*.

➤ Levine, Michael. *The Address Book: How to Reach Anyone Who's Anyone*.

➤ Peter, Lawrence, ed. *Peter's Quotations: Ideas for Our Time*.

➤ *The World Almanac*.

Surfing the Net

Cyberspace also contains some great speech stuff in Cyberspace. The Web isn't like a library where information has been arranged within an accepted set of rules, however. It's more like a garage sale, where items of similar nature are usually grouped together—but not always. As a result, you'll find treasures side-by-side with trash. And like a garage sale, the method of organization on the Web shifts constantly.

So how can you search the Web for information to use in your speeches? You have several different ways at your fingertips, each of them surprisingly easy. Here's how they work.

1. *Search engines,* which use *keywords,* help you locate Web sites. Type in a keyword, and the search engine automatically looks through its giant databases for matches.

   The more narrow the phrase, the better your chances for finding the precise information you need. For example, if you're interested in getting information about a college where you'll be speaking, don't use "college" as a keyword—you'll get millions and millions of responses. Instead, name the specific college, such as "The State University of New York at Farmingdale." This will send to you the precise Web page you need.

   It's crucial that you type in the Web address *exactly* as it appears. Pay special attention to periods, capital letters, and lowercase letters. If you are off by so much as a capital letter, you won't reach the site. So if you're not getting anywhere with your search, check your typing for spelling and accuracy.

2. The acronym *WAIS* (pronounced *"ways"*), which stands for "Wide Area Information Service," enables you to search for key words within the actual text of Web documents. This increases your chances of determining whether a document you've identified contains information on your topic.

3. *Newsgroups* are comprised of people interested in a specific topic who share information electronically. You can communicate with newsgroups through a *Listserv* (an electronic mailing list for subscribers interested in a specific topic) or through *Usenet* (a special-interest newsgroup open to the public).

4. *E-mail,* or *electronic mail,* allows you to communicate electronically with specific people. Senders and receivers must have an e-mail address in order to send mail back and forth.

Buyer Beware

Just because a source appears in print, in the media, or online does not mean that it's valid. As a result, you must carefully evaluate every source you find before you use it in your speech. As you gather your sources, evaluate them carefully. Use these three main criteria as you determine whether a source is valid for inclusion in your speech:

1. Quality
2. Bias
3. Appropriateness

Let's look at each of these criteria in detail.

Encores and Exits

Here are some of the most popular search engines:

AltaVista (http://www.atlavista.digital.com). This site processes more than 2.5 million search requests a day.

Excite (http://www.excite.com). This site has a database of 1.5 million Web pages that you can search by keyword or by concept.

HotBot (http://www.hotbox.com). You can search this site by file name, geographic location, domain, and Web site.

InfoSeek (http://www2.infoseek.com). This is a full-text search system.

Yahoo (http://www.yahoo.com). One of the most famous search engines, Yahoo lists more than 200,000 Web sites in more than 20,000 categories. You can access other search engines from Yahoo as well.

WebCrawler (http://webcrawler.com). This site is used by America Online.

Quality

As Spencer Tracey said about Katharine Hepburn in the movie *Adam's Rib*, "There's not much meat on her, but what there is is choice." Research source materials are like movie stars: quality counts.

You want only the choice cuts for your speech. If the material isn't of the highest quality, it won't support your thesis, convince your audience of your point, or stand up under your listener's scrutiny. In fact, low-quality material will have just the opposite effect. That's why it's important to evaluate the quality of every source before you decide to include it in your speech.

Check the source writer's qualifications. Is this someone you trust to give a valid opinion? Here are some other factors to consider:

➤ What is the writer's reputation?

➤ Does the author have a bias or a personal agenda to advance?

➤ Was the source well-reviewed?

➤ Is the publisher reputable?

➤ Is the source up-to-date?

➤ Is the source complete?

➤ Is the source fair, or does it contain distorted information?

Bias

Every source is biased because every source has a point of view. For example, an article on hunting published in *Field and Stream* is likely to have a very different slant from an article on the same subject published in *Vegetarian Times*. Bias is not necessarily bad, as long as you recognize it as such and take it into account as you evaluate and use the source.

How can you protect yourself from being misled by bias? Consider these issues as you evaluate a text for misrepresentation:

➤ Does anyone seem to be quoted out of context?

➤ Are facts or statistics cited in a vacuum?

➤ Does the quotation reflect the overall content of the source, or does it reflect only a minor detail?

➤ Has key information been omitted?

Speech of the Devil

Traditional research methods may not always work on the Net because everything on the Internet is constantly being updated, improved, relocated, shuffled, and cut. When you do your search, don't expect something that you found today to be there tomorrow—or even an hour later. If you find material and need it, it's a good idea to download a copy of it. And no, it's not enough to store the address under the "Favorite Places" icon, because the site can vanish.

Class Act

You can check in reference sources such as *Who's Who, Who Was Who, Something About the Author,* and *The Dictionary of Literary Biography* to find out more about an author.

Appropriateness

For a source to make the final cut, it must fit with your audience, purpose, and tone. It must be *appropriate* to the topic and occasion. How can you decide whether a source is suitable for inclusion in your speech? Try these suggestions:

➤ What makes this source fit my audience?

➤ Does this source contain information you need?

➤ Does the source suit the purpose of your speech?

Taking a Side

A child said to his friend, "Let's play doctor."

"Good idea," said the other. "You operate, and I'll sue."

Remember, there are two sides to every argument (until you take one). Once you've gathered all the facts, decide how you stand on the issue, if you haven't already. What do you want your audience to believe or do? Now it's time to develop your case. Decide which of the following appeals will best serve your purpose and audience. Some speakers decide on a stance before research. Often a speaker has already been assigned a stance, or already feels strongly about what he or she is speaking about.

Appealing to Logic

Logical arguments rely on objective facts instead of personal opinions or preferences. In turn, each logical argument in your speech must be supported by evidence: facts, statistics, expert testimony, or details about the argument. The basic organization for a persuasive speech developed on logical arguments looks like this:

Introduction: Catches the listener's attention and states your argument

Body: States each logical argument and presents supporting evidence

Conclusion: Restates your argument and summarizes your main points

Logical arguments are developed in two basic ways: by inductive reasoning and by deductive reasoning.

Inductive Reasoning

Inductive reasoning is thinking from parts to the whole by drawing conclusions from specific facts. Scientists use inductive reasoning when they state a hypothesis and then conduct tests to see whether it's valid. If repeated experiments produce the postulated result, the scientists are able to conclude that their hypothesis is likely valid.

For inductive reasoning to be solid, there cannot be any exceptions to the conclusions you draw. For example, if you saw three white cats and concluded that all cats are white, your conclusions would not be valid.

Deductive Reasoning

Deductive reasoning is thinking from the whole to the parts. Start with a general statement and then proceed to specific facts that follow from the statement.

Sometimes the deductive argument at the center of a persuasive speech can be stated in three sentences, as in this example:

Major premise: All chocolate is fattening.

Minor premise: This candy bar is chocolate.

Conclusion: Therefore, this candy bar is fattening.

To use deductive reasoning correctly, you must first make sure that the major premise is true (this is often accomplished by using inductive reasoning). If your major premise is not valid, the rest of the argument will collapse. After you have your major premise down, craft a minor premise that logically follows it. Then decide if the conclusion is sound.

Finally, make sure that any qualifications of your first statement are repeated in the conclusion. However, a speaker rarely lays out a deductive argument this neatly. In most cases, for example, the first statement will be implied rather than stated.

Use the following check list when writing a persuasive speech using logical appeals:

➤ Is my topic appropriate to my audience?

➤ Have I sufficiently narrowed my topic?

➤ Did I research how other people feel about this topic?

➤ Did I select my side of the issue?

➤ Did I make my opinion as my thesis?

➤ Did I select the most effective facts?

➤ Did I weigh both inductive and deductive arguments?

➤ Did I check my inductive and deductive arguments to make sure that they're valid?

Appealing to Emotion

An emotional appeal makes the audience want to do what you ask. A powerful speech can derive its strength from facts and logic, but reason never rely on reason at the expense of emotion. Listeners have a limited ability to appreciate a complicated argument or soak up reams of information. As a result, many effective public speakers make their case by emotional means as much as by intellectual ones.

Because speakers also have voice and nonverbal communication as part of their arsenal, a speaker can often use emotional appeals much more effectively than a writer. When speakers use emotional appeals, they seduce the audience by tapping needs we all share. Here are some of these needs:

➤ **Physical needs:** These are what you need to survive. They include the need for food, water, sleep, air, and protection from injury or harm.

➤ **Psychological needs:** These make up a person's inner life. They include the need for love, affection, security, and self-esteem.

➤ **Social needs:** These tie into a person's relationship to a group. They include status, power, freedom, approval, belonging, and conformity.

Select a persuasive strategy based on your answers to the following four questions:

➤ What do you want your audience to do?

➤ What objections, if any, is your audience likely to have?

➤ How strong a case can you make?

➤ What kind of persuasion does your organization value? Do they favor reasoning or emotional kinds of persuasion?

As strong messages and strong speakers are an uncommon luxury, good speeches are carefully crafted combinations of reason and emotion.

Class Act

Photographs and slides with an emotional slant work especially well with speeches based on appeals to emotion.

Would You Buy a Used Speech from This Person?

Fact: Speakers need their audience to identify with them if they are going to be persuasive. Want to make your speech powerful? Secure your audience's trust. Here's how.

Make the audience think that you, the speaker, are a person very much like them (or like the way they see themselves on a very good hair day). Whatever the topic of your persuasive speech, it's important to get your audience to identify with you. To do so, you need to do the following:

Establish your own credibility by...

➤ Showing that you know what you're talking about

➤ Explaining your credentials

➤ Sharing information about your background

➤ Being well-informed

Evoke their goodwill by...

➤ Complimenting the audience on its good points

➤ Identifying with a person the audience admires

➤ Speaking with confidence

➤ Using the appropriate tone

➤ Showing powerful body language

➤ Standing upright

Be properly enthusiastic by…

➤ Avoiding false bravado

➤ Believing in what you're saying

Truth or Consequences

Faulty logic can demolish even the most carefully constructed speech—and it's one of the surest ways to lose an audience. Following are the common errors in reasoning, referred to as *logic fallacies*.

Begging the Question

This logic error consists of stating a position that needs to be proven as though it has already been proven. For instance:

> The question we must resolve is whether Dr. Wilson should be granted tenure with such an inadequate publication record.

The real issue is not whether Dr. Wilson should be granted tenure. The real issue is whether Dr. Wilson has an inadequate publication record. The speaker has avoided having to prove the real allegation by assuming that it's a fact. This leads the audience to make the same assumption.

Bogus Claims

A claim can be considered *bogus,* or false, when the speaker promises more than he or she can deliver. For example, the speaker may refer vaguely to "many important experiments," or "recent clinical studies" to prove a point. The point may indeed have value, but the studies the speaker cites as proof are too fuzzy to have merit. Well-educated people are rightly skeptical about this kind of behavior.

Effective research sources use specific support, not just vague references to unidentified studies and sources. You can't evaluate "many important experiments" or "recent clinical studies" unless you know how they were undertaken, by whom, and where the results were published.

Speech of the Devil

"Well-known" information is another form a bogus claim can take. Be wary of sources that tell you that "Everybody knows that…" or "It is a well-known fact that…." If the fact is so "well-known," why is the writer bothering to cite it as support? Very likely, it's the best support the writer can muster— which doesn't speak well for the validity of the source *or* the writer.

Also be on the lookout for sources that use empty phrasing such as "statistics that show...." Statistics can be very useful in proving a point, but they can also be misleading—especially if you don't have the numbers to evaluate their validity. Ask yourself:

Does this statistic raise any unanswered questions?

Has the source of the statistics been revealed?

False Analogies

False analogies are misleading comparisons. They generally do not hold up because the items or people being compared are not sufficiently alike. For instance:

A good marriage is like a game of baseball. In baseball, if a player follows the rules, the game will be a success. Likewise, in marriage, if the players stick to the rules the partners accept, the marriage will flourish.

This is a false analogy. Marriage and baseball may have a few surface similarities, but marriage is much more complex than baseball. The relationship between "the rules" and "success" is infinitely more intricate in marriage than it is in baseball.

Loaded Terms

Suspect sources may use *loaded terms* to make their point. A term becomes "loaded" when it is asked to carry more emotional weight than its context can legitimately support. As a result, it becomes *slanted* or *biased*.

Class Act

Loaded terms are most often used in political speech.

Words with strong *connotations* (emotional responses) often show bias. For example, a speaker may refer to the governor's "regime" rather than "administration." "Regime" is a loaded term because it's most commonly used to describe oppressive military dictatorships.

Misrepresentation

This type of bias takes many forms. First, a speaker can lie outright. Or, a speaker can twist what the opponent has said. To misrepresent in this way, a speaker must use *oversimplification*: A complex argument can be reduced to ridicule in a slogan, or an important element of an argument can be skipped over. A speaker also may be more subtle by inventing false data.

And then there are misleading statistics—numbers that are true but that do not prove what the speaker claims. For example, you may have heard the advertisement that "four out of five dentists surveyed" endorse a certain brand of gum. All you know for sure is that five dentists were surveyed—not 50 dentists, not 500, not 5,000. Because these dentists may not be typical of the entire population of dentists, their answers may not provide accurate information.

Oversimplifying the Issue

When speakers oversimplify the issue, they twist the truth by presenting too narrow a range of possibilities. For example:

> Here, we have a clear-cut choice between a plan that will result in international catastrophe or a plan that will result in a thriving economy both at home and abroad.

Can two sides of an issue really be that clear-cut? It seems unlikely. Unless the speaker can back up the assertion with convincing details, the audience is likely to shake its collective head in disbelief. The argument is not valid.

A Little Latin

Post hoc ergo propter hoc is Latin for "After this, therefore because of this." It is the mistake of confusing *after* with *because*. Look at the following example:

> During the board of directors' term of office, the value of common stock has declined 25 percent; preferred stock declined by 15 percent. Should we reappoint people who cannot manage our money?

The fact that the value of the stock declined *after* the board of directors took office does not mean that it happened *because* they were in office. In order to prove that the board of directors are responsible for the dip in the stock, the speaker must show that the events are linked by a cause-and-effect relationship.

Reasoning Backward

This logic fallacy assumes that people belong to a group because they have characteristics in common with that group. Therefore, it assumes that anyone with those characteristics is a member of that group. Study this example:

> Democrats are always proposing tax increases. Governor Harriman is proposing a tax increase. From this we can conclude that Governor Harriman is a Democrat.

Clearly, people other than Democrats have proposed tax increases. This ploy comes up a lot when public officials seek re-election in a tough year.

The Least You Need to Know

➤ Effective persuasive speeches rely on appeals to logic, emotion, and trust.

➤ Assertions should be backed up with carefully researched facts, details, examples, and statistics.

➤ Facts matter: Use them to make your persuasive speeches really persuade. You can find great facts in text and electronic sources.

➤ Only use sources that are high-quality, free from bias, and appropriate.

➤ Errors in logic can destroy an argument. Logic fallacies include begging the question, bogus claims, false analogies, loaded terms, misrepresentation, over-simplifying the issue, confusing "after" with "because", and reasoning backward.

Chapter 11

The Life of the Party: Speaking to Entertain

In This Chapter

➤ What *entertaining* means

➤ Organizational patterns

➤ Research techniques

➤ Happy talk

➤ Entertaining speeches and social cohesion

A panda walked into a restaurant and ordered a sandwich and a drink. When he finished, the panda pulled out a pistol and shot up the place, scaring customers and breaking dishes, glasses, and liquor bottles before turning to leave.

Shocked, the manager said, "Hey, what are you doing?"

The panda glanced back over his shoulder and said, "I'm a panda—look it up," before disappearing out the door.

The bartender pulled out a dictionary and thumbed through it until he found an entry for "panda." The definition read: "A tree-dwelling animal of Asian origin characterized by distinct black-and-white markings. Eats shoots and leaves."

Not all speeches deal with "big," serious issues. In fact, many speeches are designed to be entertaining and ceremonial. These presentations occur at club meetings, dinners, parties, graduations, awards ceremonies, holidays, and ribbon cuttings—all our social rituals. Knowing how to give a good entertaining speech is a key element in your public and personal life.

In Chapter 8, "Types of Speeches," you learned that speeches that entertain do more than entertain: They also create social cohesion by generating good feelings. In this chapter, you'll learn the skills you need to speak effectively at a ceremonial occasion.

Playing the Crowd

Speeches that entertain are not the same as talks that inform or persuade. For one, speeches that entertain are usually much shorter than the other two types of speeches. In addition, they often take a more personal approach.

Class Act

Speeches that entertain can have a more immediate effect on your life than speeches with a more serious, lofty tone and purpose. That's because social occasions often present rich opportunities for you to score points with the audience. Those "points" are often cashed in for money for worthy causes and goodwill with business contacts and influential acquaintances.

Always start your entertaining speech by assessing your audience. This is crucial because on these occasions, your listeners are not there to learn or be convinced: They're gathered to have a good time. Think about what topic and content will ensure that the audience gets what they came for. Consider their likes and dislikes. Reflect on their level of sophistication.

Here are your big three considerations:

➤ Audience

➤ Occasion

➤ Purpose

Developing a Clear, Central Theme

Select a theme that suits the occasion and audience. Go for a theme that's novel, provocative, and original. (Not too novel, provocative, and original, though—you want to entertain, not shock.) Remember, the easiest way to stay awake during an after-dinner speech is to deliver it.

Look back over the information in Chapter 7, "Getting to Know You: Audience Analysis," for ways to slant your topic to suit your listeners.

Even when your main purpose is to be entertaining, you should still include at least one serious idea in your speech. Why? A speech that is all fluff can sometimes become tiresome and vacuous.

Remember that you want your audience to have a good time. You can't encourage other people to enjoy themselves unless you're a happy camper yourself. So, it should be plain to your audience that you're having a good time at that particular moment. Your topic should be genial, good-natured and suited to you, the audience, and the occasion. It should be a topic that you like speaking about. Finally, the overall theme of your speech should have three additional characteristics:

➤ **Optimistic.** This is not the time to share your personal problems, paint a gloomy picture of the present, or offer dire predictions for the future. Keep it light.

➤ **Uncomplicated.** Remember, people have come to be entertained. Don't make your audience strain to get your point. Develop your speech around one or two points that they can easily grasp.

➤ **Enlivened with anecdotes.** Avoid stale, familiar jokes. I recommend humorous anecdotes drawn from your own experience, about the guest of honor, or concerning the purpose of the speech. For example, a colleague once gave a very funny speech about me by parodying my spring/summer/winter/fall allergies. Every other anecdote was accompanied by a blast of sneezes and a flurry of tissues.

Speech of the Devil

While the interjection of a serious note in an entertaining speech can serve as a much-needed anchor, the seriousness should never be allowed to dominate. Keep the purpose of your speech firmly in mind: to entertain.

What about humor? If you're very comfortable with humor, go for it. Otherwise, consider taking a much simpler but equally effective course to win laughs: Play it straight. Sometimes, the best way to tell a joke is to tell it seriously. (Hey, works for me. You, too, can use this approach to get a laugh while maintaining your cool.) This is the technique Jack Benny made famous and Kelsey Grammer recycles so effectively.

Class Act

Unless you are very skilled at wordplay, don't comment on your own jokes; instead, let one story flow naturally into the other.

Doing the Heavy Lifting

A juggler driving to a performance was stopped by a policeman. "What are those knives doing in your car?" asked the officer.

"I juggle them in my act."

"Oh yeah?" said the cop. "Let's see you do it."

The juggler began tossing and juggling the knives.

A guy driving by saw this and said, "Wow, am I glad I quit drinking. Look at the test they're making you do now!"

A speech that entertains can be organized in a number of ways, so you'll have to do a little juggling to find the way that works best for your purpose and audience. Here are two methods that have proven to be especially useful to novice public speakers:

Speech of the Devil

Satirizing the host, a special guest, or any other person in attendance can be a great way to open a speech—if it's done with taste and tact. It's never acceptable to be mean, vicious, or embarrassing. Judge the room's comfort zone, and stay well within it. If you have any doubt, go with a personal anecdote, a reference to the occasion or news event, or a joke.

Method 1: Point and Proof

The *point and proof method* means that your speech is made up of a central idea supported by a series of examples, anecdotes, or amusing stories. This method of development not only entertains your audience, but also makes it easier for them to remember the main points of your speech. To create an effective point and proof speech, follow these steps:

➤ Open with an anecdote, preferably an amusing one.

➤ Explain the point of the anecdote. Describe how your speech will be organized around this point.

➤ Illustrate your point with additional anecdotes, each building on the central point. Remember to spread your stories evenly throughout your speech so the really good stuff isn't all bunched in the beginning, middle, or end.

➤ Close your speech by restating your central point. Then tell a great story to ensure a smash ending.

Method 2: Spoof Point and Proof

This method of organization lampoons the point and proof method:

➤ Start by relating an anecdote, referring to the occasion, alluding to a recent amusing event, or poking fun at the host.

➤ Present a serious problem and exaggerate it beyond all sense of proportion.

➤ Offer a ridiculous solution, illustrating it with a series of humorous anecdotes.

➤ Close your speech by lampooning an absurd call for action, telling a story to show the irony of your argument, or summarizing the silly steps of your solution.

See Chapter 13, "Getting Organized," for additional guidelines for organizing entertaining speeches.

Get the Facts!

Now it's time to gather your supporting material—examples, details, anecdotes, and jokes—that help you make your point. Think of this step as trimming your Christmas tree: The supporting material adds glitter to a solid frame.

You should always gather more material than you think you will need. It's also important to vary the supporting material you select: Your speech writing will be much less arduous if you have ample material from which to choose. Keep in mind that it's not unlikely that what looked like a sure laugh-getter while you were researching turns out to be a dud when you're writing. If you've limited your research, you might find that you don't have enough additional material when you need it.

Besides, speech writers are a thrifty lot; you'll find that any extra material, like leftover Thanksgiving turkey, rarely goes to waste. Put it in your speech-writing freezer or folder. That way, you'll have a stock of items to draw on the next time you're asked to give an entertaining speech.

As you're researching, don't panic about organization (yet). Instead, jot down the following information:

➤ Facts about the sponsoring group.

➤ Anecdotes from news stories, TV, radio.

➤ Events from fact or fiction.

➤ Good, non-offensive jokes. Always err on the side of caution: Never insult anyone.

Then zero in on the specifics. Get statistics, quotations, names, dates, and places. Ask yourself the following questions to make sure you've been thorough:

Did I look at high-interest newspapers? (Don't shun those supermarket tabloids: They contain some great stories that are perfect for entertaining speeches. Even some of the headlines can work, such as "Headless Body Found in Topless Bar.")

Did I look at family, club, or the organization's photo albums for ideas for anecdotes?

Did I skim magazines that match the audience's interests for information on the topic?

Did I call friends for information? How about audience members?

Are there any other sources I can use?

Speech of the Devil

Irony is the most difficult form of humor to carry off; all too often audiences take it seriously. Before you use irony, be sure that your audience will understand that you're being ironic.

Now it's time to make sure you know what *not* to do:

➤ Don't start your research until you have your purpose and message firmed up.

➤ Don't ignore what you already know about a topic.

➤ Don't hesitate to ask for help from research librarians and experts.

➤ Don't limit your research to similar sources, such as only newspapers or only magazines.

➤ Don't use out-of-date materials, even if they are easier to get than more reliable and timely sources.

➤ Don't write down everything indiscriminately. Pick and choose: You want only the information that's relevant to your purpose and audience.

➤ Don't write down anything you don't understand.

➤ Don't record any key piece of information without making sure that it's true. Check all crucial facts in two reliable sources.

➤ Don't write down incomplete citations. Be sure to record the author, title, date, and page number with each source. You may need it later.

Share and Share Alike

Speeches that entertain often focus on experiences that the speaker shares with the audience and guest of honor. These speeches are most successful when the speaker relates anecdotes that help the audience tap into common events.

For example, imagine that you're speaking at a retirement dinner for a colleague. If you've already retired, you can relate some of the things that the guest of honor can now share with you. If you've yet to reach that blissful (or so I'm told) stage of life, you might recall shared work experiences, such as the time the guest of honor got stuck in the snowbank trying to dig your car out of a drift.

If you're speaking at a wedding, you might want to recall your own wedding. If you're presenting an award, share some positive anecdotes about the recipient; if you're cutting the ribbon at the new library, remind the community of how people pitched in to make the dream a reality.

Class Act

Speakers often memorize entertaining speeches to make sure that the show runs smoothly.

Making Happy Talk

Whether your purpose is to entertain at a roast, toast the bride and groom, or honor a worthy award-winner, speeches that entertain build good feelings. People attend these functions to affirm their commitment to their family, service group, country, religion, or community. You can create a feel-good situation in several ways, without resorting to flowers, candy, or winning lottery tickets. Let's look at some of these techniques.

The You-Attitude

Adopting the "you-attitude" means looking at events from the audience's perspective rather than from just your own viewpoint. Using the you-attitude helps you craft an entertaining speech that delivers what the audience expects and that also respects their intelligence.

To use this method, imagine that you are sitting in the audience. What would you like to hear? What would you not want to hear? Rather than considering only what you want to say, think about what the audience wants to hear, and what the occasion requires. After all, the purpose of your speech is to entertain, not to instruct or persuade. This is the time to leave your ol' soapbox home and just concentrate on making people feel good. (This is especially important if you think the meal will be inedible instead of merely indigestible!)

Tug the Heart Strings

Another effective way to forge good feelings is through emotional appeals. This technique is a nifty way to reinforce values and unity.

An appeal to emotion reinforces the audience's identification with you by tapping the values and interests that you share. Become one of them rather than the sage on the stage.

Finally, keep your speech short (and sweet). Nothing spoils an entertaining speech like time. Make your point, illustrate your point, and summarize your point. You can generally deliver a good entertaining speech in about 10 minutes.

The Least You Need to Know

➤ Speeches that entertain must be closely linked to the audience's needs and wants.

➤ Develop a clear thesis and method of organization for these speeches.

➤ "Entertaining" doesn't necessarily mean that you have to be humorous; avoid humor unless you're comfortable with it.

➤ Do thorough, careful research; there's no substitute for hard work.

➤ Build goodwill with the you–attitude and emotional appeals.

Part 3
Writing Your Speech

Once upon a time, when writing styles were more formal than they are now, some people were very careful never to end a sentence with a preposition. Even then, however, there were stylistic mavericks who let their prepositions fall with abandon.

Winston Churchill was one of these people. His secretary, appalled, always revised the drafts of Churchill's speeches to avoid ending sentences with a preposition. Exasperated, Churchill finally sent this message to his secretary: "This is the sort of English up with which I will not put!"

Let the writing begin!

Chapter 12

Whose Speech Is It, Anyway?: Speech Style

In This Chapter

➤ Diction and word choice

➤ Tone

➤ Clichés, euphemisms, and jargon

➤ Sexist language

➤ Figures of speech: images, similes, metaphors, hyperbole, and personification

➤ Writing style and your speaking style

Four guys from Idaho, Iowa, New York, and Florida were on a cross-country road trip together. The car had been on the road for about two hours when the man from Idaho rolled down his window and began tossing potatoes from his bag out of the car. The guy from Florida asked, "What the heck are you doing?"

"We have way too many potatoes in Idaho," he replied, "and this is a great way to get rid of some."

After another hour passed, the Iowan rolled down his window, opened his duffel bag, and began tossing out ears of corn. The New Yorker asked, "Now what the heck are you doing?"

The Iowan replied, "Well, we have far too much corn in Iowa, so I figured this would be a great chance to get rid of some of it."

About two hours later, the Floridian rolled down his window and tossed out the man from New York.

When it comes to writing a speech, never throw *anything* out the window. Just because you can't use something in the speech you have to write this very minute, doesn't mean you won't want to use it in the speech you have to write tomorrow.

In this chapter, you'll learn how to write a winning speech. The following sections show you how to select the words that most accurately convey your meaning, suit your personal speaking style, and mesh with the audience and occasion. You'll discover that using words well depends on making good choices. I'll show you the advantages of using language that's simple, accurate, and appropriate. Sometimes the choices are clearly right or wrong; other times, the choices are more subtle. As you'll find out, awareness of your purpose, audience, and situation will influence your choice of words.

Speech of the Devil

Give yourself and your audience a break: Keep the sentences short. Long, complex sentences are hard to read. There's more chance that you'll trip over long sentences, lose their rhythm and pacing, and make a hash out of the whole speech. Long sentences are also more difficult for the audience to follow.

Words and More Words

A university creative writing class was asked to write a concise essay containing the following four elements:

➤ Religion

➤ Royalty

➤ Sex

➤ Mystery

The prize-winning essay read: "My God," said the Queen. "I'm pregnant. I wonder who did it."

It's best to get your point across quickly and simply right off the bat. The building blocks of all speeches are words. *Diction* is word choice. One of the most frequent questions I'm asked in my speech classes is, "Shouldn't I use long words to impress my audience? Won't I seem smarter if I use a lot of hard words?" Well, there's no doubt that some of those 25-cent words are appealing—they can make even the finest stylist act like a kid in a candy shop. So many words, so little time!

It *is* tempting to show off your vocabulary, but your point as a public speaker is to communicate a message. Pick the words that best convey your meaning. When people read, they have the time to study the words and think about them. Because listening is an oral skill, however, people can't go back to pick up something they didn't catch the first time. As a result, you should select the easier word over the more difficult one.

Talk Soup

Diction is a writer or speaker's choice of words.

Easy on the Ears

If your listeners have to work to figure out what you're saying, chances are they will lose entire chunks of your speech. By the time they decipher one sentence, you'll be three ahead. Strive for clarity, not complexity. Read over the following examples:

Hard to Understand	Easier to Understand
Precipitous	Steep
Mellifluous	Golden, mellow
Euphonious	Musical
Loquacious	Talkative
Thespian	Actor
Machiavellian	Cunning
Quahog	Clam
Salubrious	Healthy
Badinage	Joking
Obsequious	Humble

For informal speeches, use an everyday level of diction, with standard vocabulary, conventional sentence structure, and contractions. Eulogies, commencement addresses, and other formal speeches call for formal language: long, complex words; complex figures of speech; and few contractions.

To the Point

Instead of puffing up your words, give specific details, facts, and examples that prove your point. Set out the statistics that people can use as benchmarks. If you want to prove that speed-skater Bonnie Blair is an extraordinary athlete, for example, dazzle your audience with the facts:

Class Act

The fastest way to discover whether you'll trip over a word or whether a sentence is too long is to read aloud what you wrote. After all, if you can't say it smoothly, the audience won't understand it easily.

> Bonnie Blair blasted the competition off the ice in the 1994 Winter Olympics at Lillehammer, Norway. Blair won gold medals in both the 500-meter and the 1,000-meter speed-skating races, giving her a career total of five gold medals. That's one more medal than any American woman has ever won in an Olympics—winter or summer. Only speed-skater Eric Heiden, the hero of the Lake Placid Winter Games in 1980, has brought home as much winter gold for the United States.

Talk Soup

The **tone** is your attitude toward your subject and audience.

Hone the Tone

Your choice of words affects the tone of your speech. *Tone* is your attitude toward your subject and audience. Your tone can be formal, informal, or somewhere in between. Different tones are appropriate for different occasions, audiences, and purposes.

An informal tone, for example, is well suited to a brief speech at a birthday party; a formal tone, in contrast, would be more appropriate for a commencement address or a speech at a stockholders' meeting.

No matter what tone you adopt for your speech, it's not a bad idea to downplay your own importance in the Great Chain of Being. You can almost always score a few points with a little humility, while arrogance and smugness rarely play well. And try to avoid absolutes, which convey a black-and-white rigidity. Study the following chart for additional guidelines.

Alternatives for Words That Could Make You Seem Rigid or Smug

Words to Avoid	Words to Use
Always	Sometimes
Invariably	Occasionally
Constantly	From time to time
Forever	Now and then
Never	Occasionally
Never again	Once in a while
At no time	Seldom
In no way	Rarely
Certainly	Likely
Assuredly	Reasonably
Without fail	Potentially
Positively	At times
Unconditionally	At intervals
Absolutely	Not infrequently

Avoid Clichés Like the Plague

Strive to craft fresh, new phrases. As a general rule, try to stay away from *clichés*—phrases that are so shopworn that they have lost their capacity to communicate with impact. If you've heard these phrases over and over again, you can bet your audience has, too.

Here are some clichés to avoid like the plague. (That's our first one.)

➤ Dead as a doornail

➤ Gentle as a lamb

➤ Sweet as sugar

➤ Tough as nails

➤ Straight as an arrow

➤ Ripe old age

➤ Raining cats and dogs

➤ Face the music

➤ Happily ever after

➤ Hard as nails

Speech of the Devil

When you're talking to a group of fashion mavens, the difference between burgundy, crimson, scarlet, carmine, cerise, fuchsia, and cranberry matters. When you're addressing a general audience, *red* will do the trick nicely.

Sometimes, however, clichés can work for you. People tend to like to hear familiar ideas and sentiments sprinkled among new ideas, like sugar on berries.

Clichés can be an asset, if you use them cleverly. But for a cliché to work, it can't be used in its tired, old way. Instead, manipulate the cliché to make it work for you. Take the cliché "The business of America is business," for instance. (Even dinosaurs were probably sick of this one.) To give the cliché new life, try this:

> Calvin Coolidge once said that the business of America is business. That may have been true in his day, but today, the business of America is minding everyone else's business.

Avoid Euphemisms

A *euphemism* is a nice way of saying something that might offend your listener. For example, rather than saying that a student is a lazy lump, we say he is "not working up to his capacity" or is "working below his potential."

Talk Soup

A **euphemism** is a mild, agreeable phrase substituted for one thought to be offensive or harsh.

113

Euphemisms are sometimes necessary for tact in social situations. For example, most people find it more comfortable to offer condolences by saying "I'm sorry that your dog *passed away*" rather than "I'm sorry that your dog died." The euphemism "passed away" cushions the uneasy situation.

Out with the Euphemisms, In with Plain English

Euphemisms	Clear English
He came within the venue of the law enforcement establishment.	He was arrested.
Her occupation is domestic engineering.	She is a homemaker.
She announced that she was in favor of terminating the employment of the computer engineer.	She wanted to fire the computer engineer.

Talk Soup

Jargon is the specialized language of a particular organization, occupation, or group.

Avoid Jargon

Jargon is the specialized language of a particular organization, occupation, or group. Using jargon is a bad idea when it comes to speech-making because people outside your organization are not likely to understand it. All occupations have their own jargon. The following chart gives some examples of jargon from different professions or hobbies.

Jargon from Different Areas of Expertise

Stamp Collecting	Computer	Speech
Adhesives	RAM	Articulation
Sidebar	Bit	Phonation
Glassine	Chip	Resonance
Commens	Hacker	Dysphonias
Definitives	Hard copy	Aphasia
Mint	Floppy	Phoneme
Hinged	Program	Aphesis
Reprints	Windows	Apheresis
Covers	Virus	Phonic

As you draft your speech, consider your purpose and audience to decide whether a word or phrase is indeed jargon. For example, an audience of baseball fans will easily understand a speaker who refers to "RBIs," "ERAs," and "homers," but those words are jargon to an audience not familiar with baseball. They may even have a different meaning in the jargon of another group.

For example, "ERA" would refer to the Equal Rights Amendment in the jargon of the National Organization of Women. The computer jargon "virus," "program," "chip," "bit," and "floppy" also have other meanings.

Avoid Sexist Language, Baby

Sexist language assigns roles or characteristics to people on the basis of gender. The term was originally used to refer to practices that discriminated against women. Now, the term *sexist language* also includes any usage that unfairly limits the aspirations or capabilities of either sex. Read over the guidelines that follow:

➤ Avoid outdated stereotypes such as "Men are terrible housekeepers," or "Women are bad drivers."

➤ Do not describe women by their looks, age, or clothing—unless you do the same for men.

➤ Do not use a wife's first name and a husband's last name.

No: Mr. Green and his wife, Amanda

Yes: Chet Green and his wife, Amanda; or Chet and Amanda Green.

➤ Do not use the word "girls" to refer to adult women. Use the word "women" instead.

➤ Avoid using the masculine pronoun to refer to males and females together. Use a pair of pronouns, or recast the sentence into the plural form.

Class Act

English is an unusual language in that it comes from two main language families, Latinate and Germanic. Over time, the two vocabularies began to merge. Even today, hundreds of years after modern English developed, words often retain traces of their origins: German-based words tend to be shorter, more direct, more blunt, while Latin-based words tend to be long and scientific.

Speech of the Devil

In most cases, it's a good idea to avoid slang and regional expressions. Slang—words such as "rad", "deadhead," "groovy," and "neat"—pass out of usage quickly and can make your speech not only confusing, but also dated. Regional expressions consist of words particular to a specific region, such as "grinder," "poorboy," "hero," or "sub" (these are all used for a cold cut sandwich). As with slang, regional expressions can confuse your listeners.

No: An electrician cannot afford to make mistakes in *his* job.

Yes: An electrician cannot afford to make mistakes in *his or her* job.

Yes: Electricians cannot afford to make mistakes in *their* jobs.

➤ Avoid the use of "man" when women and men are both included. Try to use gender-neutral words such as "people," "humanity," and "humankind."

No: *Man* does not live by bread alone.

Yes: *People* do not live by bread alone.

➤ Avoid expressions that demean one gender.

No: Career girl, gal Friday, male nurse, lady doctor, lady lawyer

Yes: Professional woman, assistant, nurse, doctor, lawyer

➤ Avoid expressions that exclude one sex.

No: A man-sized meal, old wives' tale, the common man, mankind

Yes: A huge meal, superstition, the average person, humanity

➤ Avoid stereotyping occupations by gender when men and women are included.

No: Businessman, mailman, policeman, chairman, stewardess

Yes: Business executive, postal carrier, police officer, chair or chairperson, flight attendant

You also want to avoid racist language or language based on ethnicity. For example, the term "gypped" comes from "gypsy." As a result, "gypped" is highly offensive to gypsies because it implies that they are thieves.

Go Figure

Figures of speech (also called figurative language) are words and expressions not meant to be taken literally. Figurative language uses words in new ways to appeal to the imagination. These expressions create comparisons and connections that use one idea or image to enhance or explain another. This can make your speech especially memorable—even quotable. Figures of speech include images, similes, metaphors, hyperbole, and personification.

Illustrate with Images

An *image* is a word that appeals to one or more of our five senses. Imagery can be found in all sorts of writing, but it is most common in poetry. Imagery is important in speech because it can make your address memorable by telegraphing meaning. A memorable image can stay in your mind long after you have forgotten the rest of the speech. If you can get pictures floating through people's minds, your speech will be the one they remember.

A striking image transforms a ho-hum address into an unforgettable experience. A case in point is former President George Bush's image of "a thousand points of light" for the spirit of volunteerism. The image produced an emotional response, fulfilling the popular politician's tendency to inspire.

Here's a longer example from Martin Luther King, Jr.'s famous "I Have a Dream" speech:

> I have a dream today that one day in the state of Alabama, whose governor's lips are presently dripping with the words of interposition and nullification, will be transformed into a situation where little black boys and black girls will be able to join hands with little white boys and white girls and walk together as sisters and brothers.
>
> I have a dream today that one day every valley shall be exalted, every hill and mountain shall be made low, the rough places will be made plains, and the crooked places will be made straight....

In 1963, when this speech was delivered, it presented a waterfall of images that were within a vast audience's grasp. Many count this as the most powerful speech in their memory.

Speechmakers in any realm—business, politics, and private life, to name just a few—can apply imagery to their speeches. To find images that you can use, look at the usefulness of your topic or commodity. Trace the subject from the producer to the consumer.

Dare to Compare with Similes and Metaphors

A *simile* is a figure of speech that compares two unlike things. Similes use the words "like" or "as" to make the comparison: "A dream put off dries up like a raisin in the sun" is an example of a simile.

A *metaphor* is also a figure of speech that compares two unlike things. However, metaphors do not use the words "like" or "as" to make the comparison: "The rush-hour traffic bled out of all the city's major arteries" is a metaphor.

Hyperbole (or Overstatement) and Personification

Hyperbole is exaggeration used for a literary effect such as emphasis, drama, or humor: "If I don't get this report in on time, my boss will kill me."

Class Act

Many speakers select an important phrase from their speech and use it as a refrain. This technique is called *repetition*. If you have an important point to make, don't try to be subtle or clever: Whack the audience in the head with your mallet of repetition! Repetition makes a speech resonate, which makes it easier to remember and thus more significant.

Personification is giving human traits to nonhuman things: "This speech begged to be given." Hyperbole and personification are like spice: A little goes a long way in making a speech delicious.

Throw Out the Rule Book: A Look at Grammar

Ever have your knuckles smartly rapped because you had broken one of the cardinal Rules of Writing such as "Never use contractions in formal writing"? Fortunately for those of us who are still massaging our knuckles, a lot of these rules don't apply to speechwriting. Contractions make your speech sound more natural. Feel free to cut out all the contractions in your speech—but be ready to have it collapse under the weight of its own pomposity.

When writing your speech, it's best to capture the rhythms of spoken English. This means that you can throw out these old formal writing rules:

➤ Never use contractions in formal writing.

➤ Never end a sentence with a preposition.

➤ Never use clipped words (such as "till" for "until").

➤ Never interchange "which" and "that."

➤ Never split an infinitive. (For example, "To boldly go where no one has gone before." "To go boldly…" sounds silly.

You're always better off if your speech accommodates your natural speech patterns. (Notice that I snuck in the contraction "you're.") This is because we're most at ease when we are speaking in our normal voice, with normal speech patterns. Words and grammatical constructions that are unfamiliar are hard for speakers to deal with, even with a lot of rehearsal time.

A Final Word: Be True to Yourself

Writing and delivering a speech is especially difficult if the subject of your speech has nothing to do with your business, hobbies, or interests. For example, you may be asked to give a speech for the groundbreaking for the new dog-racing track, when you've never even owned a dog.

Why are you on the top of everyone's dance card? Maybe you look good in a suit, have a great voice, or come cheap. Whatever the reason, don't sell yourself short. You don't have to resort to greeting-card sentiments to fill the allotted time. And by all means, remember to avoid such shopworn clichés as "Do the right thing" and "Tomorrow is the first day of the rest of your life."

You don't have to pretend to be Oprah, Phil, or even Father Flanagan from *Boys' Town*. Think about what makes you important: your wisdom, common sense, and experience.

They asked *you* to speak because, know it or not, you earned it. Do keep in mind that, generally speaking, your speech will be better if it deals with concrete stories, exam-ples, and illustrations that make sense coming from your mouth. And your speech will be even better if you use natural language, brief sentences, and vivid figures of speech. You're going to do just fine!

The Least You Need to Know

➤ Select the words and level of diction that suit the audience, purpose, and occasion.

➤ Use the appropriate tone.

➤ Avoid clichés, euphemisms, jargon, and sexist language.

➤ Include colorful figures of speech and repetition.

➤ Match your words to your personality. Remember, "To thine own self be true."

Chapter 13

Getting Organized

In This Chapter

➤ Speech length

➤ The "20-Minute" rule

➤ Methods of organizing your speech

➤ Supporting material

➤ Ideas and emphasis

➤ Model speech

A woman requested that an artist paint her in the nude.

"No" he said. "I don't do that sort of thing."

"I'll increase your fee two times," she said.

"No, no thanks!"

"I'll give five times as much as you normally get."

"Okay," said the artist, "but you have to let me at least wear my socks—I need somewhere to hold my brushes."

Organization is important, no doubt about it.

Every time you make a speech, you want your audience to think about what you're saying as you say it. You want them to process the message by considering your main idea and its supporting points. And you want your speech to be memorable, too. In order to help your audience understand your points and recall them with clarity and pleasure, you need to organize your speech into a recognizable and easy-to-follow pattern.

In this chapter, you first learn about time limits. How long is an effective speech? Then you'll learn how to analyze different organizational patterns. Next, we'll discuss how to select the organizational pattern that suits your purpose, audience, and occasion. This chapter takes you through the process of organizing a topic, step-by-step.

Time Marches On

William Henry Harrison's inaugural address in 1841 was 9,000 words long. It took two full hours to deliver, and it was a freezing day. Harrison came down with pneumonia and died a month later. The moral of the story? The speaker who plans to go on for hours should not only have a mighty good speech, but should deliver it where it's warm.

Abraham Lincoln was once asked how long he thought a man's legs should be. "Long enough to reach the ground," he answered. How long should your speech be? Long enough to "reach the ground"—in other words, to accomplish what it intends. For example, Lincoln's Gettysburg Address—recognized as one of the finest speeches of all time—is a mere 265 words long.

Less is More

Once during a meeting, I was on my way back from the restroom when I ran into another member of the audience. Wondering whether it was a good time to go back into the room where the speaker was talking, I asked, "Has the speaker finished?"

"Yes," my colleague replied, "but he's still talking."

When deciding how long to speak, your first consideration should be how much time you are allocated—and you often don't have much control over this. Whatever length of time you're given, you're always better off going *under* the time limit rather than over.

Cheat on the short side—you're usually doing your audience a favor: The only thing worse than listening to a bad speech is listening to a long, bad speech.

Hello, I Came to Say I Cannot Stay

Few people resent a good, brief speech, but almost everyone resents having their time wasted. With speech, long does not equal better. If you've successfully communicated up to three points, you've done well. If you try to get too many points across, it's possible (in fact, probable) that your audience won't remember any of them clearly.

In fact, a great way to undo the effects of a barn-storming speech is to exceed your allotted time or to keep on talking after you've said your piece.

The "20-Minute" Rule

Twenty minutes is a good benchmark for the average speech in honor of the average occasion. There are exceptions, of course. Obviously, a wedding speech should be much, much shorter, while the keynote address at the Democratic National Convention will likely run a tad longer (especially if you're using it as a career builder, as Bill Clinton tried in 1988). Clinton was widely criticized for the length of his speech.

Speech of the Devil

Remember: No matter how good your speech *is*—and no matter how well you speak—people get cranky sitting in those hard wooden chairs and listening, listening, listening.

Twenty minutes is fair to both you and the audience. Of course, if you need more time to make your point, don't be afraid to take it. Just make sure you feel confident that you really do need it.

Be Sincere, Be Brief, Be Seated

Listening to a speech is very different from reading one. Because your audience can't go back to your speech and review confusing parts, it's important for you to provide an especially clear organization and to repeat your central points. Every speech needs a beginning, a middle, and an end. The following three-part structure is simple—and, best of all, it works. If you use this organization, your speech will be clear, well-organized, and powerful.

Here's the way that I recommend that you break down a 20-minute speech:

➤ Tell 'em what you're going to tell 'em. In the first part of your speech, tell your audience what your themes and major points are. This should take 1–3 minutes. (See Chapter 15, "Start at the Very Beginning: A Very Good Place to Start.")

➤ Tell 'em. Illustrate all the points that support your theme. This should take about 15 minutes. (See Chapter 16, "Body Building.")

➤ Tell 'em what you told 'em. Recap. Allow 1–2 minutes. (See Chapter 17, "Are We There Yet?: Conclusions, Revisions, and Titles.")

Class Act

Think of the first 2 minutes of your speech as an audition: It's a 120-second sample that must convince your listeners that the remaining 20 minutes are worth their time and attention.

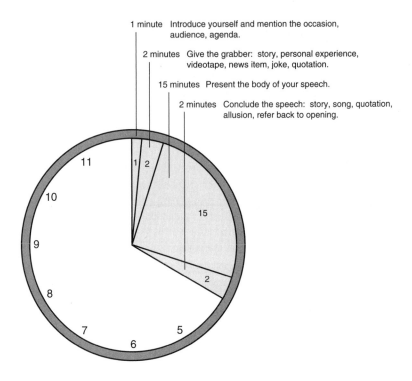

1 minute   Introduce yourself and mention the occasion, audience, agenda.

2 minutes   Give the grabber: story, personal experience, videotape, news item, joke, quotation.

15 minutes   Present the body of your speech.

2 minutes   Conclude the speech: story, song, quotation, allusion, refer back to opening.

Here's how to allocate your time during a 20-minute speech on any topic.

Another Look at Methods of Organization

Now let's turn to the body of the speech. As I explained earlier, there are different ways to organize your speech. Chapter 9, "Hear Ye, Hear Ye: Speaking to Inform," explained the organizational patterns most often used in informational speeches: alphabetical, cause and effect, chronological, numerical, problem-solution, spatial, and topical. At that time, I promised that I would discuss chronological order, problem-solution, and topical order in greater depth in this chapter—so, here they are.

Talk Soup

My definition of a good speech is one with a good beginning and a good ending—preferably close together.

Time Flies When You're Having Fun: Chronological Order

Chronological ordering works like this: Begin your speech at a certain time or date and move forward or backward. For example, you can discuss the development of the computer from 1970 to the present, or trace the methods of making plastic from start to finish. Here's the career of a colorful president arranged chronologically, for example:

The Political Career of Lyndon Baines Johnson

1. 1937, elected to Congress as a supporter of FDR.

2. 1948, elected to the Senate by a margin of 87 votes.

3. 1953, elected Senate Democratic leader.

4. 1960, lost presidential nomination to Kennedy; accepted vice-presidential spot.

5. 1963, sworn in as president after Kennedy's assassination.

6. 1964, elected president, defeating Barry Goldwater.

I Feel Your Pain: Problem-Solution Order

Sometimes, you'll want to first explain a problem with a specific situation and then offer a solution. For example, you might describe the problems with launching a new stock fund and then explain how your division can resolve these problems. Or, you might want to discuss declining blood reserves and then convince your listeners that they should participate in the company's blood drive. Here's a sample outline using problem-solution order:

Declining University Enrollment

Problems:

1. Fewer students in the region

2. Declining enrollment

3. Decreased revenue

Solutions:

1. Invite prospective students to visit campus

2. Increase advertising on television and radio

3. Place posters in high schools

4. Set up billboards on main roads

5. Establish chat rooms, a Web site, and an online admissions hot line

6. Increase scholarships

The Order of Subjects: Topical

You don't want your method of organization to be shopworn, but remember: Audiences are listening, not reading. Dividing your theme into familiar subtopics makes it easier for an audience to follow your logic. Here's how a topical speech on storms could be arranged, for example:

Storms

1. Thunderstorms

2. Hurricanes

3. Tornadoes

4. Tsunamis

5. Dust devils

Don't forget your audience! You want to make it easy for them to follow your logic. Your organizational pattern must be very apparent so they can clearly identify it. Your audience should not have to struggle to figure out what you're saying and where your speech is going.

But at the same time, your speech doesn't have to follow some boring old pattern. Instead, analyze your audience and topic to discover which pattern will help you make your point in a fresh, new way.

After you have decided on the best organizational pattern, the next step is deciding how to arrange the supporting information to maintain internal logic.

Class Act

Consider these three methods of organizing a speech in terms of your own specific theme, thesis, main points, and audience. For example, does your topic lend itself to the order of time, or would it be better served arranged by subjects? Make sure that you select the method that best helps you accomplish your purpose.

Be Supportive

There's an automotive tire dealer in town with the following motto painted in 2-foot letters on the store front: "If it's in stock, we've got it!"

You've got it, too. (And if not, you at least know where to get it.)

What's "*it*"? Supporting details, facts, and examples. Never make a point without supporting it with an example, detail, illustration, or some other form of proof. It's not enough just to include several subpoints under your main ideas. Instead, the way you use the supporting material helps create the strength of your argument, provide the information your audience needs, or give the humor or detail that makes your speech entertaining.

But you can't just set down a heap of facts. If every point in your discussion is given equal emphasis, nothing will stand out as significant. Stringing ideas together like beads is tiresome at best and confusing at worst. No matter how vivid your examples, your point will be lost unless your subpoints are correctly subordinated.

Laying the Foundation

To make your speech strong and logical, subordinate the following information:

➤ **Causes and effects.** As discussed in Chapter 9, causes and effects rarely occur individually. To clarify this relationship, list each cause and effect singly in order of importance. The most important causes of smoking, for example, might be listed as peer pressure, advertising campaigns, and an oral fixation. The most important effects might be listed as cancer, emphysema, loss of appetite, nervousness, and premature wrinkling.

➤ **Facts and examples.** What do you do with a series of facts and examples that back up your main idea? You can arrange them from most to least important, or least to most important. Or, you can put the best examples in the opening and closing of your speech.

➤ **Qualities or functions.** If you are writing an informative speech that describes an object or process, the supporting details describe how the object works or trace the steps in the process. For example, the purpose of a food processor can be described by explaining its slicing, shredding, and mixing blades. The production department of a major corporation can be illuminated by describing its functions.

➤ **Parts of a whole.** An example of parts of a whole is to discuss the modem, hard drive, floppy drives, and monitor as part of a computer; or, discuss the fabric, stitching, and finishing as part of a well-made suit.

Encores and Exits

Looking for facts and examples? Here are some useful business-related databases:

➤ **ABI/Inform:** Bibliographic information on most business-related subjects, including companies, products, and industries

➤ **F&S Plus Text International:** Information on international companies, products, and industries

➤ **Statistical Masterfile:** Index to statistical data published by the U.S. government, state governments, private companies, trade associations, and university research bureaus

➤ **ERIC (Educational Resources Information Center):** Citations and abstracts on educational research

---

Follow the Leader

Imagine that a mythical figure named Bob has been invited to speak before a rabid group of comic fans because he is a noted comic book collector with an enviable comic art and comic book collection. Bob read the first part of this chapter carefully, so he has already limited his speech to a brisk 20 minutes. His topic is, not surprisingly, comics.

After Bob does some research, he discovers that close to a ton of books exist on the subject of comics. He realizes that there's no way that he can explain everything there is to know about comics in 20 minutes, even if he speaks at super-speed like The Flash. Therefore, recalling what he already learned in this chapter about limiting his topic and remembering what he learned about analyzing his audience, Bob asks himself, "What will my audience most want to know about comics?" He decides to limit his talk to the history of comics. His narrowed topic becomes:

Comics: A brief review of their history from the 1930s to the 1990s.

Now Bob lists his points on paper to see how they can be organized. His list looks like this:

➤ Horror comics (1950s)

➤ The Golden Age of comics (1938–1950)

➤ The Marvel Age (1962–1980s)

➤ The Silver Age of comics (1952–1972)

➤ Direct market comics(1970s–present)

➤ Comics in the Mainstream (Batman, Richie Rich, Casper)

Class Act

Strong organization has another key benefit: It helps you remember what you planned to say, which is especially important if you're nervous.

The ideas are good, but there are still too many of them for a 20-minute speech. Also, there are some overlaps, especially with the Silver Age and the Marvel Age. Bob decides to combine the Silver Age with the Marvel Age to get rid of the overlap. Then he decides to delete horror comics and direct market comics to limit his topic.

Further, Bob notices that the ideas are not in any specific order that an audience could follow. Which method of organization is best suited to the topic? After looking over the list carefully, Bob decides to arrange his information in chronological order. Here's what his revised list looks like:

➤ The Golden Age of comics (1938–1950)

➤ The Silver Age of comics (1952–1972) and the Marvel Age (1962–1980s)

➤ Comics in the Mainstream (Batman, Richie Rich, Casper) (1980s–present)

Bob's next task will be to arrange his ideas into an outline. This is covered in Chapter 14, "Time to Outline."

The Least You Need to Know

➤ Everyday, garden-variety effective speeches usually run about 20 minutes.

➤ Speeches should have a clear beginning, middle, and end.

➤ Speeches should also have a clear method of organization.

➤ Three of the most common methods are chronological order, problem-solution, and topical order.

➤ Details, examples, and other back-up proofs must be subordinated to help the audience follow your main idea.

Chapter 14

Time to Outline

In This Chapter

➤ Reasons to outline

➤ Full-text outlines

➤ Key word outlines

➤ Note card outlines

➤ How to build an outline

➤ Sample outline templates

Three men die in a car crash and go to heaven for an orientation. They're all asked, "When you're in your casket and your friends and family are mourning you, what would you like to hear them say about you?

The first guy says, "I'd like to hear them say that I was a compassionate doctor and a great family man."

The second guy says, "I'd like to hear that I was a wonderful husband and teacher who made a huge difference in our children of tomorrow."

The last guy replies, "I'd like to hear them say...'Look, he's moving!'"

Want to get your speeches moving? Outlining will help you. There's no guarantee that a solid outline will solve all your speech problems (and help you lose that spare tire and bring about world peace), but a good outline *will* help you organize your thoughts in a logical manner. And that's a lot of the battle when it comes to speaking in public with confidence.

In earlier chapters, you learned how to develop and organize the ideas in your speech. This chapter explains how to take those ideas and arrange them in an outline to form the framework for a written speech. First, we'll discuss the importance of outlining for any kind of speech. Then we'll cover the different kinds of outlines. Finally, I'll share some tricks to help you prepare outlines quickly and easily.

What, Me Outline?

Why bother with an outline? Why not skip right to the speech-writing itself? There's a lot of good reasons to take the time to make an outline. And here they are:

➤ An outline shows you the entire structure of your speech. This enables you to see whether you've arranged main ideas and supporting details in the best possible way. It also helps you make sure that you have given each part of your speech enough emphasis.

➤ Outlines let you see at a glance if you've forgotten anything important.

➤ An outline helps you see clearly what you want to communicate to your audience. It's all neatly laid out for you to review.

➤ Reading your outline helps you memorize how your speech is organized. When you stand before your audience, you'll have a visual image of your speech's "bones." As a result, you'll have the confidence that comes with being well prepared. And more confidence means less stage fright.

Class Act

Like Spandex bike shorts, outlines have a startling ability to reveal deficiencies. Looking back over your outline might reveal that you have used only one kind of detail, for example, when you need a lot more.

How to Know a Good Outline When You See One

Of course, the amount of detail and arrangement of subtopics on your outline will depend on your topic, audience, and previous experience in public speaking. Often, novice speakers are more comfortable with fuller outlines; more experienced speakers go with pared-down versions. But even accomplished speakers will prepare a detailed outline when the audience and occasion demand it.

Three types of outlines are used for public speaking: The full-text outline, the key word outline, and the note card outline. Let's learn about them now, shall we?

Full-Text Outline

As its name suggests, the *full-text outline* is the complete speech in outline form. Each major idea and all supporting ideas are written out in complete sentences. This provides you with the full meaning of all ideas, as well as their relationship to other ideas. In addition, the sources for all research are included, either in the outline itself or in a Works Cited section in the back of the outline. This outline offers speakers a complete scaffolding for their speech.

Key Word Outline

In contrast, the *key word outline* provides trigger words rather than complete sentences. Every main idea and supporting detail is reduced to a key word or phrase that the speaker can remember more easily. Preparing and then skimming this type of outline can help you fix the structure and content of your speech firmly in your mind. While it does not offer as much detail as the full-content outline, it can be prepared in much less time.

Note Card Outline

You can also create an outline from your note cards. As you speak, you use your note cards as the outline. This type of outline works best in informal speaking situations that don't require a fully written speech. They're also well-suited for experienced speakers.

Outline Rules

On the road for one of his lecture tours, Mark Twain went into a barber shop.

"You picked a good time to come, stranger," the barber said. "Mark Twain's going to give a speech tonight. I suppose you'll go?"

"Oh, I guess so," Twain replied.

"Have you got a ticket?" the barber asked.

"Not yet," Twain said.

"Then you'll have to stand. Everything is sold out."

"How annoying," Twain sighed. "I never saw such luck! I always have to stand when that fellow gives a speech."

It's a good idea to know all the rules of outlining long before you're the one standing up there. Whether you prepare a full-content or a key word outline, all outlines must obey the following Official Outline Rules.

Speech of the Devil

For those rugged individualists who like to do things their own way, relax. The outline police won't get you if you don't use Roman numerals, capital letters, and cardinal numbers. You do, however, have to adopt a consistent set of numbers, letters, or symbols. Otherwise, you'll confuse yourself.

No Mix and Match: Use Uniform Letters and Numbers

Traditionally, the body of the speech is indicated by Roman numerals (I, II, III). Subheads are indicated by capital letters (A, B, C). Subdivisions under the subheads are shown by cardinal numbers (1, 2, 3).

Conventional outlines call for at least two entries at each outline level. For example, if you have Roman numeral I, you must have Roman numeral II; if you have an A under Roman numeral I, you must have a B. Follow this rule if you're going to turn in your outline for school credit. Otherwise, list only those headings, subheadings, and details that you need for your speech. Don't pad the outline just to satisfy a need for order.

As you study these sample outlines, notice that items of the same logical importance have the same letters and numbers throughout. I've followed the conventions of pairing entries, but you don't have to.

I. Main Head

    A. Subhead

    B. Subhead

    C. Subhead

        1. Subdivision

        2. Subdivision

        3. Subdivision

II. Main Head

    A. Subhead

    B. Subhead

    C. Subhead

        1. Subdivision

        2. Subdivision

        3. Subdivision

III. Main Head

    A. Subhead

        1. Subdivision

        2. Subdivision

    B. Subhead

        1. Subdivision

        2. Subdivision

    C. Subhead

I. Main Head

    A. Subhead

        1. Subdivision

        2. Subdivision

    B. Subhead

        1. Subdivision

        2. Subdivision

    C. Subhead

        1. Subdivision

        2. Subdivision

II. Main Head

    A. Subhead

        1. Subdivision

        2. Subdivision

        3. Subdivision

    B. Subhead

III. Main Head

    A. Subhead

    B. Subhead

    C. Subhead

Class Act

Use a capital I for the Roman Numeral 1, a capital V for the Roman Numeral 5, and a capital X for the Roman numeral 10.

Go Solo: Include Only One Idea Per Line

Put only one idea under each Roman numeral, capital letter, or number. Running multiple ideas together defeats the very purpose of the outline: to separate and differentiate ideas. Here's what I mean:

No-No

    I. Circumstances sometimes force people to live alone. Grown children leave the nest—they go to college, move to other cities to get jobs, or marry and move away to start families of their own.

Yes-Yes

I. Circumstances sometimes force people to live alone.

    A. Grown children leave the nest.

        1. They go to college.

        2. They move to other cities to get jobs.

        3. They marry and move away to start families of their own.

Now study this template:

Thesis statement:

I. First main idea

    A. First subordinating idea

        1. Reason or example

        2. Reason or example

    B. Second subordinating idea

        1. Reason or example

        2. Reason or example

Get Down: Subordinate Ideas Properly

It's not enough just to place each idea on its own line; the items listed as subordinate must actually *be* subordinate. This means that they must be less important in meaning, not of equal or even greater importance.

Further, ideas must be related logically. Outlines can't include subpoints unless they are directly linked to the main point under which they are placed. Here's an example:

No-No

I. Noise pollution comes from many sources.

    A. Music blasts into headphones.

    B. Music in clubs assaults the senses.

    C. Lawn mowers and leaf-blowers roar.

II. Jackhammers and other construction tools blast.

III. Noise pollution occurs in many large cities.

A. Noise pollution occurs during leisure time.

B. Radios blare.

C. Cars and buses honk their horns.

Yes-Yes

I. Noise pollution comes from many sources.

    A. Noise pollution occurs in many large cities.

        1. Jackhammers and other construction tools blast.

        2. Radios blare.

        3. Cars and buses honk their horns.

    B. Noise pollution occurs during leisure time.

        1. Music blasts into headphones.

        2. Music in clubs assaults the senses.

        3. Lawn mowers and leaf-blowers roar.

Speech of the Devil

Beware of following an outline *too* slavishly, for an outline can limit a writer's options. For example, an outline can prevent a writer from discovering the material's organic unity or from making choices that might improve the speech. An outline may also divert you from focusing on audience and purpose.

Indent Lines to Show the Relationship of Items

Each succeeding level of the outline should show more specific detail than the one before it. The more important an idea is, the closer it will be to the left margin. Traditionally, main ideas are flush left, subheads are indented 5 spaces, and subdivisions are indented 10 spaces. If an outline entry is longer than one line, the second line should be indented as far as the first word of the preceding line.

Study this template:

Thesis statement:

II. Main idea

    A. First subordinate idea

        1. Supporting evidence

        2. Supporting evidence

    B. Second subordinate idea

        1. Supporting evidence

        2. Supporting evidence

Encores and Exits

You can use computers to help you organize your research into a speech outline. All the major software companies have programs available that you can use to write outlines. They're nifty because they enable you to move ideas around quickly, resulting in better-organized speeches.

On the Straight and Narrow: Use Parallel Structure

Make all ideas grammatically parallel. This means that they should be in the same form, such as all phrases or all sentences. Further, all the phrases (or sentences) should be in the same form, such as all adjectives, all adverbs, or all gerunds (*-ing* forms). Here's what I mean:

No-No

      A. Using earplugs. (gerund)

      B. To avoid excessive noise. (infinitive)

Yes-Yes

      A. Using earplugs. (gerund)

      B. Avoiding excessive noise. (gerund)

Recipe for a Great Outline

Unlike Grandma's cooking, outlining is not a mysterious little bit of this and a pinch of that. Rather, outlining is an explicit process. Follow my recipe for a speech outline, and I guarantee great results every time!

➤ First write down your topic, purpose, audience, and audience attitude. For example:

Topic	Community's need for a library
Purpose	Persuasive
Audience	Civic association
Audience attitude	Antagonistic, unfriendly

➤ Then build the framework for your outline. The skeleton of your ideas begins with your topic and purpose. Keep these firmly in mind to guide you as you develop your outline.

Remember that the body of your speech will contain three main ideas, designated by Roman numerals. The main ideas will support the topic and purpose. Under each main head will be subheads, which relate to the main heads. Any subdivisions (1, 2, 3) under the subheads provide support. Here's a sample general structure:

    I. First main idea

        A. First subordinating idea

            1. Reason or example

            2. Reason or example

        B. Second subordinating idea

            1. Reason or example

            2. Reason or example

➤ Third, write each of the specific points you intend to cover. Study this model:

    I. Tennis is one of the best sports to play.

        A. Provides all-around exercise.

            1. Improve cardiovascular system.

            2. Build agility and stamina.

        B. Is enjoyable.

            1. Make new friends.

            2. Feel invigorated and refreshed.

➤ Finally, revise, reword, and rearrange your ideas. Go back over your outline to make sure that items are parallel and logical. See if every item is in the correct place and is subordinated properly. And make sure that you have sufficient support for each of the statements you have included.

The All-Purpose Outline

One size doesn't fit all when it comes to outlines—but in many instances it can come close. Below is a sample outline form. You can adapt it to suit the special needs of your audience, purpose, and thesis.

I. Introduction

    A. Grab your audience's attention.

    B. State your topic and purpose.

    C. Preview your speech.

II. Body

    A. State first main idea.

        1. Support

        2. Support

    B. State second main idea.

        1. Support

        2. Support

    C. State third main idea.

        1. Support

        2. Support

III. Conclusion

    A. Restate your main idea.

    B. Add a memorable conclusion.

See Appendix B for additional sample outlines.

The Least You Need to Know

➤ Outlining is an equal-opportunity skill: Any type of speech can—and should—be outlined.

➤ Outlining your speech is a crucial step in clarifying ideas.

➤ Full-text outlines describe the speech in complete sentences; key word outlines use important words and phrases to sketch the speech's contents.

➤ Outlines must use a consistent system of letters and numbers, subordinate ideas, and be in parallel grammatical form.

➤ Once you get the hang of it, outlines are not difficult to construct—and are well worth the time.

Chapter 15

Start at the Very Beginning, A Very Good Place to Start

In This Chapter

➤ Why the opening matters

➤ Open with a story

➤ Open with a question

➤ Open with a reference to the setting or occasion

➤ Open with a quotation

➤ Open with numbers—statistics or dates

➤ Open with media, such as video clips

➤ Open with humor

Are you like the mosquito at a nudist camp—you know what you ought to do, but you don't know where to begin? One of the questions I'm asked most often is, "How do I begin my speech?" In this chapter, you explore many different ways to get your speeches off to a great start. You'll also discover how to choose the method of introduction that best suits your audience, topic, purpose, and personal speaking style.

Hand-in-Glove: Intro and Speech

You can begin your speech in a number of ways. Whatever method you select, your opening should accomplish the following five tasks:

➤ Forge a bond with the audience.

➤ Establish credibility and goodwill.

➤ Create interest.

➤ Preview the speech by introducing your main points.

➤ "Hook" the audience by grabbing their attention.

Think about all the movies, television shows, and plays you've seen—they all open with a hook. The same is true of novels, short stories, and essays. And the same will be true of your speeches.

Before you write the introduction, put yourself on the other side of the lectern and think about what kind of opening would grab your attention. Would a brief anecdote do it? How about a question? A quotation? A joke? What suits your audience, purpose, and style? Let's start with the story opening.

Encores and Exits

If you're a recognized authority in your field, your reputation will automatically convey credibility. As long as your speech stays within the boundaries of your area of expertise, you're going to be trusted. If you're not recognized as an expert, the host should read off your credentials to establish your credibility.

If the host fails to share your credentials with the audience and they are important to the success of your speech, don't shy away from introducing yourself as part of your opening. Meet the situation head on by saying, "Let me tell you a little bit about myself"—and then do. This is going to mean that you'll have to adjust your prepared speech opening a little, but under certain circumstances, it's a must.

Story Time

Here's how a speaker at an insurance convention used a story to open a speech:

A patient makes an appointment to see a specialist. After a week of expensive tests, the patient gets the bill.

She rushes back to the specialist's office and screams, "Are you nuts? This bill is outrageous. There's no way I can pay this!"

The doctor replies, "Okay, so pay me half."

"Half? Half? I can't pay half!"

"Well," the doctor replies, "what amount can you pay?"

"Not a cent. I'm a poor, old woman."

The doctor let out a long sigh. "Why did you come to me, one of the most famous specialists in the country?"

"Listen, doc," the patient replies, "when it comes to my health, money is no object."

We Americans want the best health care that money can buy, but we are appalled when we get the bills. Unfortunately, these bills will only increase as the American population ages and medical tests become more complex.

(Not So) Trivial Pursuit

An off-shoot of the anecdote is the fact-ette, commonly called a *factoid*. It's that small bit of trivia that can maintain the audience's attention. *USA Today* is a great source of factoids. Here are a few that caught my eye recently (but remember, factoids have to suit the audience, purpose, tone, and your individual style).

Speech of the Devil

Never open with a fake smile and a throw-away slick line. Few things turn off an audience as quickly as a phoney-baloney opening.

➤ Lightning strikes the United States 40 million times each year.

➤ A lightning bolt has enough power—30 million volts—to light up all of New York City.

➤ The average thunderstorm is more powerful than an atomic bomb.

➤ Boris Karloff modeled his mummy face and costume in the film *The Mummy* after Ramses III.

Danger, Will Robinson

Everyone knows one really good anecdote, question, quotation, or joke stored up for just this occasion. So you've decided to take your great opening out and slap it down at the beginning of your speech. There's only one problem: It doesn't fit. It's just not right. What to do? Some speakers cram that sucker in anyway, twisting it to fit. Resist the temptation.

Class Act

News items make great openings. Keep an eye out for offbeat news stories, headlines, and other topical stories. But remember, like fish and house guests, topical news stories get old very quickly.

Clip-n-Save

Speakers in demand are constantly on the look-out for good anecdotes. The obsessive-compulsive crowd (of which I'm a charter member) keeps files of newspaper and magazine clippings, piles of photocopies, and notes from their reading. (In my defense, these files have come in handy more than once—who said all neuroses are bad?)

Join the clipping club! Start a story folder today. Cram it with clippings, and you'll have a good start for some of your speeches.

Asked and Answered

Would you like to join...

The German Philosophy Club?	I. Kant.
The Nixon Club?	Pardon me?
The Peter Pan Club?	Never. Never.
The Quarterback Club?	I'll pass.
The Compulsive Rhymers Club?	Okey-dokey.
The Pregnancy Club?	Conceivably.
The Procrastinator's Club?	Maybe next week.
The Self-Esteem Builders?	They wouldn't accept me.

One of the easiest and most effective ways to open a speech is with a question. People immediately begin to frame an answer, and then are likely to listen closely to your speech to see if their answer matches yours. Public speakers use this opening a lot because it works well. Effective questions often set up a mini-mystery and provide a personal touch. Here's how they do it.

Who Done It?

It's a good idea to open with a question that leaves the audience wondering what the answer is. Here's one that a motivational speaker used at a marketing seminar:

> "There's a buzz in this room, an electric charge in the air. I've spoken at a lot of meetings, and I'm never wrong about this. Can you feel the power? The high voltage excitement? What is it?"

The answer? "Conviction." In addition to pumping up the audience members, this opening also flattered them.

Personal Touch

Prodding the audience's ego right off the bat causes the audience to feel personally involved in your speech in a positive way. The audience members think, "Hey, this speaker is talking about me!"

Here's a personal opening tailored for a charity fund-raising event for a new hospital wing:

> "Can I trust you? Are you someone I can rely on to do the right thing? I know I can. Let me tell you why I need your trust now more than ever. It's a matter of life and death."

The most successful questions are tailored to the occasion. An expert on dieting opened her after-dinner speech with these questions: "How many calories do you think you've just eaten? How much fat? How much protein? Well, I'm going to tell you, and the real facts will amaze you." These questions grabbed the audience because they were specifically suited to the occasion. You can make your questions just as pertinent and interesting.

Greetings from the Home Team

Everyone likes to have a moment in the sun. And it's easy to make this part of your opening if you're speaking at an out-of-town event. I'm not talking about a rehash of the Chamber of Commerce pamphlet handed out at the drive-through hospitality window, but something more personal about the town. This is another version of the personal touch.

Isolate a handful of specific, representative, flattering things you have learned about the city, town, or community where you're delivering your speech. Follow these guidelines when doing your research:

➤ Read up on the town, especially in the local newspaper.

➤ Speak to people who live there. (Stop for a chat at the Blue Moose Diner.)

➤ Take a drive through the community to see what it's like.

Speech of the Devil

Be merciful when it comes to using a favorite story or a beloved quotation. Include it only if it precisely fits the audience, occasion, and purpose. If it doesn't, put it back in your folder for another day.

Then craft an opening to that shows you've taken the time to learn about your hosts and their community or organization. It will make all the difference—cross my heart.

You Could Look It Up

➤ "I'm not into working out. My philosophy: No pain, no pain." —Carol Leifer

➤ "The reason most people play golf is to wear clothes they would not be caught dead in otherwise." —Roger Simon

➤ "Anytime four New Yorkers get into a cab together without arguing, a bank robbery has just taken place." —Johnny Carson

➤ "I always wanted to be somebody, but I should have been more specific." —Lily Tomlin

Most speakers love quotations, but there is a vocal minority that won't open a speech with anything less than an original utterance. Ironically, the oft-quoted famous 19th-century American philosopher and minister Ralph Waldo Emerson was a member of the later crowd. "I hate quotations," he said. "Just tell me what you know."

Actress Marlene Dietrich, in contrast, was a standard-bearer for the quote crowd: "I love quotations because it is a joy to find thoughts one might have, beautifully expressed with much authority by someone recognizably wiser than oneself."

Controversy aside, it can be surprisingly comforting to let other people's words carry the opening of your message. Using an appropriate quote in a speech is like using good artwork in a book: It illustrates your point and grabs the audience's attention. Good quotations should be a standard part of your speech-making bag of tricks.

Quote with Class

Here are some pointers to follow when using quotations:

1. If you're quoting someone who is dead, make it clear in the speech that they are dead; that is, "In the words of the late Groucho Marx...."

2. Don't use quotations to show off what you know.

3. If you don't know how to pronounce the author of the quotation's name, don't fake it. Cop out instead. Try these lines: "A famous person once said..." or "An author once wrote..." or "It's been said that...."

4. Include context or background to make the quote more meaningful. Quotes are illuminated when the writer, date, or situation is included.

5. Quote correctly. Misquoting in the beginning of a speech shoots your credibility.

6. Be sure the quotation is relevant to what you're saying, appropriate to your audience, and fresh.

Words to Live By

When you select a quotation, remember your own personality and the impression you want to convey. Think about your audience, the subject, and the person you're quoting. To give the impression that you are the master of your material, draw quotations from material that it seems likely you would have read. (This also lessens the chance that you'll sound like a pompous fool.)

Class Act

Even if you abbreviate your notes rather than writing out the full text, be sure to write out completely any quotation that you are directly quoting. (Obviously, paraphrasing lets you off the hook.)

By now you've probably guessed that I'm an enthusiastic supporter of using quotations in the opening of a speech. But too many quotations are like too much of anything (except good-quality chocolate). You don't want your audience to spend most of your speech wondering if you actually read all the books, saw all the movies, and spoke to all the people you quote. Savvy audience members will check out your back pocket to see if that's where you hid your copy of *Bartlett's Familiar Quotations*. You want your audience to concentrate on you and your message. So think of quotes like garlic: A little goes a long way.

Looking for Quotes in All the Right Places

So where do you find good quotes? Obviously, the more you read, the more material you have to draw on.

Here are some suggestions for finding pithy quotations:

➤ Books of quotations and trivia, such as *The Guinness Book of World Records*, *The Trivia Encyclopedia*, and *199 Things Every American Should Know*

➤ Newspapers and magazines

➤ Television, especially "classic" 1950s shows

➤ Literature: short stories, essays, and novels

Speech of the Devil

Don't feel compelled to quote verbatim (the quote police won't come after you, I promise). Put the quote in your own words. Change words. Have a good time with the quote! You have to be careful, of course—not attributing a quote can be viewed as *plagiarism* (theft) in certain situations. To avoid plagiarizing, state that you're paraphrasing the quote before you attribute it to its author.

For example, you can say: "To paraphrase Kurt Vonnegut...."

➤ Witty friends with good memories

➤ Comic books and other popular literature

➤ TV and radio commercials

➤ Public personalities, living or not

Encores and Exits

Addressing a group of scholars and need some fancy quotes to open your speech? Here are some useful Latin phrases for the 1990s:

1. "Domino vobiscum." (The pizza guy's here.)

2. "Nucleo predicus dispella conducticus." (Remove foil before microwaving.)

3. "Bodicus mutilatimus, unemploymi forevercus." (Better take the nose ring out before the job interview.)

4. "Motorolus interruptus." (Hold on, I'm going into a tunnel.)

5. "Minutus cantorum, minutus balorum, minutus carborata descendum pantorum." (A little song, a little dance, a little seltzer down your pants.)

The Numbers Game

Did you know that...

➤ The total weight of all insects on Earth is 12 times greater than the weight of all people.

➤ A mosquito has 47 teeth.

➤ The average U.S. college or university student reads about 60,000 pages in four years.

➤ Because they are on opposite sides of the San Andreas fault, Los Angeles and San Francisco creep 2.5 inches closer together each year.

➤ There is enough stone in the Great Wall of China to build an 8-foot wall that circles the globe at the equator.

➤ Mailing an entire building has been illegal in the United States since 1916, when a man mailed a 40,000-ton brick house across Utah to avoid high freight rates.

As these examples show, you can also open your speeches with numbers, from statistics to dates. Here's how it's done.

Stats It!

Statistics mean numbers, but numbers are meaningless unless they are taken as part of a whole. This means you have to place the numbers in the context of something understandable to your audience. Your task is to cut and stitch them to fit the fabric of your speech. Never, never distort the numbers; instead, make them work to suit your audience and purpose.

Here are some example statistics from the *1995 Information Please Almanac* about traffic fatalities.

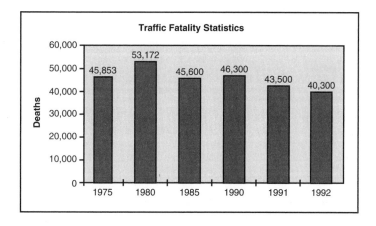

Well, that was depressing and dull. Can you imagine the reaction you would get if you started a speech that way? You would have to go from table to table, picking heads off plates. It's more interesting to rephrase the statistics this way: "Motor vehicle collisions cause one death every 13 minutes, and one injury every 14 seconds." That's better, but I'm still not jumping up and down to hear more, are you?

Here's how then-President Harry Truman used statistics successfully in 1947 to open a speech before a highway conference:

> When I was in the Senate...I found at that time more people had been killed in automobile accidents than had been killed in all the wars we had ever fought, beginning with the French and Indian War. This is a startling statement. More people have been permanently injured than were injured in both the world wars from the United States.

Truman put the numbers into a meaningful context. He used them to shock his audience into an awareness of the seriousness of the problem.

Date Night

You might try opening your speech by linking the date with the subject of your speech. Here's how one speaker used dates for this slight tongue-in-cheek opening for a review course for standardized college admissions tests:

> "Did you know that today is the 50th anniversary of the first standardized test? Yes, on this very day the Army administered a standardized test to sort its recruits. That was the only widespread standardized test that existed. Think how far we've come in only 50 years. Now we give these tests all the time. Now, don't you feel lucky?"

Speech of the Devil

For generations, speakers have opened their presentations with "Good evening, ladies and gentlemen." Openings like this are usually fluff. Unless you feel compelled to include it or you feel that your audience will be appalled by its absence, skip it and get right to the real opening of your speech.

How can you find these great dates? Look through reference books about great discoveries, publications, performances, wars, sports events, films, personalities, and culture. One of my all-time favorite sources is *Timetables of History*.

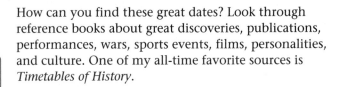

Sex, Lies, and Videotapes

If you have the resources, videotapes and other equally sophisticated audio-visual materials can make great openings. In this age of visual images, the old saying "A picture is worth a thousand words" is more valid than ever before. Clips from old movies make especially good openings. (Some speakers are uneasy about relying on visual aids because of possible technical problems, a problem that's covered in Chapter 25, "A Thousand Words: Visual Aids.")

Class Act

Sharing a personal experience, giving some biographical information, praising the audience, and using definitions are some other effective ways to open your speeches. Remember to pick the method that suits you, your audience, and your purpose.

Laugh In

Humor is an excellent way to relax both the audience and yourself. It serves to plunge your listeners right into the topic while simultaneously establishing instant rapport. Humor is also a nonthreatening way to get to a moral or lesson.

But if you decide to open with a joke, be very sure that it is appropriate to the occasion. Remember, few things are as painful as a joke poorly told. *Always* stay away from ethnic, racist, and religious jokes (no priests, rabbis, and ministers in rowboats, please). See Chapter 18, "Ever Hear the One About?: Using Humor," for a detailed discussion of using humor appropriately.

Whatever type of introduction you use, keep it short. After all, you're dealing with your introduction, not the body of your speech. The introduction or opening hook should be no more than 1–2 minutes long. That's allowing 1 minute for a formal greeting (if you must have one) and 2 minutes for the "grabber."

The Least You Need to Know

➤ Open your speech with a bang by using a method suitable to your audience, topic, and purpose.

➤ Possible openings include anecdotes, questions, a reference to the setting or occasion, and quotations.

➤ You can also use statistics or dates, media, or humor.

➤ Use an opening that fits your natural style.

Chapter 16

Body Building

In This Chapter

➤ How to allocate writing time

➤ The writing process

➤ Organization: alphabetical order, cause-effect, chronological order, numerical order, problem-solution, psychological needs, and spatial order

➤ Supporting information: anecdotes, comparisons and contrasts, examples, facts, statistics, and testimony

➤ Unity through transitions

➤ Keyboarding the speech

Someone once said that speeches are like steer horns: a point here, a point there, and a lot of bull in between.

Not mine—or yours! In this chapter, you'll learn all about making the body of your speech clear, powerful, and enjoyable. You'll also learn how to craft a forceful statement of your beliefs and personality.

This chapter starts with a description of the writing process. Then it explains how to select an organizational pattern that you think will best appeal to your audience, most clearly convey your ideas, and most successfully accomplish your purpose. Next, you'll learn how to flesh out this framework with effective details, examples, and support. Finally, you'll discover how to unify your ideas with transitions and other rhetorical devices.

Class Act

The body of your speech is the heart of your message. It's the burger in your bun and the cream in your cupcake.

Write Away

Graceful, logical speeches seem artless. As any good speech writer will tell you, in reality they are the result of great practice, attention to detail, and intense concentration. In other words, it's hard work.

If you're writing an informational speech, the body is where you provide the audience with facts. If you're writing a persuasive speech, the body is where you move your audience to action or belief. If you're writing an entertaining speech, the body is where you beguile, delight, and divert your listeners.

The body of your speech is the longest part of your talk. As a result, you'll most likely spend the most time writing it. I recommend that you write it first—before you write your introduction.

You Got the Time, I Got the Place

For best results, spend only about a third of your writing time actually writing. Spend the first third of your time analyzing your audience and purpose and researching back-up information. Spend the last third evaluating what you've written. Study this diagram for a more detailed description of time allocation.

If you have three hours to write your speech, divide your speech-writing time this way to maximize your efforts.

1. **1 hour**
   Analyze audience
   Analyze situation
   Consider purpose
   Research information
   Gather facts
   Organize information

2. **1 hour**
   Actually writing

3. **1 hour**
   Revise the speech
   Adjust to audience
   Adjust to purpose
   Check word choice
   Fix grammar errors
   Check typos

Write On

Let's take a closer look at the steps you should follow as you write your speech:

➤ **Preparing.** In this stage, formulate your topic, analyze your audience, define your purpose (to inform, persuade, or entertain), and think of ideas.

➤ **Getting it all together.** Here's where you physically gather all the material that you need. Do your research by hitting the books, the CD-ROMs, or the Internet. Talk to your sources. Select a method of organization and prepare your outline.

➤ **Writing.** Hammer out a formal first draft of your speech.

➤ **Evaluating.** Read your speech and think about what you wrote. Measure it against your audience and purpose. Is your speech informative? Convincing? Entertaining?

➤ **Getting Comments.** It's showtime. Recruit a willing participant or two, and have them read your speech. Don't be shy about asking for help; no doubt you'll soon be in a position to offer constructive criticism about the draft of a speech to the friend who read yours.

➤ **Revising.** Make the changes you need based on your evaluation or those suggested by your readers. Here's where you'll add, subtract, rearrange, revise, and reshape the speech to suit your needs.

➤ **Editing.** Check the speech to make sure that you used standard written English. Fix all spelling and writing errors. This is important even if no one else is going to read your speech. Why? Because it will help you make sure that you read and pronounce each word correctly.

➤ **Proofreading.** Check the final copy to make sure that there are no typos.

Tailored to Fit

Most likely, you won't be able to say everything you want to say because it just won't all fit in one speech. "But my topic is so important," you protest. "How can I not say it all?"

No doubt, your topic is important and you probably are very knowledgeable about it. After all, you've done a great deal of serious research about your topic, so you most likely know your stuff.

But recognize right from the start that you can't fit everything you want to say into the body of your speech: You have neither the time nor the room. And if you try, you'll end up getting very little of anything across to your listeners.

Speech of the Devil

Don't skip the editing and proofreading stages, no matter how pressed you are for time. Speeches are often reprinted in conference proceedings, posted on the Internet, and used in committees and companies. Who wants a sloppy speech circulated for others to read?

Instead of cramming your speech with everything you know about the topic, zero in on the audience, purpose, material, and key point (yes, that's singular) you want to make. If you focus on one central idea, your audience will be much more likely to get your point. No matter what your topic, you must limit, focus, and organize your material. Fortunately, there are many different ways to do this. Select the method that best suits your topic, purpose, audience, and personal speaking style. These guidelines will help:

➤ Select the major point of your speech.

➤ Arrange your supporting information in a logical manner.

➤ State your thesis in a simple sentence.

➤ Make your point clear with explanations, details, facts, and examples.

➤ Restate the idea you have explained.

Now take a closer look at some of the most common organizational speech patterns.

Class Act

If at all possible, show how the method of organization you have selected directly relates to your audience's life. For example, if you're using chronological order, you might illustrate how the historical changes you describe directly affect the quality of life for your audience. Or, if you're using numerical order, link the numbers to key social and political events, such as the Great Depression, World War II, and Kennedy's assassination. That will make the events important to your listeners.

It's as Simple as A, B, C

Don't dismiss alphabetical order because it's too simple and clear. Simple and clear are very good in speeches. This method works especially well with individual points, such as the names of people, places, and things. Besides, there are times that alphabetical order is the only logical and effective way to arrange your information.

Cause-Effect

Use this organizational style when you're tracing the reasons why something happened and what happened as a result. For instance, did you start a community program with something specific in mind that produced clear results?

Suppose that you secured a federal grant to establish a summer Youth Council program. The program offers free athletic, educational, and enrichment programs to the kids in your area. As a result of your efforts, 100 kids are involved in a six-week theater program; 300 kids in summer sports; and 75 kids in computer, writing, and science classes.

Explain the effects: helping children by reducing the number of latch-key kids, and having fewer kids involved in accidents.

Time Travel

Here, you take the audience from the beginning to the end. This method is effective because it unifies and connects ideas. Explaining a process, tracing a historical event, and giving directions are all well suited for this organizational plan.

You Can Count on It

You can use numbers as transitions to walk the audience through your speech. You can go from the highest numbers to the lowest, or from the lowest numbers to the highest. Whichever way you order your numbers, stick to just a few of them, such as 1, 2, 3, or 1–5.

As explained in Chapter 13, "Getting Organized," follow this general format: "Tell 'em what you're going to tell 'em; tell 'em; and then tell 'em what you told 'em." This means that you'll likely announce something like: "There are three stages to my plan. Let me present them one at a time. First...."

Problem-Solution

In this way of approaching a speech, you start with the questions and move to the answers. For instance, is there a problem with the shipping procedure used in your company? First explain the problem and then offer one or more solutions. If you have multiple solutions, offer them from least effective to most effective. Always try to finish with your best shot—it will be what your audience remembers.

Also, don't hide the problems. Speak with honesty. Odds are, your audience is already aware of the problems, so hiding them could damage your credibility.

Speech of the Devil

If you say the word *first*, you have to say *second*; otherwise, you're leaving your audience dangling. If you announce that there will be three steps, be sure to say one, two, and three. Otherwise, your audience will confuse your point.

Let's say your company faces a serious problem, and you've been selected to speak about it. Here's how to structure a problem-solution speech that addresses this situation:

➤ Start by presenting some facts that show how serious the problem is. Let the facts speak for themselves: Don't underplay or overplay them.

➤ Discuss possible ways to solve the crisis. For example, you might propose limited layoffs, benefit givebacks, or increased hours.

➤ Invite audience members to suggest other solutions. Make it clear that everyone must pull together for any solution to work.

Gas, Food, Lodging

Another way to organize your speech is according to the psychological needs of your audience. What issue concerns them the most? Place that issue first. What issue concerns them least? Cover that issue last.

You can also start with the issue the audience finds the most acceptable and work toward the issues they find least acceptable. This will help you establish credibility and win over your audience early on—before you have to deal with thorny topics that are apt to spark resentment.

Assume you are a labor leader addressing management. There's apt to be more than a little resistance to your point of view. As a result, you should open your speech with the point that's likely to cause the least resentment, such as a comment about the high quality of the product.

Class Act

The psychological method of organization requires the most thorough audience analysis. Consider where your audience stands on the issues. Start with common ground and move to differences of opinion.

Map It Out

Spatial order is geographical order: east to west, north to south, right to left, up to down. For example, say that you have to give a speech to evaluate the success of your hospital's outpatient program. You can arrange the facts region by region and area by area. Or, you might survey the district from the northernmost point to the southernmost point. Discussing a shipping plan? Arrange the speech according to the route that a delivery truck might take.

Cast and Crew

Where do you find a no-legged dog?

Right where you left him.

Where do you find the information you need to support your points? Read on to find out.

But first, remember this: The supporting material in your speech proves the accuracy of your statements, illustrates points of interest, or entertains the audience. You'll use these verbal supports to reinforce and clarify your statements. This is how you build understanding and audience support.

Once Upon a Time

Anecdotes are brief narratives, stories, or verbal illustrations that provide vivid support for your point. These stories can be drawn from personal experience, the experience of others, or your reading and research. If you have more than one anecdote, be sure to distribute them throughout the body of the speech so that the really good stuff isn't grouped in the beginning, middle, or end.

Comparisons and Contrasts

A *comparison* points out the similarities between something that is already known and something that is not. A *contrast* shows the differences between two things. Comparisons and contrasts illuminate the unknown. For example, a speaker can explain the unfamiliar game of cricket to Americans by comparing and contrasting it to a familiar American game: baseball.

Because comparisons and contrasts draw a judgment based on a single instance, it must be a valid analogy to be believable. The two objects being compared must be closely alike in all essential respects. The question you must ask yourself is, "Do the similarities between the items outweigh any differences that might be important to the conclusion I am trying to draw?"

Examples

An *example* is a type of support in which you state several specific, brief instances or facts. It recounts an incident that brings out the point you're making. Sometimes an example describes a typical instance; in other times, it depicts an actual situation.

There are two main types of examples: *factual* and *hypothetical*. The former tells what *actually* happened; the latter, what *could* happen. To be convincing, a hypothetical example must make sense and match the facts. Hypothetical examples make abstract explanations more vivid and specific, and they're especially useful in explaining a complicated plan. Instead of just outlining the details, you can create a hypothetical situation and trace the process.

Speech of the Devil

Never make a major point in a speech without presenting at least one form of support to clarify, illustrate, or support it. The substance of what you say rests in the examples, details, facts, and testimony you include. The most powerful speeches use a combination of sources, including these:

➤ Anecdotes

➤ Comparisons and contrasts

➤ Examples

➤ Facts

➤ Statistics

➤ Testimonies by authorities

Often, one or more of these forms of support are combined, as when anecdotes are used to provide examples or when facts are added to personal experience.

Class Act

Break down a major topic into its components or subtopics. For instance, health care can be subdivided into types and costs. Discuss each topic in turn.

Facts

Facts are statements that can be proven. Factual examples describe situations that have actually happened. Facts make for a particularly effective means of support because they cannot be easily refuted. The incident becomes vivid to the audience; because it is true, it has great persuasive power.

Furthermore, facts create credibility. They help convince your audience that you know what you're saying and that you deserve to be taken seriously.

Consider these points when selecting facts:

➤ Is the fact clearly related to the main point of the speech?

➤ Is the fact a fair example? Select representative facts and examples; details drawn from left field have little power because they are anomalies.

➤ Is the fact vivid and impressive?

Figure It Out

Not all figures are statistics; some are just numbers. *Statistics* are numbers that show comparison or the relationship between ideas and things. They point out how something gets larger or smaller and illustrate how one circumstance affects another. Statistics impress an audience because they back up your claims. Take a look at some examples:

➤ Today, about 60 percent of first marriages end in divorce.

➤ According to the most recent statistics, the median age at a first marriage for women is 24.1; for men, 26.3.

➤ In 1970, the federal government collected $195,722,096 in taxes; by 1998, the number had jumped to $1,176,685,625 collected.

Source: 1998 Information Please, Almanac

Like your mother-in-law, a little statistic goes a long way. Masses of figures are difficult for an audience to understand, so follow these guidelines when using statistics as support:

➤ Round figures off to make them easier to understand.

➤ Slow down when you present statistics. Emphasize the importance of the numbers by your voice and gestures.

➤ Copy the statistics onto handouts, or present them on overhead projectors.

Speech of the Devil

In order to maintain your credibility, you must be sure that the statistics you cite are accurate. Consult only reputable, up-to-date, recognized sources, such as the latest almanacs, government documents, or statistical abstracts. Also cite the source of your statistics in your speech to build an even stronger credibility.

➤ If you saturate your speech with too many statistics, you're likely to lose your audience.

Order in the Court!

You may wish to cite another person's opinions to reinforce your point of view. When a speaker cites the opinions of others word-for-word or nearly verbatim, it's called *testimony*. Testimony can clarify an idea or supply proof.

To be most effective, testimony should come from a recognized expert or authority. It's not enough that you know the authority—the audience must recognize the person as well. Also, if the testimony is overly influenced by personal interests, it will appear prejudiced and weaken your credibility.

As you present testimony, state the person's name and qualifications so that your audience can be sure of the authority's specific expertise in the subject area.

Class Act

Be sure to present statistics in terms that your audience can grasp. For example, saying "At 525 feet tall, the new Union Hall will be the largest building in the area," is virtually meaningless. To give the statistic meaning, compare it to something the audience can grasp: "The new Union Hall will be as tall as the Washington Monument."

Go with the Flow: Transitions

No matter which method you use, make sure that your ideas are arranged logically and smoothly. As you move from one point to the next, give your listeners some clear toeholds so they can easily follow your points. Information that may seem evident to you may be muddy to your audience; leaps of logic that appear perfectly reasonable when you wrote them may leave your audience stranded in mid-air.

Never *assume* that your audience will see the connections that you see between arguments, facts, and anecdotes. Lead your audience from point to point, example to example, and issue to issue. Your goal is to create your conclusions for your audience.

A speech is logical and coherent when its sentences and ideas are related to each other. You typically make decisions about coherence after you write the first draft of your speech, when you begin to see how the ideas fit together. One of the best ways to make it easy for your audience to follow your points is to include *transitions*—words and phrases that signal how ideas are connected. Each transition shows a specific relationship between ideas. The following chart lists different kinds of transitions you can use to convey different kinds of relationships between ideas.

Talk Soup

Transitions are words, phrases, and sentences that link related ideas and parts of a speech.

Transitions to Link Your Ideas

Relationship	Transitions
Place	At the side, adjacent, nearby, in the distance, here, there, in the front, in the foreground, in the back, in the background
Summary	In brief, in conclusion, finally, on the whole, as a result, hence, in short
Result	Therefore, thus, consequently, so, accordingly, due to this
Time	Meanwhile, subsequently, immediately, at length, eventually, in the future, currently, before, soon, later, during, first, second, third, next, then, finally, afterward
Concession	Of course, to be sure, certainly, naturally, granted
Contrast	On the other hand, but, yet, however, nevertheless, nonetheless, conversely, in contrast, on the contrary, still, at the same time
Comparison	Similarly, likewise, in like manner, in the same way, in comparison
Example	For example, for instance, thus, as an illustration, namely, specifically
Addition	Also, in addition to, moreover, and, besides, further, furthermore, equally important, next, then, finally

Class Act

You can also link ideas by using (1) deliberate repetition, (2) parallel structure, and (3) pronouns. Deliberate repetition deals with selecting a key word related to the main idea and repeating it at important points to help the listeners follow your ideas. Parallel structure is matching grammatical forms. And using pronouns that clearly refer to nouns helps your listeners follow the bridges you build between sentences.

Getting It on Paper

Let's briefly focus on the mechanics of getting your speech on paper. I recommend that you type your speeches to reduce the chances that you will misread your handwriting.

As you type, follow the accepted rules of capitalization: Capitalize proper nouns, proper adjectives, and the first word in a sentence or direct quotation. Avoid typing your speech in all capital letters: Capital letters can make your speech confusing to read by giving you the impression that you're delivering a telegram.

Use at least a 12-point font to make your speech easy to read. Select a clear, standard font, such as Courier or Times New Roman, and avoid elaborate fonts.

You should also leave at least 3 inches blank on the bottom of the paper. That way, you won't be forced to lean your head all the way down to your chest to read the paper and thus muffle your voice. In addition, leave generous margins—at least 2 inches—on the top and sides. This helps keep your head focused straight ahead at your audience. And be sure to number the pages to keep the order clear!

The Least You Need to Know

➤ Savvy speechwriters make effective use of their time by dividing their task into three parts: planning, writing, and revising.

➤ Like a good undergarment, a method of organization supports the whole speech. Pick the method of organization that suits your purpose, audience, and material.

➤ Don't skimp on the details, examples, statistics, facts, and other back-up information. That's what makes your point or entertains your audience.

➤ Use transitions and other rhetorical devices to create unity and coherence.

➤ Be complete, but exhaust neither the topic nor the audience.

Chapter 17

Are We There Yet?: Conclusions, Revisions, and Titles

In This Chapter

➤ Techniques for drawing your ideas to a satisfactory close

➤ Appeal, illustration, inducement, quotation, and summary

➤ Order of composition

➤ Reading and revising

➤ Memorable titles

An engineer had an exceptional gift for fixing all things mechanical. After serving his company loyally for over 30 years, he happily retired.

Several years later, his company had a seemingly impossible problem with one of their multimillion-dollar machines. In desperation, they called on the retired engineer who had solved so many of their problems in the past.

The engineer reluctantly took the challenge. He spent a day studying the huge machine. At the end of the day, he marked a small "x" in chalk on a particular component of the machine and said, "Here's your problem." The part was replaced and the machine worked perfectly again.

The company received a bill for $50,000 from the engineer for his service. They demanded an itemized accounting of his charges. The engineer responded briefly:

One chalk mark $1

Knowing where to put it $49,999

Your conclusion may be the only part of your speech that people remember, so it's crucial that you make it memorable—in other words, put the "x" in the right spot. And as with every other part of your speech, writing a good conclusion requires a lot of effort.

In this chapter, you'll learn how to end a speech with power and assurance. You'll also see how revising and editing can help you avoid making mistakes during showtime. Finally, you'll learn how to select a suitable—and memorable—title.

End Game

A conclusion has three main goals:

➤ To restate the main points you made in your speech

➤ To focus on your desired response

➤ To leave the audience with a sense of completion

Let's take a look at each purpose in detail.

To be effective, the ending of your speech should make your point clearly and forcefully. To do so, it often sums up the individual subpoints you've made in the body of your speech. The summary can hammer home your point, or it can be more subtle—but it *must* reinforce the purpose of your speech.

Class Act

One way to make sure that your conclusion is focused is to read your thesis statement aloud. Then think of your conclusion as the thesis in more emphatic words. To give your conclusion the proper emphasis, consider using parallel structure, repetition, and brief, forceful words.

At the same time, your conclusion should leave your audience with the feelings you want them to have. For example, if you're giving a persuasive speech, you want your audience to be cheering for your ideas when you finish talking. If you want your audience to think deeply about what you said, your conclusion should leave them in a calm, reflective mood.

Of course, the conclusion also should convey a feeling of finality. Your words must give the audience the sense that your speech is over. Few things annoy an audience as much as a false ending. Sensing that the speech is coming to a close, the audience begins to gather up its psychological and physical belongings, only to find that the speaker has taken a deep breath and started anew. False endings cheat the audience and destroy much of the effect of a speech. An effective conclusion ties together all the strands of your speech while telegraphing to the audience that the end is indeed in sight.

Some of the most practical methods you can use to end your speeches involve the use of these elements:

➤ Appeal

➤ Illustration

➤ Inducement

➤ Quotation

➤ Summary

It's rare that these methods are used in isolation: Adept speechwriters often combine two or more methods. For example, quotation works extremely well with summary and appeal; an inducement is sometimes prefaced with a summary. Nonetheless, the following sections present these methods one at a time. That way you'll be able to pick out the specific elements of each conclusion. However, notice that some of the examples do indeed combine methods—just as you will, if they serve your purpose and audience.

Help Me, Rhonda: Using Appeal

Using the appeal technique allows the speaker to directly remind the audience of its responsibilities to take action or to follow a specific belief. To be successful, the appeal must be powerful and commanding. Folded within it should be the main ideas that support the reason why the appeal is valid.

Here's how the famous abolitionist William Lloyd Garrison ended his 1831 appeal to abolish slavery. Notice that he gives his listeners a specific direction to follow by describing exactly what he wants them to think and do. Garrison uses strong, biblical diction to marshal the forces of right on his side.

> **Speech of the Devil**
>
> Remember that your speech is being written to be heard, not read, so write for the ear, not the eye. Speech is straightforward and conversational, so it calls for short, familiar words, active verbs, personal pronouns, contractions, and subject-verb-object order. You can even use incomplete sentences if they convey your meaning well.

> What then is to be done? Friends of the slave, the question is not whether by our efforts we can abolish slavery, speedily, or remotely—for duty is ours, the result is with God; but whether we will go with the multitude to do evil, sell our birthright for a mess of pottage, cease to cry aloud and spare not, and remain in Babylon when the command of God is "Come out of her, my people, that ye may not be partakers of her sins, and that ye receive not her plagues." Let us stand in our lot, "and have done all, to stand." At least, a remnant shall be saved. Living or dying, defeated or victorious, be it ours to exclaim, "No compromise with slavery! Liberty for each, for all, forever! Man above all institutions!

Picture Perfect: Using Illustration

An *illustration* is a detailed example of the idea or statement you're supporting in your speech. When you give an illustration, you're recounting an incident to make a point. To be effective, the illustration must be vivid and memorable. Recall that illustrations can be true or hypothetical. (True illustrations are called *facts*.)

Just as you can open your speech with an illustration, you also can close with one. The following surrender speech by Chief Joseph, leader of the Nez Perce Indians, is a quietly eloquent illustration of the need for peace. In 1877, a dispute between the Native American tribe and the federal government erupted into war. Hoping to join forces with the Sioux, Chief Joseph led his people on a long march from Oregon to Canada. The tribe was heavily outnumbered by government troops; on October 5, Chief Joseph was forced to surrender.

The speech centers on the factual illustration of his tribe's situation. Notice the powerful effect of the repetition, parallel structure, and simple words. The speech is reprinted below in its entirety. Notice especially how the conclusion uses an illustration of the fate of his people.

> Tell General Howard I know his heart. What he has told me before, I have in my heart. I am tired of fighting. Our chiefs are killed. Looking Glass is dead. Toohoolhoolzote is dead. The old men are dead. It is the young men who say yes or no. He who led on the young men is dead. It is cold, and we have no blankets. The little children are freezing to death. My people, some of them, have run away to the hills and have no blankets, no food; no one knows where they are—perhaps freezing to death. I want to have time to look for my children and see how many I can find. Maybe I shall find them among the dead. Hear me, my chiefs. I am tired; my heart is sick and sad. From where the sun now stands, I will fight no more forever.

Class Act

Read your speech aloud as you revise and edit to hear—as well as see—any rough spots that need polishing.

Might Makes Right: Using Inducement

You can also conclude a speech by revisiting the key ideas and then supplying one or two additional examples for accepting the belief or taking the action you proposed.

See how the writer of the following speech combines summary and added inducement to urge the use of mandatory air bags in cars.

In conclusion, there is no doubt that air bags save lives and prevent serious injuries. The Johnson/Juarez study I cited earlier demonstrates the effectiveness of airbags in sharply reducing vehicular casualties and injuries. In addition, the cost of including them in all cars is minimal. Further, having airbags in your car may reduce your insurance costs. The only argument that can be raised against air bags is their cost, which shows how casual many people are about their safety and survival. Even if you're willing to take chances with your own life, you owe this additional safety to your family. Only buy cars that come with airbags, and insist that car manufacturers install them in all cars.

What's the Good Word? Using Quotations

Quotations are another good way to end a speech—but they only work if the quotation directly relates to the main points that you made in your speech. A quotation can be direct or slightly paraphrased.

This method is notably effective if you opened your speech with a quotation. Matching the opening and closing format gives your speech unity and cohesion. It also subtly serves to remind your audience of your opening points.

Following is the entire text of the speech Justice Oliver Wendell Holmes wrote for his 90th birthday tribute. Holmes delivered the speech over the radio on March 7, 1931. Notice the effectiveness of the quotations.

Talk Soup

An **inducement** is an incentive to sway a person to act or think in a certain way.

In this symposium my part is only to sit in silence. To express one's feelings as the end draws near is too intimate a task.

But I may mention one thought that comes to me as a listener-in. The riders in a race do not stop short when they reach the goal. There is time to hear the kind voices of friends and say to oneself, 'The work is done.' But just as one says that, the answer comes: 'The race is over, but the work never is done while the power to work remains. The canter that brings you to a standstill need not be only coming to rest. It cannot be, while you still live. For to live is to function. That is all there is to living.'

And so I end with a line from a Latin poet who uttered the message more than 1,500 years ago: 'Death plucks my ear and says, Live—I am coming.

The Grand Finale: Using Summary

In this method of ending a speech, the speaker reviews the main points of the speech and draws conclusions from them. This type of ending is especially well-suited to the informative speech because it helps remind your listeners of your argument's main points. It also works very well with a persuasive speech because it allows you one last chance to go over the main arguments you presented.

Following is an excerpt from the speech that playwright-dissident Vaclava Havel delivered when he became president of Czechoslovakia. Havel gave this speech when he assumed office on New Year's Day 1990. Notice how he reiterates the most important elements of his speech in his conclusion. See if you can tell from this conclusion whether Havel is speaking more to inform or persuade.

> In conclusion, I would like to say that I want to be a president who will speak less and work more. To be a president who will not only look out the windows of his airplane, but who will always be among his fellow citizens and listen to them attentively.
>
> You may ask what kind of republic I dream of. Let me reply: I dream of a republic that is independent, free, and democratic; a republic with economic prosperity yet social justice; a humane republic that serves the individual and therefore hopes that the individual will serve it in turn; a republic of well-rounded people, because without such people, it is impossible to solve any of our problems, whether they be human, economic, ecological, social, or political.

Class Act

Craft your conclusion with words that convey strength. Use memorable imagery, words, and phrases that appeal to the senses. Also use *alliteration*, the repetition of initial consonant sounds. Abraham Lincoln used alliteration in the opening line of "The Gettysburg Address": He repeated the initial "f" three times: "Four score and seven years ago our fathers brought forth on this continent...."

Body Shop: Matching the Conclusion to the Speech

If you write your opening and closing first, chances are they won't be an integral part of your speech. On the other hand, by writing the introduction and conclusion after you write the body, your speech will be much more cohesive and logical.

For a brief speech, start with a catchy opening that refers to your topic. In the body, present all the supporting information. Close with a challenge, summary, or appeal. With a longer speech, you may wish to start with a less direct opening, such as a quotation. After you develop your main idea, close with the same method you used in the opening. The structure of the body remains the same, but the introduction and conclusion have been dovetailed to your audience, purpose, and subject.

Reading and Revising

As you learned in Chapter 16, "Body Building," the three final stages in writing your speech are revising, editing, and proofreading.

➤ Revising entails adding, subtracting, and changing material in response to self- or outside evaluation.

➤ Editing involves checking for mechanical errors: spelling, punctuation, grammar, and usage. These are the errors that might make you slip up as you deliver the speech, or that might cause you embarrassment if the speech is later reprinted.

➤ Proofreading is the last step. Here's where you make sure that your speech is typed, printed, or written correctly. Remember to type the speech with upper- and lowercase letters, and triple-space the manuscript for ease of reading.

Crafting a Title

Speech titles have two purposes: They suggest the general contents of the speech while simultaneously grabbing the audience's attention. Think of the title as an advertisement. If successful, the title should make the listener want to hear more. A good title has these characteristics:

➤ Relevant

➤ Intriguing

➤ Brief

Speech of the Devil

Even if you are only going to use a small part of a quotation, always check the entire quotation—then double-check it! I once heard a story about a speaker who finished his address to a prominent public figure with two lines from John Dryden:

> A man so various he seemed to be
>
> No one but all mankind's epitome.

The honoree liked the conclusion so much that he went back to check the rest of the quote. Here's how it goes:

> Stiff in opinions, always in the wrong
>
> Was everything but starts and nothing long;
>
> But in the course of revolving moon
>
> Was chemist, fiddler, statesman and buffoon.

Relevant means timely or up-to-date. As a general rule, avoid recycling titles. Unless the fit is perfect, your speech will seem dated. Avoid last year's slang and local expressions that are apt to be misunderstood.

Intriguing means pleasantly puzzling. For example, if you're addressing a community group that's opposed to sidewalks being installed in the neighborhood, consider "A Walk on the Wild Side," "An Important Community Issue," or "The Issue of Sidewalks."

Encores and Exits

There's no magic bullet that works for all speech writers all the time. Nonetheless, effective speech writers are most likely to adopt these approaches:

➤ Accept that the first draft will have to be revised.

➤ Break their writing into manageable tasks.

➤ Focus clearly on audience and purpose.

➤ Seek feedback and weigh it carefully.

➤ Be flexible in their approach to writing.

Class Act

Write the title last, after you have finished the entire speech. Creating a title that is both intriguing and suitable will be easier after you have written the rest of the speech.

Brief means that the title must be punchy. The title should be as short and to the point as possible. Senator Margaret Chase Smith realized this when she called her speech against Senator Joseph McCarthy a "Declaration of Conscience." The only exception is scientific talks, for tradition demands that those speeches be prefaced by long, descriptive titles. It's a good idea to title your speech even if you think no one will ever see it, just to be in the habit and just in case you need one at the last minute.

The Least You Need to Know

➤ Powerful conclusions restate the main points you made in your speech, focus on your desired response, and leave the audience with a sense of completion.

➤ You can end a speech in several different ways. Select the method that best suits your audience and purpose.

➤ Time spent revising and editing is time well spent.

Chapter 18

Ever Hear the One About...?: Using Humor

In This Chapter

➤ When to use humor—and when not to

➤ Rules for using humor

➤ What makes a good joke

➤ How to find effective jokes

➤ Jokes that work

➤ Jokes that never work

A doctor made it his regular habit to stop off at a bar for a hazelnut daiquiri on his way home. The bartender knew of his habit, and would always have the drink waiting at precisely 5:03 p.m. One afternoon, as the end of the work day approached, the bartender was dismayed to find that he was out of hazelnut extract. Thinking quickly, he threw together a daiquiri made with hickory nuts and set it on the bar. The doctor came in at his regular time, took one sip of the drink and exclaimed, "This isn't a hazelnut daiquiri!"

"No, I'm sorry," replied the bartender, "it's a hickory daiquiri, doc."

The most popular way to begin a speech is with humor. That's because a good story entertains the audience. It convinces them that you're an everyday person, a person just like them—but with a good sense of humor. Experienced speakers know that the perfect comedic line can immediately get the audience on your side. The audience feels safe and relaxed; with one suitable joke, you've taken command.

However, the key word here is *suitable*. Few things are as dismal as a bad, tasteless, or otherwise unsuitable joke. Humor must be handled correctly for it to succeed. Furthermore, some jokes are right for some occasions and dead wrong for others. In this chapter, you'll learn how, when, and why you should use humor. We'll discuss jokes that work and those that don't, and we'll also cover how to match your natural speaking style to the demands of humor.

Laugh In

A woman's husband had been slipping in and out of a coma for several months. She stayed in his hospital room every day and every night. When her husband came to, he motioned for her to come nearer. As she sat by him, he said, "You know what? You have been with me all through the bad times. When I got fired, you were there to support me. When my business failed, you were there. When I got shot, you were by my side. When we lost the house, you gave me support. When my health started failing, you were still by my side. When I think about it now, I think you bring me bad luck!"

Humor is a key element in all but the most gloomy speeches and occasions. But you must consider your own natural style before you decide how much humor—and what kind—to use. Some people, like Jay Leno and David Letterman, are naturally funny and have great timing . Other people are not blessed with this gift.

The standards for humor also are rising. With comics like Robin Williams and Jim Carrey plying their trade, audiences have gotten used to great topical jokes that are perfectly delivered. Few of us are that talented, but there's no need to despair: The audience is on your side. People gathered to hear a speech are often already primed to enjoy themselves.

Speech of the Devil

Never insult your hosts or audience. A line like, "Could you sit up a little straighter, please? These jokes are going over your head," serves only to alienate your audience. Don't bite the hand that pays your fee!

Humor 101

Let's explore the basic rules of using humor in speeches.

➤ **Social conventions.** Jokes depend on a shared frame of reference. You and your listeners must understand the social background of the joke, or you'll fall flat.

➤ **Audience analysis.** The humor must fit the audience. Jokes that work with the Parent-Teacher Association likely won't crack up the annual shareholders' meeting.

➤ **Appropriateness.** Use humor only when it is appropriate. For example, you don't want to use too much humor when delivering a funeral eulogy or breaking the news about poor corporate performance.

➤ **Personal style.** The joke you tell must suit your specific style. Few women can pull off the tough personas of Rosie O'Donnell and Roseanne; button-downed stockbrokers generally shouldn't attempt to impersonate Rodney Dangerfield. Some comedians can work against type, but this requires years of practice.

➤ **Make a point.** When used effectively in a speech, humor does more than just entertain the audience, it makes a point. It supports your thesis. Audiences might forget the actual joke, but they remember the point it was meant to reinforce.

So The Joke's Not On You...

Ask yourself the following questions before you decide to use a joke in a speech:

1. Is the joke genuinely funny?
2. Can I comfortably tell this joke?
3. Does this joke match the mood of my speech?
4. Does this joke fit with the purpose of my speech?
5. Will my audience understand the joke?
6. Will my audience appreciate and like the joke?
7. Is the joke tasteful?
8. Is the joke fresh?

If you answered "no" to any of these questions, play it safe and avoid the joke. Follow this iron-clad rule: When in doubt, cut it out. If you answered "yes" to all these questions, read through these detailed ways to make humor a part of your public-speaking style.

What Makes a Good Joke?

You can't tell a joke successfully without understanding how the joke works. What makes a joke funny? In part, it's the way the joke is constructed. Try this one:

> In my neighborhood, we have a word for sushi: *bait.*

The humor comes from the contrast between the expectations that "*sushi*" sparks: delicious little expensive morsels of fish, compared to the stinky reality of "bait." By placing the word "sushi" in the same sentence as "bait," the contrast is underscored.

Class Act

What should you do if a joke falls flat? Nothing. Never explain a joke. You're apt to notice that some audience members didn't get your joke, but even if the entire audience seems baffled, don't retreat. Let it go and move on with your speech.

The colon (":") allows the speaker to pause for effect. This pause sets up the punch line (or in this case, the punch word).

Rewrite the same words in a different way, and the joke falls flat. Here are some examples:

> In my neighborhood, we call sushi something else. We call it bait.

> In my neighborhood, we call sushi bait.

> Some people in my neighborhood call sushi bait instead of calling it sushi, but it's really the same thing.

This isn't to say that there's only one way to word a joke. This *is* to say, however, that you must think about the way you arrange the words to achieve the greatest punch and laughter. Play around with the wording until the joke works for you. Then try it out on people whose judgment you respect—preferably people with a good sense of humor. If they laugh, you'll know that you're on to something. If they don't, either find some new friends or go back to the drawing board.

Be of Good Cheer

So what's funny to most people most of the time? Toastmasters International recommends a number of ways to develop humor in speeches. I've adapted some of these and added some advice of my own. Here they are, as recommended by four out of five joke-meisters.

Speech of the Devil

Be judicious in your borrowing. Don't take a joke from the previous speaker on the agenda—unless you have a topper and want to one-up the last speaker. In my experience, an audience will only find a joke funny once per occasion. And one-upping can be dangerous.

Borrow Good Jokes

It's okay to take a little bit of well-tested material from people you know are funny. Just make sure that the jokes suit your audience, purpose, and individual style. Tried-and-true humorists include Will Rogers, Mark Twain, Robert Benchley, Woody Allen, and Dave Barry. The first three are better suited for an older audience; the last two for younger audiences.

What about wading through stacks of joke books to find a nugget of humor? I don't recommend it. Reading through scores of joke books to find one good joke is like reading the telephone book for fun. By the time you find something that you think will work for your speech, you'll probably be so numb that you won't even know what's funny any more. It's like eating a whole bag of cookies: By the time you finish, you're slightly green.

But First, a Little About Me

The safest kind of humor consists of jokes that use the safest target: yourself. For example, a child once asked John F. Kennedy how he became a war hero. "It was absolutely involuntary," he answered. "They sank my boat." The linguist S. I. Hayakawa once opened a speech by saying, "I'm going to speak my mind because I have nothing to lose."

Take a page from the masters. Poke fun at yourself before you poke fun at someone else.

Live at Five

Many events that happen to you, people you know, and people in the news are funnier than anything you could make up or find in a joke book. These events also have the advantage of being fresh, original material. As a result, you won't have to worry that everyone in the audience heard a variation of your joke last week on Leno or Letterman.

Original stories from your own life can be especially effective. They bring your audience closer to you because your listeners appreciate that you can poke fun at yourself.

Think about things that set you off from the audience. I sometimes make jokes about being a Long Islander. For added humor, I use a little "Lawn Guyland" pronunciation. Here's a true story I used in a speech about the need for patience and tolerance in marriage:

Speech of the Devil

Avoid drawing from stories that are too prominent in the news, because they're apt to be overworked. It's likely that most clever speakers have thought of using them, too.

> One night, my husband and I were sitting in the local diner talking about the week's events over huge slabs of cake. As a member of a large and voracious family, I quickly polished off a slice of cheesecake the size of an ocean liner. My husband, raised in a smaller, more restrained bunch, was taking more human bites out of his apple pie. Batting my lashes at my long-suffering husband, I poised my fork over his pie. When he protested, I said, 'I bore your children.' He replied, 'You bore a lot of people. Take your fork out of my pie.'

If necessary, embellish your stories with a little fact-stretching. Stay within the confines of reality and reasonableness, however.

Play with Words

For entertaining speeches, my method is to go to the utmost trouble to find the right thing to say, and then to say it with the utmost humor. Yogi Berra is a great inspiration to me. Here are two of my favorite Yogiisms:

➤ "I don't mind being surprised, as long as I know about it beforehand."

➤ "It's deja vu all over again."

Take the time to craft and polish your joke. A well-phrased witticism can go a long way toward building audience goodwill, even if your delivery is a little stiff.

Encores and Exits

Yiddish is a language suited to indigestible food, serious complaining, and great curses. No one curses like Yiddish speakers. (Okay, maybe the Greeks.) Take a look at some of my favorite Yiddish curses:

➤ Corns should grow on your nose.

➤ May a band of gypsies camp in your belly and train bears to dance on your liver.

➤ May all your enemies move in with you.

➤ May your sex life be as good as your credit.

➤ May all your teeth fall out—but one that shall ache.

Making Humor Work for You

An effective storyteller has many ways of reinforcing humor, such as facial expressions, exaggerated lines and gestures, and pauses. But even if you're not a natural comedian, you can tell a joke successfully. Follow my tricks of the trade:

1. **Don't apologize for your inexperience.** Never use lines like "I'm not much of a comedian" or "I don't tell jokes too well, but I'll do my best." This destroys your joke before you start.

2. **Stick to the basics.** If you clutter up your joke with unnecessary details, your audience will lose interest. Include only the elements you need to make your joke work.

3. **Don't overplay your hand.** If you promise the audience the moon, they are going to expect the moon. Avoid lines like "This is the best joke you ever heard" or "Wait until you hear this one." Don't promise; just deliver.

4. **Enjoy yourself.** Smile and look happy. Your mood will be contagious, making it that much easier to get a laugh.

5. **As you tell the joke, look the audience members in the eye.** Shift your gaze around the room, pausing to focus on specific individuals.

6. **Keep your jokes short.** Dragging out a joke can often spoil the humor of it.

7. **Leave the audience enough time to enjoy the joke.** If you rush the laughter, you'll undercut the effect you worked so hard to achieve.

8. **Speak slowly and clearly.** Make sure the audience can understand every word of your joke—especially the punch line!

Jokes That Never Work

After visiting "Silent Cal" Coolidge at the White House, the speaker for the evening, Ring Lardner, confided to friends, "I told him the funniest story, and he laughed so hard you could hear a pin drop."

So, there you are at the podium rattling away from your prepared speech when you notice that a number of people seem to be nodding off. You think, "Perhaps I should come up with a great joke to get their attention."

Think again.

All too often, humor in speeches backfires because the speaker doesn't use humor correctly. The speaker instead tells jokes that are insulting, stupid, or just not germane to the speech, without considering the ramifications of the remarks.

The most dangerous kind of humor is the kind that makes fun of other people. Avoid these topics:

➤ Religion

➤ Race

➤ Sexuality

➤ Intelligence

➤ Birthplaces

➤ Handicaps

➤ Ethnicity

➤ Sexual orientation

➤ Religious leaders

Class Act

Sarcasm and irony can backfire, creating sympathy for the opposite point of view. This can lead to bad press for you and the group you represent.

➤ Childlessness

➤ Physical appearance

➤ Political leanings

Speech of the Devil

Speakers almost never have the chance to try their material out in front of a real audience. Is it worth the gamble that you might upset your audience with an offensive joke? Nope.

These jokes have a way of blowing up in your face, even if they are genuinely funny. Here's an example of what I mean:

> The first speaker asks, "John, why do people take such an immediate dislike to me?"

> The second speaker answers, "Because it saves time."

This is funny, but it's also nasty—and being nasty usually doesn't make it, either. What is acceptable at a roast, for example, won't cut it at a commencement speech.

The fact that insulting material has been written, rehearsed, and performed to an appreciatively laughing audience would seem to give it some legitimacy. You might be tempted to use one of these jokes. "After all," our beginning speaker might think, "it worked on television, so it should work in my speech."

What you don't see is the stack of irate letters from viewers, the scores of enraged telephone calls, and the list of canceled advertisements. Play it safe.

The Least You Need to Know

➤ Successful jokes are built on a common frame of reference.

➤ Your humor must fit your audience, purpose, topic, and personal style.

➤ Avoid any joke that demeans, insults, or might make anyone in the audience uncomfortable.

➤ If you're still uneasy about making an attempt to be funny, you're better off using relatively little humor in your speeches.

Taking the Show on the Road: Multicultural Concerns and International Speeches

In This Chapter

➤ Cultural values, beliefs, and practices

➤ Say it correctly in any language

➤ The demands of a foreign audience

➤ Translators

Experts agree: To succeed in America today and in international business, you need an understanding of other cultures, beliefs, and patterns of acceptable behavior. Communicating with people from other cultures and in other countries is crucial if you want to manage a multicultural workforce or do business abroad.

➤ Frank Perdue's chicken slogan, "It takes a strong man to make a tender chicken," was translated into Spanish as "It takes an aroused man to make a chicken affectionate."

➤ Scandinavian vacuum manufacturer Electrolux used the following slogan in an American campaign: "Nothing sucks like an Electrolux."

➤ When Parker Pen marketed a ball-point pen in Mexico, its ads were supposed to have read, "It won't leak in your pocket and embarrass you." The company mistakenly thought that the word "embarazar" (to impregnate) meant to embarrass, and the ad wound up reading: "It won't leak in your pocket and make you pregnant."

Experts agree: To succeed in America today and in international business, you need an understanding of other cultures, beliefs, and patterns of acceptable behavior. Communicating with people from other cultures and in other countries is crucial if you want to manage a multicultural workforce or do business abroad.

In this chapter, you'll learn how to avoid these blunders while also learning how to make speeches that meet the needs of international audiences—both at home and abroad.

Vive la Difference

In the past, Americans used the metaphor of the "melting pot" to describe the assimilation of different cultures into the whole. Today, the metaphor has become a "mosaic" or "quilt" to more accurately reflect the country's cultural diversity.

Take this test to find out how attuned you are to successful intercultural communication. Check the items that apply to you, then score your test by giving yourself one point for each question you checked.

Yes No

❏ ❏ 1. Are you aware that your values are influenced by your culture?

❏ ❏ 2. Do you think your values are not necessarily the "right" values?

❏ ❏ 3. Are you flexible and open to change?

❏ ❏ 4. Are you sensitive to nonverbal clues?

❏ ❏ 5. Are you knowledgeable about the values, beliefs, and practices of other cultures?

❏ ❏ 6. Can you perceive differences among individuals within a culture?

Score Yourself

5–6 checks	You're ready to address the UN.
3–4 checks	You could serve cookies at the UN.
1–2 checks	You should think about visiting the UN.

Even if you never leave the United States—and maybe not even your own hometown—at some point you'll most likely deal with people whose culture and background differ from yours. That's because America is becoming an increasingly multicultural society.

John/Jean/Juan Q. Public

In the last census, about one-quarter of the people living in the United States identified themselves as minorities. For example, there are 2,000 Hmongs from Laos living in Wisconsin, and nearly half of all Californians are African-American, Latino, or Asian.

According to one estimate, there are roughly twice as many Muslims as Episcopalians in the United States today. And the 350 employees at the Digital Equipment Corporation plant in Boston come from nearly 50 countries and speak 19 different languages; the plant's announcements are printed in English, Portuguese, Haitian Creole, Vietnamese, Spanish, and Chinese. As you can see from these examples, it's not as easy to make assumptions about a potential audience as it once was.

Class Act

Colors don't convey the same meaning in every culture. In America, for example, brides wear white; in China, in contrast, brides wear red. In Mexico, purple flowers are left on coffins. In Korea, red ink is used to record deaths, but never to write about the living.

Do You Have Anything to Declare?

Unfortunately, few speakers have much experience dealing with multicultural audiences or know much about the special needs that come with these speeches. As a result, they approach the podium with great trepidation. How many of these concerns worry *you*? Read the following list of common questions to get an idea:

➤ Will I make a cross-cultural blunder?

➤ Can I use humor effectively?

➤ How can I show respect for my host's culture?

➤ How can I show respect for my foreign hosts?

➤ How can I show pride in my own heritage?

➤ How can I be sure that my message is understood?

➤ How can I meet the special demands of a foreign audience?

➤ How can I use translators effectively?

All these worries are valid ones. But don't worry—this chapter will help familiarize you with some specific ways to deal with the special problems that international speeches bring.

Ways to Get Your Message Across in Any Language

Cultural awareness has a tremendous impact on speaking situations. Successful diplomats, for example, thoroughly prepare before meeting with diplomats from other cultures.

Encores and Exits

Learning another language involves more than words—even laughing can be different. In Japan, for example, polite laughter is conveyed by holding your arms at your sides, shoulders forward, head bowed, with a hand covering your mouth. In contrast, Americans generally laugh with a more open body position. Usually the head is back and the mouth open. And in the United States, loud laughter is acceptable—even expected—when something is genuinely funny.

The following suggestions can help you communicate with people from other cultures.

1. **Declare your pleasure at speaking to this foreign audience.** Acknowledge the honor of addressing a cross-cultural audience. At the opening of the speech, state your positive feelings about being invited to speak to people from another country or of another culture. The acknowledgment should be direct and sincere, not obsequious or hollow. For example, you might say, "I am most grateful for the honor of being the first representative from the XYZ Company to address a Japanese audience."

2. **Cite an expert from your guest's country or culture.** If possible, find an authority from the host's country or culture whose views match the theme of your speech. Possibilities include educators, respected public officials, writers, artists, or famous historical figures. As with any authority you cite, be sure that the reference is appropriate to the speech and that the figure is indeed admired by the members of your audience.

3. **Include a quotation from your guest's country or culture.** Select an apt quotation from a well-known, well-respected source that reinforces your message and flatters your audience. Consider quoting a popular person or work of literature from your host's culture, for example. Be sure to include context or background to make the quote more meaningful.

4. **Make references to your own culture.** Focus on your culture's shared values. Emotional appeals help bridge gaps between customs and traditions by showing that people share common feelings, no matter how diverse their backgrounds.

5. **Deliver your most powerful line in the audience's language.** Learning a line or two of your speech in your audience's language makes an impression that's much greater than the effort required. This illustrates in an especially dramatic way the importance of intercultural understanding. Don't overthink it; the line can be as

simple as, "My country extends its thanks to everyone here." Your guests will appreciate the effort you expended to learn a few words of their language. It's also an effective way to build rapport with your audience.

6. **Use the country's measurement terms.** America is one of the few places in the world that does not use metric measurements. If you are delivering a speech in a country that uses metric terms, translate your figures into metric. It's a small touch that goes a long way toward impressing an audience.

7. **Check your timing.** If you are delivering a major speech in another country, try to adjust the time of your presentation to accommodate everyone's internal clock. Avoid speaking when you—or members of your audience—are jet-lagged. Also, if the speech is going to be carried in the media, try to time it so that it can be broadcast at home as well as locally.

8. **Reinforce the need for intercultural communication.** Address the issue of cultural diversity head-on to reassure your audience that everyone is singing from the same hymnal (Case in point, some audiences won't understand expressions such as "singing from the same hymnal!"). You can cite statistics, specific examples, and vivid anecdotes that stress the need for international understanding. This data should be easily available in up-to-date reference texts such as an almanac.

Class Act

In North America, clothing conveys nonverbal messages about competence, success, and influence. In Japan, clothing denotes the occupational group as well as status. Company badges include rank; workers wear different colors when they go on strike.

Read over these examples to illustrate this point:

➤ The United States has more than $500 million invested abroad. The bulk of America's foreign investments are in the European countries, including Belgium, Denmark, France, Germany, and Italy.

➤ Foreign countries have nearly $500 billion invested in the United States. Five countries account for more than 75 percent of the direct foreign investment. In order from most to least, these countries are the United Kingdom, Japan, the Netherlands, Canada, and Germany.

Stroll Through the Cultural Minefield

When Pepsi entered the Chinese market, its slogan, "Come alive with the Pepsi generation" was translated into Chinese as "Pepsi brings back your dead ancestors."

The great increase in international communication has resulted in scores of linguistic blunders. Elevators seem to be at special risk for garbled translation:

➤ This sign was seen in a Bucharest hotel lobby: "This lift is being fixed for the next day. During that time, we regret that you will be unbearable."

➤ In a Leipzig elevator: "Do not enter the lift backwards and only when lit up."

➤ In a Belgrade elevator: "To move the cabin, push button or wishing floor. If the cabin should enter more persons, each one should press number of wishing floor. Driving is then going alphabetically by national order."

➤ A Paris elevator: "Please leave your values at the front desk."

Encores and Exits

It's tempting to lay all the blame on people, but a technological approach doesn't always get out all the translation bugs, either: A United Nations translating computer translated the cliché "Out of sight, out of mind" as "invisible insane."

You Can Check Out Anytime You Like, But You Can Never Leave

Hotel signs are also susceptible to gibberish when translated. For example, a Tokyo hotel posted this sign in something sort of resembling English: "It is forbidden to steal hotel towels please. If you are not a person to do such a thing, please not to read notis." The same hotel tried to explain the mechanics of bathing this way: "Please to bathe inside the tub." This sign was seen on the door of a Moscow hotel room: "If this is your first visit to the USSR, you are welcome to it."

Here are some more famous international bloopers concerning hotels:

➤ You might want to have your laundry done in this Yugoslavia hotel: "The flattening of underwear with pleasure is the job of the chambermaids."

➤ This Vienna hotel is prepared for fire: "In case of fire, do your utmost to alarm the hotel porter."

➤ This Athens hotel has a clear policy on criticism: "Visitors are expected to complain at the office between the hours of 9 and 11 a.m. daily."

Our Neighbors Across the Pond

Even British and American English can involve translation bloopers because the two languages often use different terms to convey the same meaning. Many people in Europe, Asia, Africa, and the Caribbean have learned British English, not American English. Study this chart to avoid embarrassment in a language closer to home:

American English	British English
Legal holiday	Bank holiday
White-collar job	Black-coat job
Attorney in non-court work	Solicitor
Attorney who goes to court	Barrister
Ground floor	First floor
Elevator	Lift
Hood	Bonnet

Shop 'Til You Drop?

Shopping signs overseas can make it tricky for even the most intrepid mall-crawler:

➤ In a Hong Kong supermarket: "For your convenience, we recommend courteous, efficient self-service."

➤ A Tokyo shop advises: "Our nylons cost more than common but you'll find they are best in the long run."

➤ A tourist found this sign in the shop of a Swedish furrier: "Fur coats made from ladies with their own skins."

➤ Seen in a Hong Kong tailor shop window: "Ladies may have a fit upstairs."

➤ An Athens tailor had this sign posted in his shop: "Order your summer suit. Because is a big rush will execute customers in strict rotation."

➤ Even trendy Paris boutiques are not exempt from the terrors of bad translation: "Dresses for street walking," the sign in a chic shop window read.

➤ And to add insult to injury, a sign in a Moroccan shop window bragged: "Here speaching English."

Class Act

If you are writing a speech that will be translated, leave about one-third more white space than you would on an English document. When text is translated from English into most other languages, it usually takes up more space.

And what about keeping your purchases clean?

➤ A Bangkok dry cleaner gets right to the heart of the matter: "Drop your trousers here for best results."

➤ A Roman laundry likely didn't mean exactly what they wrote on this sign: "Ladies, leave your clothes here and spend the afternoon having a good time."

The size of the transaction doesn't seem to affect the skill of the translator, as the following sign spotted in a car rental firm in Japan shows: "When passenger of foot heave in sight, tootle the horn. Trumpet him melodiously at first but if he still obstacles your passage, then tootle him with vigor."

Speech of the Devil

Be completely, totally sure that the phrase you have selected to speak in your audience's language accurately expresses your sentiments. Study with a competent foreign speaker to make sure that you are pronouncing every word correctly. Few things are as embarrassing as making a fool of yourself in a language you don't even understand.

When in Rome (or America Today)

Tourist attractions are equally apt to fall under attack by the language-impaired, as these examples show:

➤ An ad for donkey rides in Thailand reads: "Would you like to ride your own ass?"

➤ A Budapest zoo cautions: "Please do not feed the animals. If you have any suitable food, give it to the guard on duty."

➤ A sign in Germany's Black Forest states: "It is strictly forbidden on our camping site that people of different sex, for instance men and women, live together in one tent unless they are married with each other for that purpose."

➤ A Czech tourist agency suggests: "Take one of our horse-driven carriage tours. We guarantee no miscarriages."

And woe be to those who dare to drive, fly, or otherwise try to get around in a foreign land:

➤ A Japanese detour warns: "Stop. Drive Sideways."

➤ A sign in a Copenhagen airline ticket office: "We take your bags and send them in all directions."

➤ This sign was spotted in a Chinese railroad station: "Please keep cleanness. Sanitary important."

Eat, Drink, and Be Merry

Eating abroad can be imperiled by bad English:

➤ A Swiss restaurant menu reads: "Our wines leave you nothing to hope for."

➤ A Swiss inn's sign reads: "Special today—no ice cream."

➤ An Acapulco hotel assures its diners: "The manager has personally passed all the water served here."

But it goes both ways. Armed with a German-English dictionary, one tourist ordered a "heisser hund," a literal translation of the American "hot dog." Unfortunately, the literal translation just didn't cut the mustard. What did it mean? "A dog in heat."

You don't want to get sick, either, as the following two signs show. A sign in the window of a Roman doctor reads, "Specialist in women and other diseases." A Hong Kong dentist posted this notice: "Teeth extracted by latest Methodists."

Lingua Franca

These mistranslations serve to illustrate one of the toughest aspects of translating from one language to another: keeping idioms intact. Many times, idioms cannot be translated from one language to another. Skilled translators can help you avoid these blunders. Let's take a look at how to use translators.

As the number of people speaking languages other than English has grown in America, so has the need for translators. Translators are called upon to translate courtroom testimony, operating manuals, and business contracts, among other things.

Unfortunately, there is a huge difference between someone who happens to speak a foreign language and someone who has the ability to translate between speakers and writers of different languages. The first is an amateur; the second, a professional. Competent, effective public speaking requires a professional.

If at all possible, take your own translator when you travel to another country on business. Discuss with the translator ahead of time the nature of your work abroad, the speech or speeches you will be giving, and any technical terms you will be including.

Speech of the Devil

Beware of foreign slang. Then-President John F. Kennedy got tripped up with his famous "Ich bin ein Berliner" line. JFK *wanted* to say, "I am a Berliner," but he *really* said, "I am a jelly donut." That's because the correct phrase is "Ich bin Berliner"—"I am Berliner"—without the article "ein" ("a"). Adding the article results in the slang phrase for a donut.

Class Act

A good translator can help you interpret nonverbal behavior and negotiating strategies.

How can you find a translator who can do the best possible job for you? Start by word of mouth: Ask people in your field for recommendations. Unfortunately, people tend to guard good translators with the same zeal they use to safeguard trusted child-care workers, cleaning help, hairdressers, and the last of the super-premium ice-cream. If no one steps forward with a recommendation, consider advertising for a translator.

In any event, carefully interview all candidates.

During the interview, see if you feel comfortable with the candidate. If you feel uneasy, this is not the right translator for you—no matter how good the individual's reputation and skills are. Remember, you are essentially trusting this person with your reputation. You want to select a person you can work with easily. See if the person projects the image you want: Is the candidate professional, well-groomed, and competent? Use this checklist when interviewing translator candidates.

➤ How did you learn the language?

➤ Where did you study?

➤ What was the nature of your training?

➤ Did you ever live in this foreign country?

➤ What are your teachers' credentials?

➤ How long have you been a translator?

➤ How often do you work?

➤ What types of materials do you feel most comfortable translating?

➤ What were your last three translating jobs? Request specific details: length of assignments, types of materials, clients, fees, and so on.

➤ Have you ever translated speeches within my particular industry or field?

➤ Why do you want this job?

➤ What do you see as your complete role as a translator?

➤ What references can you offer?

The Least You Need to Know

➤ The world is changing—be there or be square.

➤ It's easy to make a big boo-boo when you're addressing multicultural or international groups. Check and recheck your speech for possible blunders.

➤ It's crucial that you learn the traditions, attitudes, and beliefs of the people you deal with at home and abroad.

➤ Use a competent translator to help you deal with speeches in other languages.

➤ It's a small world after all.

Part 4

Take It On Home: Tackling Specific Kinds of Speeches

Ever see a Marx brothers movie, such as A Night at the Opera *or* A Day at the Races? *If you've ever seen one of these classic flicks, you know that Groucho was the brother with the big mustache and the bigger cigar, Chico was the brother with the outrageous Italian accent, and Harpo was the curly-haired brother who played the harp and spoke by honking a horn. No one ever heard his voice on film. As a result, people assumed that he couldn't speak.*

Years after the Marx brothers stopped making movies, Harpo would occasionally host charity functions. His standard opening line was to step onto the stage, sidle to the microphone, and say, "Unaccustomed as I am to speaking in public...."

This section of the book shows you how to craft speeches that work so that you *won't shock people with your eloquence.*

Chapter 20

Informational Speeches

In This Chapter

➤ Conduct process analysis

➤ Train and teach

➤ Interview and be interviewed

➤ Testify in court

➤ Give (and get!) criticism

➤ Describe an object, person, or place

➤ Define a concept

The inscription on the metal bands used by the U.S. Department of the Interior to tag migratory birds had to be changed. The bands used to bear the address of the Washington Biological Survey, abbreviated:

Wash. Biol. Surv.

That was until the agency received the following letter from a Texas camper:

Dear Sirs:

While camping last week, I shot one of your birds. I think it was a crow. I followed the cooking instructions on the leg tag, and I want to tell you, it was horrible.

Talk Soup

More than ever before, we're compelled to inform and be informed. When you try to clarify a concept or process for your audience, define terms and relationships, or in any way expand their knowledge, the object of your speech is to **inform**.

The bands are now marked *Fish and Wildlife Service.*

We live in an information society. As a result, good communication skills are more important than ever. In this chapter, you'll learn how to give clear and effective speeches that inform. That way, you won't be the one eating crow—even if it *is* boiled to perfection.

Insert Tab A into Slot B: Explaining a Process

Tech Support: What does the screen say now?

Person: It says, 'Hit ENTER when ready.'

Tech Support: Well?

Person: How do I know when it's ready?

Can you explain how to operate a computer to a technophobe? Can you describe your plan to revitalize the town park to your mayor? Can you describe the steps your colleagues must take to install new software applications, order materials, or complete an accident report?

You might often find yourself in the position of having to explain a *process*, whether as simple as ordering flowers or as complex as installing a fax modem. Whatever the process is, your explanation should have three parts: introduction, body, and conclusion.

➤ In the *introduction,* explain why the process is important and what steps you will be describing.

➤ In the *body,* explain the steps one at a time. Demonstrate or illustrate each step as you discuss it. As you speak, look at your audience to be sure they understand what you're saying. If your audience doesn't seem to be following you, repeat the step and explanation. Try to use different words when you restate it to help your listeners grasp the ideas in another way.

➤ In the *conclusion,* briefly go over the steps again. Remind your listeners about any important rules, safety regulations, or cautions. To make sure that your audience understands the process, consider asking them to restate the rules in their own words. You can do this at the end of the process or after each step.

Working Nine to Five: Job-Training and Teaching Sessions

Job-training sessions are unique informative speech situations because in this situation, audience members learn by doing, not just by viewing and listening. As a result, when you run job-training sessions, you should encourage your audience to become actively involved. Getting your audience involved in the process leads to questions and, ultimately, more give and take. This creates a more effective session. At many job-training meetings, the speaker functions more as a moderator, so don't be afraid to let go of the reins.

You're probably sick of hearing this by now, but like all other kinds of speeches, it's important to thoroughly prepare for job-training sessions in advance. These sessions should be longer than other kinds of speeches, however, because the require a lot more audience involvement. Also be sure to save some time for audience members to go over what they learned.

Strong speaking skills are especially important in teaching sessions because these presentations too easily become boring and tend to be filled with too much information. Follow these guidelines to make your teaching sessions clear and effective:

Class Act

It's a good idea to join Toastmasters International if you have to do a lot of informational or persuasive speaking. Toastmasters provides an ideal forum to hone and improve the skills you need to make these kinds of speeches. Look in the telephone book to find the chapter of Toastmasters closest to your home or office.

Speech of the Devil

When you're explaining a process, be sure to keep your sentences short. Use vivid, concrete language and precise terminology.

1. Decide what knowledge is most important. You can't cover everything (nor should you want to).

2. If a number of people are speaking, review all the presentations beforehand to see if they can be pared down.

3. Arrange the information you'll be imparting in a logical fashion. The order of time (first to last) or the order of importance (most to least important) works best.

4. Be precise in presenting measurements, sizes, numbers, colors, time, and other technical facts.

5. Present complex or crucial technical information by using visual aids. This is explained further in Chapter 25, "A Thousand Words: Visual Aids."

6. Consider utilizing small discussion groups to cut down on information overload and to allow your audience time to digest crucial facts.

The Corner Office: Interviews

Before you even get to an interview, you have make an initial inquiry about the job. It's likely that most of the job inquiries you make will be oral rather than written. For example, you may telephone about a job you have seen advertised, or you may speak in person to a personnel manager or job recruiter. Whether you find out more about a job by phone or in person, use this Interview Preparation check list to make a good impression on your prospective employer.

Check off each item on this list as you complete it.

Class Act

Remember to always keep your audience firmly in mind and to consider their needs and goals. It helps to recall that public speaking is an audience participation event (if it weren't, it would be called *private speaking*).

Interview Preparation Checklist

❑ Prepare a list of questions about the job.

❑ Know the name and title of the person you need to contact.

❑ Have a pencil or pen and paper ready to take notes on your conversation.

❑ Identify yourself at the start of the conversation. Then explain why you are calling.

❑ Give the person any helpful information about prior meetings or contacts, such as "We talked last week at Ted P. Skimmer's party."

❑ Follow up the conversation with a phone call or letter.

Power to the People

So you've made your inquiries, sent a follow-up letter (and perhaps a résumé and cover letter), and have landed an interview. You should know that today, many employers expect you to be more aggressive during the interview than was common in the past. The key is to present yourself as qualified, assured, and personable. Follow these guidelines:

1. Do your research: find out as much as you can about the job, company, and industry. Read stock reports, newspaper articles, and magazine pieces. If possible, speak to people you know in the company and industry to get additional information.

2. Leave yourself plenty of time to get to the interview. This will help prevent you from rushing in all frazzled.

3. Dress neatly and appropriately.

4. Bring an extra copy of your résumé, a list of references, and a pen. It's also a good idea to have identification, such as a social security card or a driver's license.

5. Be ready to answer questions about your education, experience, job qualifications, and interests.

6. Be confident and polite, and convey your enthusiasm.

7. Ask intelligent, thoughtful, well-researched questions about the job.

8. Leave the gum, elaborate jewelry, overpowering perfume, nose ring, and other distracters at home.

9. Watch for cues that the interview is over. To signal the end of a meeting, many interviewers look at the clock or their watch, push back their chairs, or shuffle papers.

10. Thank the interviewer for his or her time.

Whack 'Em and Stack 'Em

Interviewing candidates for a job is one of the touchiest areas of informative speech because what an interviewer should and should not say at an employment interview is now subject to strict federal guidelines. For example, in the United States it is illegal to ask job applicants about their race, religion, or marital status. Some topics may be perceived as illegal or legal, depending on how they are asked. For example, it is illegal to ask, "How old are you?" but it is legal to ask, "Can you prove that you are over 18?" However, all questions must be relevant to the job and must be asked of all applicants.

If you are employed by a major corporation, speak to your human resources department to obtain a copy of these guidelines and the company's interview policy. In many companies, it's mandatory that a representative from the human resources department sit in on all job interviews.

If you belong to a small company or run your own shop, be sure to obtain a copy of the federal guidelines and study them carefully before you conduct a job interview.

Speech of the Devil

In court cases, companies have been at fault when women have been discouraged from applying for jobs, when African-Americans have been judged solely by a group of whites, when interviewers have not been trained, and when companies have not kept adequate records.

In the Hot Seat: Giving Testimony

More than 14 million people are arrested every year. Given the high number of bad guys, it's likely that at some point in your life you'll be required to testify under oath. In addition to appearing at a trial, you may be called to testify before an investigative committee or commission.

The purpose of testimony is to present facts and evidence from which other people will draw conclusions. These "other people" may include judges, juries, and committee members. As a witness, you should follow these rules:

1. Listen carefully to the entire question before answering.

2. Do not interrupt the person asking the question or anticipate what the questioner has to say.

3. If an objection is raised, wait to hear the court's response to the objection before answering.

4. Be sure that you understand the question before you answer.

5. If you do not understand the question, ask for an explanation.

6. Give precise, factual answers. Cite dates, times, and other specific details, when possible.

7. Answer only what was asked in the question. Do not elaborate.

8. Do not offer your own opinion unless specifically asked to do so. In these instances, back up your opinion with specific details.

9. Answer carefully. Take the time you need to make sure that your answer is correct and concise.

10. Keep your cool. Don't lose your temper, even if you are being baited.

Let's Get Critical

Like the common cold, criticism knows no bounds. But unlike the common cold, criticism serves a useful purpose, especially when you are evaluating an employee. Constructive criticism points out the weaknesses in people's work and suggests ways they can improve their performance.

Class Act

When testifying, tell the complete truth. Do not withhold facts that should be part of your response. (Recall that you promised to tell the "whole truth.")

Use this check list to help keep your criticism helpful, not hurtful.

❏ Did I limit my criticism to one specific aspect of the job or assignment?

❏ Did I focus on the behavior, not the personality?

❏ Did I make my criticism helpful, saying things like, "Please proofread your typing," rather than, "You're a poor administrative assistant"?

❏ Did I listen closely to the person's defense? Did I understand the other person's point of view?

❏ Did I include praise by telling the person what parts of the job he or she does well?

Can you take it as well as you dish it out? Constructive criticism can come from a superior, colleague, or subordinate. When you accept criticism, listen carefully. Be sure you understand what specific criticisms the person is making. Then think about whether the criticism is valid. Don't rush to defend yourself. Instead, ask for specific suggestions for improvement, and jot down these ideas.

Then, correct your performance according to the other person's suggestions. Evaluate your progress by politely running your work by that person again. (Keep in mind that wording such as , "Is this closer to what you had in mind?" is better than "Is this good enough for you now?")

Listen Up: Describe an Object, Person, or Place

The key to describing a person, place, or thing is organization. With these speeches, it's a good idea to select and arrange your points systematically, taking care to make your organization of ideas clear. The audience must be able to follow your description without any problems.

Speech of the Devil

Remember: More trouble is caused in the world by indiscreet answers than by indiscreet questions.

The most common method of organizing these descriptive speeches is space sequence, using location or position as the basis for arrangement. For instance, you might arrange your details from top to bottom, bottom to top, inside to out, and so on. An outfit might be described from top to bottom, a building from bottom to top, and a home inside to out, for example.

Define a Concept

One of the most common informative speaking tasks falls under defining a concept. Why? Because it is often necessary to define an obscure term or establish a special meaning you wish to attach to a particular word or phrase before you can explain anything further. If you neglect to define key concepts, you'll fail to communicate your meaning adequately, no matter what else you may say down the line.

Five main ways exist for clarifying a concept. Let's look at each one:

➤ **Dictionary definition.** To use this method, place the concept or term you're defining into a category or general class. Then, carefully distinguish the concept from other members of this class. For example: "Democracy is a system of government by the people, of the people, and for the people."

➤ **Etymology.** What's the history of the concept you're explaining? How was the word created? What is its background? Etymology clarifies the meaning of a concept by providing the history of the word or phrase. For instance, a pandemic disease is one that is very widespread, such as the viral influenza that caused thousands of deaths in 1918. A less serious example is the common cold, which seems to always be circulating. *Pandemic* means "general, universal, affecting most of the people." The concept comes from two Greek roots: *pan*, which means "all," and demos, which means "people." When you break a word down this way, you are using etymology.

➤ **Negation.** Negation clarifies the meaning of a concept by telling you what it's *not*. For example: "By socialism, I do not mean communism, which supports the common ownership of the means of production."

➤ **Example.** An example illustrates the meaning of a concept by giving an instance of its meaning: "The new Skydome on the parkway is an example of modern architecture."

➤ **Use in a sentence.** Sometimes, the best way to clarify the meaning of a concept is to use it in a sentence. Putting a concept in this context can make the meaning concrete to your audience: "*Rad* is a slang term, meaning exceedingly fashionable or trendy. It has a positive connotation. For instance, if I say, What a *rad* haircut, I really mean, What a stylish haircut."

Each of these methods can help you write precise and useful informative speeches. Suit the method or methods to your audience and style, as you learned earlier in this guide.

The Least You Need to Know

➤ Informative speeches explain concepts, define terms, and explain processes.

➤ Process-analysis speeches always contain an introduction, body, and conclusion.

➤ Job-training and teaching sessions call for a logical arrangement of ideas, precision, and visual aids.

➤ Be careful what you say when interviewing a candidate. Certain questions and topics are legally off-limits.

➤ Learn to give and take criticism well.

➤ The key to describing a person, place, or thing is correct organization.

➤ Describe a concept by using its dictionary definition, etymology, negation, examples, or context.

Chapter 21

Persuasive Speeches

In This Chapter

➤ Speeches of fact, speeches of value, and speeches of policy

➤ Purposes of persuasive speeches

➤ Sales presentations, using direct and indirect approaches

➤ Eulogies

➤ Persuasive speeches that solve problems

➤ Campaign speeches and candidate nominations

A woman with twin boys gives them up for adoption. One of them goes to a family in Egypt and is named "Amal." The other goes to a family in Spain, who name him "Juan." Years later, Juan sends a picture of himself to his biological mother. Upon receiving the picture, she tells her husband that she wishes she also had a picture of Amal. Her husband responds, "But they're twins—if you've seen Juan, you've seen Amal."

Persuasive speeches, however, can look a lot different from each other than Juan and Amal. In this chapter, you'll learn how to construct important and useful types of persuasive speeches. You'll learn specific techniques that will help you convince a wide variety of audiences in a wide variety of situations.

True to Type

What do the following situations have in common?

➤ Political candidates wooing voter support and TV commercials pitching the latest toothpaste

➤ Salespeople urging you to buy their widget and a charity trying to convince people to donate money

➤ A committee trying to iron out a difficult problem and two people working together to solve a dilemma

Talk Soup

Persuasive speeches aim to move an audience to belief or action.

All involve forms of *persuasive* public speaking. When your purpose is to influence your audience or alter their beliefs or attitudes, you're speaking to persuade.

Whether you're selling wares or ideas, effective persuasion is based on accurate logic, powerful appeals to emotion, and trust. Persuasive speeches include making sales presentations, selling budgets and ideas, solving problems, delivering eulogies, running for election, and nominating a candidate for office.

Three on a Match

Three types of persuasive speeches exist:

➤ **Speeches of fact.** Here, you try to prove that something is or is not so, or that something did or did not happen. "Our candidate has always supported the family farmer," would be the thesis for a persuasive speech of fact.

➤ **Speeches of value.** In this speech, you try to prove better or worse, good or bad. "This movie is superior to its sequel," could form the basis for a persuasive speech of value.

➤ **Speeches of policy.** In this case, you try to prove that something should or should not be done. "You should not buy real fur," is a common theme for a speech of policy.

Strategic Air Strikes

All persuasive speeches have three main purposes:

➤ To provide enough information to create an effective foundation for your stance.

➤ To overcome the listener's objections.

➤ To move the listener to belief or action.

Select a persuasive strategy based on your answers to the following four questions:

➤ What do I want people to do?

➤ What objections, if any, will people have?

➤ How strong a case can I make?

➤ What kind of persuasion does my organization or audience value (fact, value, or policy)?

Now, it's time to apply these techniques to specific types of persuasive appeals.

Sales Presentations

It's either money or love that makes the world go 'round (or that wins over an audience). In the first instance, you must sell the company's widget; in the latter, you must sell yourself. Here are some guidelines to make this public-speaking task easier and more likely to succeed.

1. **Tell a story.** Do your research in categories (such as a competition analysis), but know that when it's time to deliver your speech, you'll get the client's attention more quickly if you organize your information in story form to support your overall message.

2. **Don't inundate.** Don't bombard the client with data just to prove you've done your homework. Remember, more isn't always better.

3. **Be flexible.** If interest flags, move on. If the client is ready for closure, give it to him or her. Being able to adjust in midstream shows that you're responsive as well as confident.

4. **Show, don't tell.** Create conceptual visuals to illustrate major relationships, use message heads on graphs and charts, and explain the graphic in terms of the story.

5. **Deliver, don't read.** Your speech is not a bedtime story. The last person who deliberately read to you was probably your mother, and she was trying to put you to sleep. A comatose client cannot be a happy client.

6. **Look and listen.** Much of communication is nonverbal. Body language, facial expressions, and tone of voice can reveal far more than actual words. Too often we take the absence of outright hostility as audience acceptance. Pay attention to nonverbal signals.

7. **Act professional.** Your body language counts, too. Maintain an "up" posture; use open hand gestures (with elbows away from the body), look directly at the client, and show him or her (through facial expressions, voice, and energy) that you feel confident and positive.

Speech of the Devil

If clients can't see the slides, they won't get the message.

Class Act

Too many speakers become abstract and machine-like when presenting. Be human: Use a conversational tone and casual language. Smile when appropriate.

8. **Plan ahead.** Don't rely on handouts that are still warm from the copying machine when you deliver your speech. While you're at it, avoid writing your speech in the taxi on the way to the client's office. You want to get your sales pitch down before it's time to rush over to the client's office.

Sales presentations demand special persuasive techniques. Your appeal can be direct or indirect—and your choice of technique depends largely on your audience and the amount of resistance you expect to encounter.

In the next two sections, you'll learn how to apply these techniques to two common sales tasks: selling an idea and selling a budget. The following sections explain the direct approach as it applies to selling an idea, and the indirect approach with regard to selling a budget. Then you can apply each technique to your specific needs in each individual case.

Up Close and Personal: The Direct Approach

The direct approach works best when your audience is receptive to your ideas. This persuasive technique allows you to present all your ideas at once. Here's how.

Encores and Exits

In other cultures, making a direct sales pitch might backfire. Brazilians, for example, are often offended by a direct solicitation. Even supervisors are expected to suggest instead of request. In India, people often assume that a direct request conceals a more subtle message. Often, people ignore the direct statement and focus on the supposed "subtext."

Open your speech with a hook that will catch the audience's attention. In the body, provide a list of reasons why people should act on your idea. Finish with a handle: Tell the audience what to do and why they should do it now. Let's take a look at each part in detail:

1. **Hook:** Provide a 1-minute introduction that grabs your audience.
2. **List:** Give the audience the information they need to support your idea. Include specific reasons why your idea is worth their support.

3. **Handle:** Make the action sound easy. Give the audience a positive reason for supporting your idea. Avoid closes that use "if" and "why not"—they lack positive emphasis and might even encourage your reader to say no.

Through the Side Door: The Indirect Approach

Use an indirect approach when you expect resistance from your audience. This pattern allows you to demobilize your opposition by showing them all of the evidence that supports your position *before* you give your audience a chance to say no.

Speech of the Devil

Don't skimp on the details. The more you tell, the more you sell.

Follow these steps:

1. **Start by establishing common ground.** For example, show how the budget is beneficial to both sides.

2. **Define the problem you share, and then show how your budget will solve it.** Your task is to convince your audience that something must be done before you can convince them that your budget is the solution.

3. **Explain specifically how your budget will solve problems.** Keep personalities out of the discussion; don't use the words "I" or "my."

4. **Show how the advantages of your budget outweigh the disadvantages.** Depending on your budget, possible disadvantages might include a decrease in personnel, supplies, office space, or vacation time. Possible advantages might include greater profits, market share, promotions, office space, or vacation time.

5. **Tell the audience members what you want them to do: support your budget.** Get your audience to act quickly, perhaps by offering an additional incentive. For example, "By passing the budget now, we can avoid laying off additional people this quarter," or, "We can move into the new office space this year instead of next if we pass the budget now."

Checkpoint Charlie

"Would you buy a used car from that person?" Use the following checklist to ensure against anyone saying that about your sales presentation.

Styles Presentation Checklist

❑ Did I analyze my audience?

❑ Did I meet my audience's needs?

❑ Did I adjust my speech to deal with changing needs?

❑ Have I used specific facts and figures?

❑ Did I effectively answer questions about the product?

❑ Did I remember that "the customer is always right"?

❑ Did I speak with enthusiasm and confidence?

❑ Did I know when to stop talking?

Class Act

A persuasive speaking strategy that works in one situation may not work in another. Some organizations expect direct requests; others, a more indirect approach. Study role models and solicit advice when selecting a persuasive approach for selling a budget or an idea.

Talk Soup

A **eulogy** is a speech given in praise of a person. Eulogies are most often delivered at funerals, but they can also be given at any occasion that honors someone.

As you edit and revise your sales speech, check off the important elements you completed or considered.

Dead, But Not Forgotten: Eulogies

Under the sod and under the trees
Lies the body of Jonathan Pease.
He is not here, there's only the pod:
Pease shelled out and went to God.

—Nantucket, Mass., c. 1880

A *eulogy* is a speech given in praise of a person. Speakers often deliver eulogies at funerals and memorial services. In addition to fulfilling a very important business and personal function, delivering a eulogy also can be an important part of your own healing process.

Every eulogy has three main goals:

➤ Express regret for the loss: "We are poorer for the loss of Joe Schmo...."

➤ Celebrate the life: "Joe loved people...."

➤ Find meaning: "When we think about Joe, let us remember how fully he lived his life."

For the most powerful eulogies, concentrate on a few specific qualities of the person being honored. For example, a eulogy for a retiring volunteer firefighter might concentrate on the effect of the person's bravery by giving instances when he or she helped others.

Take a look at these ten key strategies and some practical tips for writing and delivering a memorable tribute.

1. Keep yourself out of it. Reach out to comfort as well as to honor. For example, instead of saying, "I was amazed by the tremendous outpouring of love and support Joe Schmo received," say, "Joe Schmo was touched and amazed—we were all amazed—by the tremendous outpouring of love and support he received from scores of people."

2. Speak honestly and pay attention to rhythm. Check the flow of your writing by reading your speech aloud as you write it. Make sure the rhythm captures the cadence of natural speech.

3. Include a balanced look at the person's life. Don't ignore some obvious facts about the person's life, such as his nine former wives (especially if most of them will be in the audience).

4. Relieve tension with anecdotes. The stories should be specific and illustrate important aspects of the person's life. Former President Jimmy Carter used this anecdote in his 1977 eulogy for Hubert Humphrey:

> "And I'll never forget sitting in the front presidential suite of the Georgia governor's mansion, a very beautiful room, trying to talk to Senator Humphrey, and she [Carter's daughter, Amy] climbed up on his lap without any timidity at all. In a very natural way, he put his arm around her as though she was his own grandchild. And I'll always remember Senator Humphrey sitting there talking to me about politics and about the campaign, smiling often, with brownie all over his face. And each time he frowned, brownie crumbs fell to the floor. And Amy loved him then and has loved him ever since. But I think she recognized in him the qualities that have aroused the love of so many people."

5. Reach out to all your listeners. Try to touch them all, even Aunt Hortense—the one no one has spoken to since she called the IRS on your Uncle Joe.

6. Weave background information into the stories you tell so that the newest friends feel included.

7. Make long-time friends and colleagues a part of your tribute by quoting them.

8. Write from your heart. Avoid lofty, overblown sentences. See how Robert F. Kennedy opened his 1968 eulogy for Martin Luther King Jr. with these words from his heart:

> "I have bad news for you, all of our fellow citizens, and people who love peace all over the world, and that is that Martin Luther King was shot and killed tonight."

9. Address people directly. Use their names, as in "Seymore Glass said that...."

10. End on an emotional, memorable, quotable note. Secretary of War Stanton's words on the death of Abraham Lincoln have become famous for their tightly packed emotion: "Now he belongs to the ages."

Here's a model eulogy for Beat poet Allen Ginsberg:

In the death of Allen Ginsberg, we have lost a teacher, a friend, and an example of how to be a genuine poet in the larger social and political community. Allen did not invent anything about himself; he was the real thing. He was forthright, brilliant, cranky, generous, and unapologetic. He did what few, if any, literary, social, or political figures are able to do; he brought his work off the page and dared to be himself.

For the past 40 years, his work has encouraged, enraged, and served all of us as physical evidence of the vital role of the poet in society. It has defended our existence; that artists are a necessity, not a luxury.

Allen showed us that as writers, artists, and performers, we must speak our individual truths and defend the First Amendment with who we are, not just with what we do. He has been an example to those of us struggling to stay awake, to truly breathe freely in our own skins, with our own names, and to leave this often dark and intolerant world a bit better than we found it.

He pried open the door to the room where poetry has enough power to change the world. He put his body in the door jamb, using his own life, his own voice as the proving ground for what he believed.

He used his 70 years, in part, to block that door open so others might walk through. So you and I might walk through. So we may breathe life and change into a world that desperately needs it. So we might make a difference.

As a mentor he is irreplaceable; as a living symbol of the kind of freedoms we are daily denied, he will live on. He believed in the power of Art to raise buildings and shift armies, to conjure love, make us laugh, and turn the soul to catch the light.

He will be remembered.

He will be missed.

He will not be forgotten.

—Anonymous

Proactive Problem-Solvers

Whether you're a student, an employee, an employer, or a community volunteer, you need to be able to work with others to solve problems. Working with others often sets off tempers, making it more difficult to reach an equitable resolution. When you're speaking for a group, try these guidelines to keep the waters calm:

Class Act

Write possible add-on sentences on sticky notes along the edge of note cards, in case you need them.

1. In your speech, describe and understand the problem. Define the scope and causes of the problem.

2. Be sure to isolate criteria to use in order to judge possible solutions. Establish standards for evaluating solutions.

3. Identify all possible solutions. Keep an open mind; don't discard any possibilities as you speak.

4. Evaluate each possible solution according to the standards that were set earlier.

5. Select the best possible solution and present it in your speech.

6. Address people from every involved group. To solve a work-related problem, for example, be sure to address the needs of union workers, sales associates, and management in your speech.

7. To make sure that no one is left out in the cold, don't withhold any relevant information as you speak.

8. Don't let personality conflicts infringe on your address. Work to maintain the group's cohesiveness and ability to work together after you finish speaking.

Vote Early and Often

You campaign in poetry, but govern in prose.

Even though people have individual differences in temperament and ability, their responses to persuasive appeals are surprisingly similar—so similar, in fact, that politicians have been able to develop a fairly standard pattern for campaign speeches.

Savvy candidates follow these three caveats:

1. **Be factual.** Don't stretch the truth—not even a little.

2. **Be specific.** Give details to support your claims.

3. **Be reliable.** Don't promise what you can't deliver.

Nearly all candidates attempt to create dissatisfaction with existing conditions to convince the audience that these conditions need to be changed—and that they can actually do it. Candidates craft speeches that point out flaws and failure.

Follow these steps when you write and deliver a campaign speech:

Direct Appeal	Election Campaign
1. Tell the audience what you want.	"Elect me."
2. Give them the information they need to act on your request.	"We're paying too much in taxes. I can lower taxes."
3. Tell the audience what you want.	"Vote for me."

But people don't make decisions based on logic alone. Emotional appeals make the audience want to do what you ask. When combined with direct requests, emotional appeals make surprisingly strong election campaigns. Think of the drunk driving and adopt a foreign child campaigns.

Nominating a Candidate

A speech to nominate a candidate has two aims: to explain why your candidate is qualified for a specific office, and to whip up support for your candidate. The excitement of your speech should carry over to the voting. Try these guidelines when you prepare a nominating speech:

➤ First, list the requirements for the office.

➤ Then, explain how well your candidate's training and knowledge fulfill each requirement.

➤ Don't provide the candidate's entire life history. Instead, provide examples of your candidate's positive qualities, such as judgment, loyalty, energy, and intelligence.

➤ Link each character trait to one aspect of the office.

➤ Reinforce the positive character traits you listed by using the candidate's name often.

➤ Speak with conviction and vigor.

➤ Don't attack the other candidate.

➤ Keep your speech short.

➤ End the speech with your candidate's name and a flourish to create excitement.

The Least You Need to Know

➤ Persuasive speeches include speeches of fact, speeches of value, and speeches of policy.

➤ All persuasive speeches aim to provide enough information to convey to the listener what to do, to overcome the listener's objections, and to move the audience to belief or action.

➤ Use a direct approach when your audience is receptive to your ideas; use an indirect approach when they are not.

➤ Eulogies—speeches given in praise of a person—express regret for the loss, celebrate the life, and find meaning.

➤ Election speeches are factual, specific, and reliable.

Chapter 22

Entertaining Speeches

In This Chapter

➤ Introducing a speaker

➤ Giving a graduation speech

➤ Hosting toasts and roasts

➤ Presenting and receiving an award

➤ Speaking at retirements

➤ Speaking at conventions

➤ Speaking at birthdays and weddings

➤ Dedicating an imposing edifice

Speaking to the Young People's Society in Greenpoint, Brooklyn, in 1901, Mark Twain advised, "Always do right. This will gratify some people and astonish the rest."

For centuries, speakers have been called upon to speak at various social events. Sometimes these speeches help create greater unity within an organization. Other times, they honor individuals or fulfill part of a social ritual or special ceremony. What makes these speeches different from the others described so far is their purpose: They don't inform or persuade. Instead, they entertain.

In this chapter, you'll learn how to write speeches that build goodwill, create social cohesion, and delight audiences. First, you'll learn how to introduce a speaker, give a graduation speech, and present and receive an award. Next, we'll cover speaking at conventions, birthdays, anniversaries, weddings, retirements, and reunions. Finally, we'll discuss how to dedicate a building. In each section, you'll learn how to make your natural style and grace work for you in public speaking situations.

The Host with the Most: Introducing a Speaker

Brevity is the soul of wit, but nowhere is this more true than when you're introducing a speaker. Remember, you're not the head weenie at this roast. Keep your remarks short so you don't steal the main speaker's thunder.

What's a short introduction? A 2- to 3-minute speech is ideal—and certainly your speech should be no more than 5 minutes long. The object is to get the speaker and the audience together as quickly as possible, without appearing too rushed.

Your introduction should include these elements:

➤ The title of the speech that the speaker will give

➤ Why the speaker is qualified to speak on the topic

➤ The speaker's name—preferably mentioned several times so that the audience remembers it

Class Act

Have you ever heard someone go to the podium and say, "And here's Mr. Henry Huggins and his good wife Sylvia"? How about, "We're delighted to have Mr. Horatio Hornblower and his better half, Estelle"?

These phrases were once accepted as the norm, but today they're considered tacky, rude, and disparaging. Instead, say, "I would like to introduce Herbert and Hortensia Huffnagle."

How can you get the information needed to satisfy these elements? Ask the speaker for his or her résumé. This should provide you with more than enough information. But getting your hands on a speaker's biography also carries temptation—should you use the résumé or vita as your speech? No. No. No.

Coming Attractions

Draw what you need from the speaker's résumé. The elements should then be woven into a profile, not ticked off like an obituary. Anything that unites the speaker and the audience is fair game.

Sometimes, the speaker will provide you with the introduction he or she wants used. If you're lucky, the introduction you're provided with will be a good one. If you're unlucky, the introduction will be canned and stale.

In most situations, you're under no obligation to deliver the speaker's introduction as written. Edit it to answer the three key questions listed earlier in this section.

Delete ho-hum lists of professional organizations, and fill it with lively stories that show why the speaker was invited to address the organization and why you're delighted to be making the introduction. Many times a professional speaker will supply a professionally written introduction that is designed to achieve specific goals. This introduction should *not* be edited.

Use the following check list to help you introduce a speaker with poise and self-assurance. Check off these items as you prepare and deliver your introductory speech.

Speech of the Devil

➤ Don't try to summarize the speaker's presentation.

➤ Don't try to fake it—be prepared.

➤ Don't point out any negative situations about the room, audience, or speaker.

➤ Don't say anything that will embarrass the speaker.

Speaker Introduction Checklist

❏ Pronounce the speaker's name correctly—practice beforehand.

❏ Research the person's background and achievements.

❏ Repeat the speaker's name several times.

❏ Zero in on what makes the speaker specifically qualified to address this audience.

❏ Praise the speaker (but don't embarrass him, her, or yourself).

❏ Use the format of the speech to inform (see Chapter 20, "Informational Speeches").

❏ Speak with warmth and vitality.

❏ After delivering your speech, applaud until the speaker reaches the podium.

❏ When the speaker talks, listen closely—especially to the opening. You might have to respond to mention of your name or thanks.

❏ Be sure to talk with the speaker ahead of time about what you're both going to say, so there are no surprises.

Always-Fail Clichés

Except for death, taxes, and getting great seats at the ball game the day that it rains, few things are certain in life. Here's something else to believe in: speech openings that will always flop. Trust me on this one, and don't even try 'em.

1. "It is indeed a great privilege to introduce..."

2. "On this most ceremonial occasion..."

3. "Gathered here together at this memorable affair..."

4. "We are truly honored to have with us today…"

5. "Ladies and gentlemen, heeeere's…"

6. "Without further ado…"

7. "We are truly a fortunate audience because we have with us none other than…"

8. "Ladies and gentlemen, here's a speaker who needs no introduction…"

9. "As we stand at the crossroads of this momentous occasion…"

10. "Four score and seven years ago…"

Making the Grade: Giving a Graduation Speech

Graduation speeches are plum speaking jobs because the audience is almost guaranteed to be in a good mood. Parents are finished paying astonishing tuition bills; graduates have yet to start repaying their loans; professors are glad it's all over until September.

Not only that, but everyone looks pretty good in a graduation gown.

Don't spoil the good feelings: Keep your remarks short and snappy. The most effective commencement speeches are between 10 and 15 minutes long. After that, the audience will start to fidget. A wit once said: "The greatest achievement of the graduate is sitting through the commencement address." Don't let this observation apply to *your* speech.

Try to be memorable. Keep in mind that you want your speech to be easy to remember—and easy for the press to quote.

For example, in his later years, Winston Churchill was asked to give the commencement address at Oxford University. Following his introduction, he rose, went to the podium, and said, "Never, never give up." Then he took his seat. Here are some topics to consider—and some to avoid.

Class Act

Remember that the weather in May and June is capricious. If the graduation is being held outdoors, watch for rain clouds. If you see anything threatening on the horizon, cut your remarks short.

Good Bet Speech Topics	Bad Bet Speech Topics
➤ Career issues	➤ Nuclear war
➤ Political topics	➤ National disasters
➤ Social themes	➤ Ecological cataclysms
➤ Civic subjects	➤ Automotive safety defects
➤ Economic questions	➤ The lousy job market for graduates
➤ Graduates' dreams	➤ Your recent surgical procedure

Here's an outstanding graduation speech delivered on May 21, 1998, by Jennifer L. Joyner-Lebling, the valedictorian of the graduating class at the State University of New York College of Technology at Farmingdale. Notice how Ms. Joyner-Lebling graciously credits others.

Voyage of Discovery

Chairman Mastroianni, Dr. Cipriani, honored members of the college council, faculty, staff, fellow classmates, family, and friends, I am honored to have been selected Valedictorian of the graduating class of 1998. I am honored to represent your commitment, dedication, and accomplishment in achieving your goal to be here today.

Congratulations to all of you. As our celebrations end later today, consider tomorrow and realize that graduation is just one giant step in a very important direction. For some of us, this step has been a struggle full of obstacles, barriers, and distractions...for others it has not been that easy. However, through our struggles we have still accomplished our goal, and we are here today to celebrate our achievements—this awesome achievement we have made together, as well as the individual achievements of our team members.

Like Karen Conner, the Valedictorian for the Associates degree, who was awarded the National Scholarship from the Institute of Management Accountants.

And like Michael Rodriquez of the Aerospace program, the recipient of the John L. Godwin, Memorial Flight Scholarship awarded by the National Air Transportation Association Foundation. Each are receiving Chancellors Awards for Student Excellence.

And like Ornamental Horticulture graduates Pat Haugen, Elizabeth Boruke, Melissa Rigo, Steve Langella, Jessica Bottcher, Matt McFadden, and Steve Noone, who were members of a team which took first place at the Mid-Atlantic Horticultural Field Day at Suffolk Community College.

Today is the culmination of a lot of work, a lot of sweat, a lot of tears, and a lot of money...but we are not finished. This is not final. It is, however, a significant milestone in our voyage of discovery. We have just emerged on a whole new level. You are all outstanding representatives of our graduating class. But none of us accomplished these feats alone. We had our families, partners and friends...and we had the tutelage and guidance of some pretty incredible teachers. Before you leave today, be sure to thank at least one teacher from whom you have learned while at SUNY Farmingdale, and let them know that they are appreciated.

Thank you Dr. Gary Brown for your enthusiasm and passion for your subjects and for your interest in and concern for your students.

Thank you Dr. Richard Iversen for your never-ending support, encouragement, and mentoring. You have both made a substantial impact on my education and on my future.

Thank you Gary, Fred, Debbie, and Danielle for your guidance and friendship.

French novelist Marcel Proust once said, 'The real voyage of discovery consists not in seeking new landscapes but in having new eyes.' In receiving our diplomas today, we are receiving 'new eyes.' Use what you have learned here at SUNY Farmingdale to see things in ways in which you have never noticed before. Continue to learn. Open your minds to new ideas and concepts. We leave here with the ability to make a change, the capability to make a difference, and the responsibility to make a contribution. Congratulations to you, my fellow graduates, and good luck to you as you continue on your voyage of discovery.

Speech of the Devil

Never upstage the honoree by being too funny. Also avoid stealing the honoree's material, relying on memory or ad-lib, or faking a close relationship with the honoree. It's also bad form to put the honoree on the spot.

Put Your Hands Together For...

Mark Twain answered a "Toast to the Babies" at a Chicago banquet in 1879 this way: "We haven't all had the good fortune to be ladies; we haven't all been generals, or poets, or statesmen; but when the toast works down to babies, we all stand on common ground."

The term *toast* dates back to the 1600s and refers to a chunk of bread dipped in drinks. The term then came to refer to a drink in honor of a favorite lady and, soon, a drink in honor of just about anything you could hoist one to. The custom took off so quickly that by the 18th century, Pennsylvania was fining its residents and visitors for excessive toasting.

As the custom began to hit the upscale joints, toastmasters took some pains to craft their speeches. Their toasts were often printed on the dinner menu and became part of the permanent record of many organizations.

Today, toast and roast masters are expected to set the tone for the entire event. With toasts and roasts, the skill of the speaker is really put to the test. Toastmasters are expected to be sharp and witty (which of course you are, or you wouldn't have been invited to be the host).

But no rule says that you have to spend miserable hours hunting for great jokes. You're much better off not telling any jokes at all than telling a joke poorly. On the other hand, if you've got any talent in the joke department, now's the time to display it.

Toasts

Follow these guidelines to make your toasts memorable:

➤ Make a general statement about the theme of the gathering.

➤ Introduce the head table. (Don't introduce the speaker; that will be done later.)

➤ Have the audience hold their applause until the end.

➤ Make sure your toast is appropriate.

➤ Invite the guests to join in a toast to the honoree(s).

➤ Ask a designated person at the head table to introduce the speaker.

➤ When the speaker is finished, express thanks.

And Roasts

Follow these guidelines for hosting a successful roast:

➤ Probe what you know about the honoree to find a fresh slant on his or her life and accomplishments.

➤ Provide specific examples of your honoree's character and accomplishments.

➤ Suit your remarks to the general tone of the evening.

➤ Err on the side of good taste; no matter how good a line may be, skip it if you—or the honoree—might regret it in the morning.

➤ Avoid humor if you are not comfortable with it.

Talk Soup

The **toastmaster** is the chairperson, the host. The toastmaster has three important tasks: to run the program smoothly, to hold the audience's attention, and to discourage strife. A **roastmaster** is a type of toastmaster; a roastmaster presides over a roast or honorary event.

The Envelope, Please: Presenting an Award

We all deserve recognition for a job well done. Saving someone's life, saving the company some money, saving customers' time: They all merit public acknowledgment.

Keep your speech factual and straightforward. This is even more important if you have to present an award to someone you've never met. In this situation, don't pretend that you are the honoree's best buddy. Instead, interview the person's friends, family, or colleagues to get some information that shows why the person deserves the award. Share this information with the audience, acknowledging your sources.

In Grateful Appreciation

You can use these questions as you prepare a speech to present an award.

Award Presentation Checklist

❏ Can I be generous with my praise?

❏ Can I use true anecdotes from the person's life to make my speech personal?

❏ Can I give specific reasons why the person deserves this award?

❏ Can I make it clear how this person's involvement made a difference to others?

❏ Is my speech earnest?

❏ Does my speech have an uplifting, inspirational tone?

Take the Money and Run: Receiving an Award

Follow these steps to accept an award with your usual good grace and taste:

➤ Thank and praise the giver of the award.

➤ Acknowledge the help you got from others.

➤ Explain how much the award means to you and why.

➤ Speak directly and to the point so the audience doesn't become restless.

➤ Explain the positive values you see in the award.

Class Act

Speaking at a retirement? Follow the directions for presenting an award. And under no circumstances should you let anyone sing "My Way."

Speaking at Conventions

The featured speech at a convention is called the *keynote address.* The *keynote* is the music on which a system of tones is based; similarly, the keynote address sets the tone for the entire convention.

To decide what to include in your keynote address, consider the mood of the convention, the type of organization, and the kind of business being transacted. This list will help you make sure to include all the important elements of a keynote address:

➤ Did I summarize what has happened since the last convention?

➤ Are my remarks and tone suitable to the aims of the organization?

➤ Have I established a feeling of camaraderie?

➤ Is my speech brief?

➤ Is my speech original?

Happy Birthday to You!

If you suspect that you'll be asked to speak at an event where a large cake will be prominently featured, it's a good idea to have a few short lines memorized. There's the old story about the groom who was asked to say a few words to his bride. Everyone raised their glasses when the unprepared groom staggered to his feet and stammered: "Ladies and gentlemen, I... I don't know what to say. This thing was forced on me...." (How the bride responded is not on record.)

Here are some birthday celebration lines you can use or adapt:

➤ You're not as young as you used to be / But you're not as old as you're going to be / So watch it!

➤ Another candle on your cake? / Well, that's no cause to pout, / Be glad that you have strength enough / To blow the damned thing out.

➤ May you live a hundred years—with one extra year to repent.

➤ Here's to a friend. He knows you well and likes you just the same.

➤ Here's to our friends—and the strength to put up with them.

➤ "The secret of staying young is to live honestly, eat slowly, and lie about your age." —Lucille Ball

➤ At age 52, Lady Astor said, "I refuse to admit that I'm more than 52, even if that does make my sons illegitimate."

➤ "The years between 50 and 70 are the hardest. You are always being asked to do things, and yet you are not decrepit enough to turn them down." —T. S. Eliot

Try these lines at an anniversary party:

➤ Here's to you both—a beautiful pair—on the birthday of your love affair.

➤ The best way you can surprise a woman (or man) with an anniversary gift is to give her (him) just what she (he) wanted.

Speech of the Devil

It's never a good idea to reuse a speech, but it's especially important to write new material for a toast. You want this speech tailored to the person being honored.

Going to the Chapel: Speaking at Weddings

Few will dispute the widely held opinion that having to make a wedding toast is one of the scariest kinds of speech-giving. But toasting doesn't have to be tense—as long as you're well prepared.

Relax, baby: You're in good hands! Here are specific directions for toasts that the best man, father of the bride, and the groom will deliver.

Class Act

Asked to speak at your reunion? Focus on experiences shared by everyone in attendance, like the time the gym teacher fell off the donkey at the basketball game. These speeches are most successful when the speaker is able to tell stories that will help the audience recall shared events. They also need to have a central theme as a unifying element.

The Best Man

1. Thank the bride and groom for asking you to be the best man.

2. Praise the bride and groom. Choose a theme or main idea, and center your speech around it. Remember to mention any close friends or relatives who were unable to attend and who propose a toast to the bride.

3. Wish the bride and groom well in their new life together.

4. Thank your hosts on behalf of the guests, and introduce the next speaker.

Father of the Bride

1. Welcome the groom's parents by name, followed by other relatives of both families. Then welcome friends, and any distinguished guests, by name if appropriate.

2. Thank the special services by name such as caterers and voluntary helpers.

3. Praise the bride—both her appearance and her achievements—and thank her for her part in your family.

4. Welcome the groom into the family with words of praise.

5. Offer words of wisdom to newlyweds; these are usually light-hearted and humorous. Wish the happy couple well.

6. Propose a toast to the bride and groom.

The Groom

1. Thank the bride's parents for the reception (if applicable), and supply a few words of welcome into the family.

2. Thank your own parents for their family life and your upbringing.

3. Thank the best man for his services. Add a few humorous comments about the best man.

4. Praise your bride to the sky. You'll also need to toast her. Here's a sure-fire winner: "A thing of beauty is a joy forever. Here's to you, my beautiful bride."

And what about the recipient of a toast? Don't stand, raise your glass, or take a sip of your drink. Do thank the toasters, or at least smile and graciously nod. You are not obliged to propose a toast in return.

Encores and exits

At Jewish weddings, the groom usually speaks last, after the best man. The same sequence is followed in England and Scotland, but in Ireland, anybody who wishes to speak gets up and hoists one aloft. Irish weddings are l-o-n-g affairs.

How to Make Sure That Rice Is the Only Thing That Gets Thrown

Now you know the form—but what about the context? Exactly what should you say when you make a toast at a wedding?

Weigh the nature of the nuptials and your own reputation when deciding to make your speech serious or humorous. The most successful speeches usually combine both elements, but this depends on your comfort zone. One clever speaker toasted a slice of bread and placed it in his inside coat pocket. When it was time for the toast, he said, "I have a toast for the new husband and wife...." Then he reached into his pocket, pulled out the toast, and handed it to them. After the laughter, he gave a heartfelt, serious toast. In any event, always keep it short, simple, and, of course, sweet.

If your temperament and the tone of the wedding are serious, look to serious material. Consider this quote from Shakespeare: "Look down, you gods, and on this couple drop a blessed crown."

Here are some other serious lines you may wish to weave into your wedding toast or speech:

225

➤ The love you give is the love you keep.

➤ Let's drink to love, / Which is nothing / Unless it's divided by two.

➤ Love doesn't make the world go 'round. It's what makes the ride worthwhile.

➤ A toast to love and laughter and happily ever after.

➤ Here's to the Bride and Groom! / May you have a happy honeymoon, / May you lead a happy life, / May you have a bunch of money soon, / And live without all strife.

➤ May their joys be as deep as the ocean / And their misfortunes as light as the foam.

➤ Marriage—the high sea for which no compass has yet been invented.

➤ Marriages may be made in heaven, but most of the details are worked out on earth.

➤ To keep the fire burning brightly, there's one easy rule: Keep the two logs together, near enough to keep each other warm and far enough apart—about a finger's breadth—for breathing room. Good fire, good marriage, same rule.

Class Act

Make sure that all glasses are filled before you propose a toast. Raise your glass with your right hand. In addition, be sure to hold the glass straight from your shoulder.

Again, use only material that you can deliver comfortably. If you're at ease with comic material, you might want to offer an admonition from such respected experts on marriage as Zsa Zsa Gabor: "A man in love is incomplete until he is married. Then he is finished." Phyllis Diller has some equally trenchant advice for newlyweds: "Never go to bed mad. Stay up and fight." Here are a few more lines to get you started:

➤ Before marriage, a man will lie awake all night thinking about something you said; after marriage, he'll fall asleep before you finish saying it.

➤ Here's to our wives and lovers. May they never meet.

➤ I told my wife that a husband is like a fine wine—he gets better with age. The next day she locked me in the cellar.

➤ My wife and I have a perfect understanding. I don't try to run her life, and I don't try to run mine.

Above all, don't steal the spotlight. You don't need to fill up the toast with funny stories about you and the groom fishing and playing baseball as kids, and how it has affected your life. The focus shouldn't be on you.

Encores and Exits

It is traditional to clink glasses after the toast has been proposed and before taking a drink. This tradition is rooted in earliest human history: Older cultures made a noise, such as the ringing of a bell or the clinking of a glass, to frighten away evil spirits. Toasts can be sealed with a sip of champagne, wine, a mixed drink, or non-alcoholic punch, but never with tea, coffee, or water. Whatever the beverage chosen, it should be served to the bride first, then the groom, then the maid of honor, then parents, and lastly the best man.

Cutting the Ribbon: Dedicating an Imposing Edifice

Here, your function is to pull together a community. The people who are part of the ceremony are there to reaffirm their commitment to the community and to help preserve the community's most important values.

As a result, emotional appeals and efforts to increase the audience's identification with the speaker win out over the use of logic. To ensure a good speech, appeal to the interests and values that you share with the audience.

The Least You Need to Know

➤ When you introduce a speaker, keep your remarks short.

➤ Graduation speeches should be brief, memorable, and quotable.

➤ When you present an award, be factual and straightforward. Never upstage the honoree.

➤ When you speak at weddings, suit the speech to your style and the occasion. Always err on the side of good taste.

➤ Speeches that mark endings and beginnings focus on common experiences.

Chapter 23

Speaking
Off-the-Cuff

In This Chapter

➤ The three basic rules of impromptu speaking

➤ Preparing an impromptu speech: research and experience

➤ Organizing an impromptu speech

➤ Staying on the topic and speaking in complete sentences

➤ Dealing with question-and-answer sessions

➤ Having nothing to say

➤ Overcoming stage fright

Mark Twain's knees were shaking so violently that few people in the audience believed he would be able to deliver his first lecture, but he won the day when he suddenly said, "Julius Caesar is dead, Shakespeare is dead, Napoleon is dead, Abraham Lincoln is dead, and I am far from well myself."

In the speech biz, speaking at a gathering with very little preparation and without the use of notes is called *impromptu speaking*. In everyday life, it's often called "hell" and a few other terms we can't print here. But despite its terrifying reputation, impromptu speaking need not be likened to trial by fire.

Being a good impromptu speaker is very beneficial because of its everyday usefulness. Mastering this skill will help you feel more comfortable thinking—and speaking—on your feet. You will also be better able to say what you mean. And after you finish this chapter, you might even find that you *enjoy* being asked to speak off-the-cuff. Really.

Been There, Done That

Impromptu speaking follows three basic rules:

1. Have something important to say.

2. Make your audience understand or believe it.

3. Speak simply, directly, and meaningfully.

Believe it or not, you already know how to speak off-the-cuff. You've been doing it for years, probably since you were a toddler. For example, when you go to the post office, nobody hands you a prepared speech. You simply go to the clerk and tell him or her what you want. When you go to the hairdresser, you're rarely at a loss for words (well, maybe after your hair is cut, but not before). You go about your daily business without writing speeches. And you do just fine at it.

So when you're asked to speak off-the-cuff at a business conference, Rotary meeting, PTA gathering, or annual convention, it helps to remember that you're drawing on decades of experience.

Below are some ways to tap your well of experience so you can make smooth, effective, and memorable impromptu speeches.

Know Your Stuff

An electrical engineer, a chemical engineer, and a Microsoft engineer were riding in a car. Suddenly the car stalled and stopped by the side of the road. The three engineers looked at each other with bewilderment, wondering what could be wrong.

The electrical engineer suggested, "Let's strip down the electronics of the car and try to trace where a fault might have occurred."

The chemical engineer suggested, "Maybe the fuel has become emulsified and is causing a blockage somewhere in the system."

The Microsoft engineer said, "Why don't we close all the windows, get out, get back in, open the windows again, and see if it works."

One great advantage of impromptu speaking is the fact that it automatically sounds natural and spontaneous. But don't be fooled: That "natural and spontaneous" effect is often the result of meticulous planning (and you thought this was the one kind of speech you wouldn't have to plan). Impromptu speaking is easy, as long as you follow one rule: *Know what you're talking about.* This isn't the time to rely on luck: You can't just open and close the windows and hope for the best.

If you're going to a meeting where there is the slightest chance that someone might ask you to speak, go the Boy Scout route: Be prepared. Make some notes about the topics that might come up in the discussion. Jot down ideas throughout the presentation or panel discussions.

A Method to This Madness

There are two ways to get the off-the-cuff territory down: by *research* and by *experience*. Bob Rozakis, a brilliant public speaker and my husband, used the research method when he suspected that he would be called upon to make an impromptu speech at a friend's 50th birthday party. The friend's name is Peter Goldsmith, he's a printer, and he lives in New York City. To prepare, Bob gathered facts about famous New Yorkers named Peter. He then considered how he could spin these facts to apply to Peter Goldsmith. Here are a few of his comments:

Class Act

When you prepare for an impromptu speech during someone else's presentation, concentrate not only on the speakers but also on the room and the conference theme. You'll need to keep these in mind as well.

➤ In 1626, Pieter Guldensmitt paid 60 Guilders—about $24—in cloth and trinkets for this very island. We're not quite sure which Indian tribe he paid, but he did manage to get the contract to print all the maps.

➤ Then, in 1647, using the name Peter Stuyvergoldsmith, he arrived to take over the city. At the time, he found that 18 different languages were being spoken—obviously there were fewer taxi drivers then—and so he immediately started printing translation guides.

➤ The next time we find information about Peter appears to be 1898, the time of his first trip to the Caribbean. According to accounts, Peter was seen rushing up San Juan Hill waving his American Express Gold Card and shouting "Charge!" Teddy Roosevelt was unimpressed with Peter during this time and refused to rename the island *Peter Rico*.

➤ You've all heard the stories about John D. Rockefeller walking around New York and handing out dimes. Well, Peter decided to outdo him by handing out dollar bills. Unfortunately, Peter had printed those bills himself.

The speech was a smash hit.

On-the-Spot Organization

Now that you know what you're going to talk about, here's a never-fail method for organizing an impromptu speech:

1. State the point you're making. Remember, you only get one central idea.

2. Support you point with appropriate examples.

3. Summarize and restate your point.

Encores and Exits

Some talented speakers are not above resorting to tricks to make their speeches seem less rehearsed. One such story concerns the late New York Mayor Jimmy Walker. A journalist once saw Walker dazzle an audience by saying, "Ladies and gentlemen, I arrived here this evening with some written remarks, but I've decided to discard my prepared speech and speak to you from the heart." With that, Walker balled up the paper he had been holding and tossed it aside. He went on to deliver an electrifying speech.

After Walker and his entourage had left, the journalist picked up the discarded "speech" and looked at it. The paper was nothing more than an advertisement. Walker had spoken from memorized remarks freshened with observations he had made about the people, theme, and event. And so can you.

This method of organizing is a speech is nothing fancy—in fact it's the tried-and-true method of organizing a speech you've learned earlier in this book. Memorize this method, and you'll always have a framework upon which to arrange your remarks—even if you're on the spot.

Lost in Space

Novice speakers find that one of the most difficult aspects of impromptu speaking is staying on the topic. The longer they speak, the greater their tendency to drift into other issues. Soon, they find themselves cruising through the clouds. The audience, meanwhile, is having a well-deserved snooze.

Very few speakers can resist the temptation to wander off-track. In everyday speech this is not a hanging offense, but in formal speech situations it can be disastrous to life, limb, and reputation. For example, digressions are rarely appreciated when people are reporting serious accidents, giving testimony, or proposing marriage.

Speech of the Devil

It's especially crucial to keep your speech simple when you're speaking off-the-cuff. The simpler your remarks, the less your chance of making a blunder.

"How can I properly arrange an impromptu speech?" you might ask. Here's how:

1. Quickly decide what you are going to talk about.

2. No second-guessing with spur-of-the-moment speeches: Once you've picked the topic, stick with it.

3. Don't digress.

4. If necessary, pause for a few seconds to gather your thoughts.

5. Present only two or three facts, proofs, or supporting statements.

6. Try to wrap it up with a good punch line. People tend to remember a strong exit.

7. Don't drag it out. Remember, you're not the main attraction here—if you were, you wouldn't be speaking off-the-cuff.

Uh, Like, Wow: Speak in Complete Sentences

A vast number of teachers, store clerks, and telephone operators would no doubt argue that speaking in complete sentences has become a lost art in America. "Not me!" you cry out in mock alarm. Actually, you're probably as guilty of speaking in fragments as the next person. To prove my point, take a look at the following two messages:

Class Act

To get good at spontaneous speech-making, practice, practice some more, and keep on practicing.

What you *think* you're saying:

> Fourscore and seven years ago our fathers brought forth on this continent a new nation, conceived in liberty, and dedicated to the proposition that all men are created equal.

What you're probably *really* saying:

> Like…uh…a long time ago, like maybe fourscore and seven years ago, you know. Our fathers…em…made, you know, on this like place like a continent a new nation…uh…conceived in, you know, like liberty and…uh…and dedicated to the like idea that all…uh…men, but I don't want to forget like women, like they are really important too because they make up over half the population, you know, are like sort of like created equal.

Of course, this is an exaggeration—but it's not as exaggerated as we'd like to think. Even the most highly trained newscasters sometimes slip into dead-air fillers such as "uh," "eh," and "like"—especially when the pressure's on.

You may be one of the very fortunate few who are able to speak lucid, well-formed sentences without any advance preparation—if so, you're reading this chapter for pleasure. Most of us, however, need a little help.

Audiences will indulge you in a certain amount of incoherence, but it must be kept to a minimum. Try these suggestions for speaking more smoothly:

1. Practice impromptu speaking until you feel more comfortable with it.

2. Repeat tricky phrases, names, and words until you have them down.

3. Work at eliminating distracting, "throat-clearing" phrases such as "uh" and "em."

4. Get rid of intrusive words and phrases such as "like," "you see," and "you know."

5. Tape-record yourself to monitor your progress. Remember that pauses punctuate thought. Just as commas, semicolons, and periods separate written words into thought groups, so pauses of different lengths separate spoken words into meaningful units. Remember, though, that the haphazard use of pauses when you are speaking is as confusing to the listener as the haphazard use of punctuation in written matter is to the reader.

Nowhere to Hide: Question-and-Answer Sessions

Unless questions are submitted in advance, question-and-answer sessions also call for impromptu answers. Be sure to arrange beforehand with your hosts about whether time should be set aside for questions and answers—and, if so, how much time.

If questions *are* to be allowed, decide whether you want spoken or written queries. With a small audience, questions from the floor are relatively easy to deal with; with a large audience, spoken questions can become very difficult to hear and to answer.

Speech of the Devil

Be sure that your pauses come between thought units and not in the middle of them. And don't be afraid to pause whenever a break in your speech will help clarify an idea or emphasize an important point.

If you're answering questions this way from a large audience, you may wish to repeat each question to make sure that everyone can hear it. But rather than simply repeating the questions, try reworking them. If possible, deliberately revise the wording to make the question easier to answer. Keep the rewording close enough to the original to be on the topic, and remember: You're under no obligation to respond to any questions that embarrass you, your hosts, or your company. If possible, save your close for after the Q & A. This way you will finish strong. If no one asks a question, be prepared and say "Something I am usually asked is…" and then give your answer.

When the Well Runs Dry

But what happens if you follow all this great advice and you still find that you have absolutely nothing to say?

Perhaps the most nerve-wracking situation occurs when someone at a meeting asks you for your opinion and you're caught completely off-guard. The question you're asked is virgin ground to you; you've never given it a thought. You have nothing prepared at all, neither fact nor figure anywhere near your fingertips. You're dead meat, right?

Actually, you might still be able to rescue yourself. Take a deep breath, stand up straight, look ahead, and make a rational comment. No one likely expects to experience final, total enlightenment as a result of your thoughts, but they would like logical sentences that fit the bill. If you draw a complete blank, say, "I don't know. I'll look into the issue and get back to you." Then do so.

Class Act

If you tell the truth during a Q & A session, you don't have to remember any lies. This can prevent tacky and embarrassing misstatements down the road when someone checks the statistics you casually—and erroneously—tossed off.

Probably the worst thing you can do is apologize for not being prepared. Never say something like, "Gee, I'm really sorry. I feel really terrible. No one ever asked me anything like that before. I don't have the slightest idea about what to say." When it comes to speaking in public, it's a good idea to abstain from running yourself down. After all, you can't really want your audience to believe what you're implying about yourself.

Prime the Pump

Here are some tricks you can use when you're stuck for an answer or comment:

➤ Open with a broad generalization to buy yourself a few extra seconds of scrambling.

➤ Stall for extra time by repeating the question.

➤ Ask yourself, "If I were in the audience, is this what I would like to hear?"

A Deer in the Headlights

Unfortunately, stage fright is to impromptu speaking what caffeine is to sleeplessness, especially when you're at a loss for a response. I've already discussed how you speak with scores of people every day. Yet you rarely worry whether your daily conversations are perfect and polished like a shiny stone. On the contrary, you and your listeners *expect* a few hesitations, pauses, repetitions, rephrasings, or silences.

If you approach impromptu speeches worrying about perfection, of course you will be rigid with stage fright. Wake-up call: Common sense tells you that your goal is impossible. Repeat the following chant:

➤ I am involved with my subject.

➤ I care about my audience.

➤ I know my subject.

➤ I recognize that impromptu speeches are not perfect.

➤ I'll do great.

If that doesn't work, you can always try, "I'm smart enough, I'm good enough, and people like me!" (Yes, we're kidding.)

Practice Makes Perfect

Use the following activity to help you gain experience with impromptu speaking. This will help you develop the ability to make choices through reasoning. Write your answers to the questions on paper, then draft a speech as instructed.

1. You are forced to give up the following modern conveniences:

    ➤ Radio

    ➤ Stereo

    ➤ CD player

    ➤ Refrigerator

    ➤ Telephone

    ➤ Washing machine

    ➤ Dishwasher

    ➤ Microwave oven

    ➤ Bathroom

    ➤ Television

2. In what order will you sacrifice each item? Arrange them from most to least important.

3. Jot down some reasons for your choices.

4. Give the speech.

Use the following checklist to prepare for an off-the-cuff presentation. Check off each item to help you assess each impromptu speaking situation.

Impromptu Speaking Checklist

- ❏ Who will be at the meeting?
- ❏ What will probably happen at this meeting?
- ❏ What is the likelihood that I will be asked to speak?
- ❏ How much do I know about the topic of the meeting?
- ❏ What should I prepare at home?
- ❏ What should I prepare at the meeting?
- ❏ What comments are likely to spark controversy?
- ❏ Should I use these comments or avoid them?
- ❏ How can I organize my remarks?
- ❏ How can I make my remarks impressive?

Class Act

It's better to write and practice a speech that you may not need than to not have a speech when you do need it. Preparation is a great way to beat stage fright.

The Least You Need to Know

➤ Decide what you're going to say, develop one main idea, and stick with it.

➤ Keep your speech simple.

➤ Don't go off on tangents.

➤ Speak in complete sentences, without distracting words such as "uh" and "um."

➤ Prepare and memorize a just-in-case speech if impromptu speaking terrorizes you.

Chapter 24

Debate and Parliamentary Procedure

In This Chapter

➤ The proposition of a debate

➤ The affirmative and negative sides in a debate

➤ Steps in preparing a debate

➤ Three common debate formats

➤ Debate rules

➤ Parliamentary procedure

Four friends met at a restaurant for lunch. For quite a while, no one said a word. Finally the first man mumbled, "Oh, boy!" To which the next one said, "It's awful." The third then muttered, "What are ya gonna do?"

"Listen," exclaimed the last friend, "if you guys don't stop talking politics, I'm leaving."

There's more to politics than mumbling and mind-reading, which is why debate is a crucial skill for politicians interested in swaying opinion and accomplishing the business of government. But debate is also important for people involved in business, civic, and social affairs, because the rhetorical skills debaters use carry over into all public speaking situations.

In this chapter, you'll learn how to prepare and conduct a formal debate, from the proposition to the actual speeches. Along the way, you'll learn all about the affirmative and negative sides, how to write a brief and evidence cards, and how to work with a partner. The chapter finishes with an overview of the basics of parliamentary procedure.

Point/Counterpoint

A formal debate pits one side against the other in order to discover the best side of a controversial issue. During a debate, both sides are tested under pressure, which makes debate one of the most challenging forms of oral communication.

Talk Soup

A **formal debate** is a contest in which two sides argue an issue that has only two sides. Formal debate follows a clear-cut set of rules.

Let Me Proposition You

The debate issue is called the *proposition*. It's restricted to issues that have only two clear-cut sides. As a result, a question such as "What should be done about the speed limit?" can't be debated because it has more than two sides. A workable revision would be, "The speed limit should be decreased by 10 miles per hour to cut traffic fatalities."

Here's a good proposition: "The United States should privatize Social Security." Or, try this one : "Compulsory high school shall be extended one year, from four years to five years." Or how about: "The President of the United States should be impeached for high crimes and misdemeanors." You get the idea.

Evaluate the Proposition

How can you recognize a suitable proposition? Here's what to look for:

Talk Soup

The **proposition** is the issue being debated. Propositions have two sides—no more—and can be answered in the affirmative or the negative.

➤ It is worded as a statement, not a question.

➤ It is phrased to allow only "yes" (for) and "no" (against) responses.

➤ It is worded to allow each side an equal shot at making a valid argument; it's not biased toward either side.

➤ It addresses a current, controversial issue that people care enough about to argue.

➤ It uses neutral but specific language.

If your proposition meets that criteria, it's suitable for debate.

Assume the Position

The two sides in a formal debate are called the *affirmative side* and the *negative side*. Although each side may be represented by any number of speakers, usually only one or two people on each side make the case.

The affirmative side has two jobs:

➤ To attack the status quo

➤ To argue that a specific change should occur

Because the affirmative side in a debate proposes a change in policy, it must prove not only that a problem exists, but also that the solution stated in the proposition would be an improvement over the present situation. This is called the *burden of proof*.

The affirmative side starts with the *prima facie case*, an overall argument that would convince any reasonable judge who has not yet heard the response from the other side.

The *negative side* has only one task: to disprove the affirmative side. To do so, the negative side refutes the attacks on the status quo made by the affirmative side. There are four main ways to do this:

1. Attack the affirmative side's argument by asserting that the status quo is completely satisfactory.

2. Attack the affirmative side's plan, arguing that the affirmative plan would create more serious problems than those currently being experienced.

3. Attack the logical link between the affirmative's need and plan. This is called a *need-plan wedge case*.

4. Attack all parts of the affirmative case. Called a *running-refutation negative case*, it is the most common method of attack.

Class Act

Debate is a contest between two opposing points of view; **discussion** involves agreement between sides. As a result, debate is adversarial rather than cooperative.

Talk Soup

The **burden of proof** is the responsibility of the affirmative side to prove that a problem exists and that their solution is better than the current situation.

Doing Hard Time

Formal debate is rigorous public speech, so it demands extra careful preparation. Follow these steps.

1. **Analyze the proposition.** The first speaker for the affirmative side will begin by defining the terms, so decide which terms need to be defined and how you interpret them.

2. **Get the background on the proposition.** Read up on both sides of the issue. Whether you're arguing the affirmative or the negative side, you'll need to know everything you can about the issue.

Talk Soup

In debate, **case** refers to a side's arguments on any given proposition.

Class Act

Evidence cards are ideally suited for the negative side because they help make you more nimble in your response: Individual cards can be added or subtracted depending on the affirmative's approach.

3. **Focus on the issues.** The issues form the cornerstone of any debate, since they're the key arguments on which the proposition's acceptance or rejection rests.

4. **Build a case.** Each side's arguments on any given proposition is called its *case.* To build your case, you can either prepare a brief or evidence cards. *A brief* includes a full outline of your case, with all the analysis and reasoning that you'll use. *Evidence cards,* in contrast, are note cards that contain only the points you intend to make. Think of the brief as the big picture and the evidence cards as the close-up.

   As you participate in your first few debates, consider preparing both a brief and evidence cards because the former will give you the logic of your case; the latter, the proof you need during the debate itself.

5. **Consider the opposition.** As you gather evidence, always consider how the opposition will refute each of your points. This will help you build the strongest possible case.

In Brief

Here's a model you can use to structure your brief:

Introduction

Proposition: _____

_____

   I. Justification for the debate

     A.

     B.

     C.

     (etc.)

II. Background of the proposition

    A.

    B.

    C.

    (etc.)

III. Definition of controversial terms in the proposition

    A.

    B.

    C.

    (etc.)

IV. Waived issues

 V. Conceded issues

VI. Primary issues

    A. Affirmative side

        1.

        2.

        3.

        (etc.)

    B. Negative side

        1.

        2.

        3.

        (etc.)

Discussion

    I. First main contention _____ for

        A. First subcontention _____ for

            1. Evidence _____ and

                a. _____ and

                b. _____ and

        B. Second subcontention _____ for

            1. Evidence _____ and

                a. _____ and

                b. _____ and

            (etc.)

   II. Second main contention _____ for

  III. Third main contention _____ for

        (etc.)

Conclusion

    I. Since _____ , and

   II. Since _____

    Therefore (affirm or deny the proposition)

Are Three Enough? Are Six Too Many?

A note about evidence: When you write an informative, persuasive, or entertaining speech, you normally gather only the evidence you need. Why stockpile extra proof, evidence, and facts? After all, no one is going to grill you on your presentation.

Just the opposite is true when it comes to debate. When debating an issue, figure on having three times the amount of material that you think you'll need. Why? Because you never know what rabbits your opponents are going to pull out of their hats. And when it comes to debate, the team with the greater amount of sound evidence usually wins.

Me and My Shadow

Most debaters work with a partner. As a result, teamwork is crucial to the success of your debate, no matter which side you're on. As you work with your partner, be sure to discuss the following issues:

➤ What strategy to adopt

➤ Which issues to stress

➤ How the brief will be prepared

➤ When you'll rehearse the actual presentation

Nothing can damage your chances of winning a debate as much as strife between partners, so it's important that you and your partner get along with each other. You don't have to make plans to marry, but you *do* have to make a conscious effort to set aside any differences you might have to create a united front. Try these ideas:

Speech of the Devil

Warning: Debate *is* adversarial, not cooperative. Be paranoid: When it comes to debate, the opposition *is* out to get you.

1. Recognize one partner as the leader. Follow that person's lead.

2. Make sure you have a way of reaching your partner when you're not together. Get a phone number or e-mail address.

3. Discuss ahead of time what each partner is expected to do—and never assume that the requirements of the debate are clear to your partner.

4. Divide the responsibilities into a series of smaller steps or parts.

5. Put the responsibilities into a time sequence—in what order must each step or part of the debate be done?

6. Agree on a time table—when must each part of the debate be finished?

7. Divide the responsibilities fairly. Make sure that neither partner feels put-upon or disenfranchised.

8. Agree about what to do up-front if you or your partner falls behind and won't be able to meet a deadline. Use some of your meetings to review what you and your partner have accomplished already.

9. During the debate, listen carefully when your partner is speaking. Make sure everything you say agrees with what your partner has said.

10. Resolve disagreements quickly—and privately. Don't air your grievances in public.

Debate Format

Many different formats can be used during a debate. The choice of format depends on the amount of time available, the nature of the issue, and the number of debaters on each team. The

Class Act

Set new expectations and deadlines as appropriate. Debate partners usually discover as the project moves along that the original time table and division of labor need to be modified. This helps ensure that the work doesn't all pile up at the end.

three main formats of debate are the standard format, the cross-examination format, and the Lincoln-Douglas format. Let's look at each one.

Standard Format

With the standard format, the two speakers on each team make two different types of speeches. Each speaker gives a constructive speech and a rebuttal. The constructive speeches, used to develop the major points for each team's case, are long, usually 8–10 minutes each. Rebuttals, used to refute the opposition's arguments and answer arguments to one's own case, are about half that length. Here's the breakdown of task and time:

Part	Time
First affirmative constructive speech	10 minutes
First negative constructive speech	10 minutes
Second affirmative constructive speech	10 minutes
Second negative constructive speech	10 minutes
First negative speaker's rebuttal	5 minutes
First affirmative speaker's rebuttal	5 minutes
Second negative speaker's rebuttal	5 minutes
Second affirmative speaker's rebuttal	5 minutes

Cross-Examination Format

With the cross-examination format, two speakers represent each side. Here, constructive speeches come first, followed by cross-examinations. A member of the opposing team will then try to reveal the weaknesses in each speaker's arguments by asking the speaker questions. This is how it shakes down. Notice that the debates following the cross-examination format are different from the debates following the standard format in only one respect: Each constructive speech is followed by a cross-examination period.

Part	Time
First affirmative constructive speech	8 minutes
First negative speaker cross-examines	3 minutes
First negative constructive speech	8 minutes
Second affirmative speaker cross-examines	3 minutes
Second affirmative constructive speech	8 minutes
Second negative speaker cross-examines	3 minutes

Part	Time
Second negative constructive speech	8 minutes
First affirmative speaker cross-examines	3 minutes
First negative speaker's rebuttal	4 minutes
First affirmative speaker's rebuttal	4 minutes
Second negative speaker's rebuttal	4 minutes
Second affirmative speaker's rebuttal	4 minutes

Lincoln-Douglas Format

In a Lincoln-Douglas debate format, each side is represented by only one speaker. In effect, a Lincoln-Douglas format is a modification of the standard cross-examination format. The resolutions always begin with the word *Resolved.*

Lincoln-Douglas debates usually deal with propositions of value rather than those of policy. For example, the proposition "Resolved: the recent increase in property tax should be revoked," would not fit this format, but "Resolved: the recent increase in property tax would prove harmful to the county" would fit. And since there's no policy issue, there's no plan for the affirmative case to argue.

A Lincoln-Douglas debate is also less formal and more philosophical than other debate formats. It depends more on reasoning and analysis than on evidence. As a result of its style and function, mastering the Lincoln-Douglas debate format is superb preparation for dealing with the informal debates that we often have on the job, in civic groups, and at home.

The structure looks like this:

Part	Time
Affirmative constructive speech	6 minutes
Negative cross-examination	3 minutes
Negative constructive speech	7 minutes
Affirmative cross-examination	3 minutes
Affirmative speaker's rebuttal	4 minutes
Negative speaker's rebuttal	6 minutes
Affirmative speaker's rebuttal	3 minutes

The Rules

Because debate is a special kind of public-speaking situation, it has some special rules. Here they are.

247

Encores and Exits

The Lincoln-Douglas debate format takes its name from the series of seven famous debates in 1858 between Illinois senatorial candidates Abraham Lincoln and Stephen A. Douglas. The debates, which propelled Lincoln into national prominence, largely concerned the issue of slavery in the territories. Throughout the debates, Douglas maintained his belief in "popular sovereignty," the right of the territories to determine local institutions. Lincoln argued the contrary and asserted that slavery was an absolute wrong. In so doing, he fused the Abolitionist concept of slavery as a moral evil to the platform of a major political party and changed the course of American history. Defeated in the Senate race, Lincoln was elected President two years later. See why debate is a crucial skill to acquire?

1. You're trying to convince the judge, not your opponents, so address the judge rather than the opposing team.

2. To help you maintain eye contact with the judge, know your material cold.

3. Even though you're under time constraints, don't be a speed demon. Use the same rate of speech you'd use for any pubic speaking situation.

4. Go for quality over quantity. Don't try to squeeze in extra arguments (though you do want to have extra arguments handy, just in case).

5. Be dynamic and forceful when you present your case.

6. Never lose control. No matter how outrageous the attack, keep your cool.

Speech of the Devil

When you debate, attack the issues, not your opponent. *Never* make personal attacks.

Parliamentary Procedure

A veteran congressman was asked what he had learned in the rough-and-tumble of the political arena. "Well," he said, "I found it wasn't so much whether you won or lost, but how you placed the blame."

While we're on the issue of speaking in formal groups, let's take a peek at parliamentary law, a system of public speaking rules designed to make it easier for people to work together effectively and to help groups accomplish their purposes. Parliamentary law helps eliminate the Blame Game so that people can actually get some work done.

Traditionally, parliamentary law was used to run meetings of non-profit groups, community organizations, and governmental agencies. Increasingly, however, it is being used for in-profit companies because it provides a way for people to conduct their business quickly, efficiently, and fairly.

Parliamentary law is used to run meetings in an astonishingly wide variety of organizations today. Here's just a sampling:

➤ Government   ➤ School and library boards

➤ Labor unions   ➤ Civic associations

➤ Co-op boards   ➤ Historical societies

➤ Youth groups   ➤ Charitable groups

➤ Shareholder meetings   ➤ Service clubs

➤ Academic departments   ➤ Any deliberative assembly

Peace in Our Time

Parliamentary law is a series of rules created to aid the transaction of business and to promote harmony and cooperation within an assembly. Parliamentary law is also referred to as "Robert's Rules of Order," after Henry Martyn Robert's famous 1876 book by the same name.

Take A Walk on the Mild Side

The overall rules of parliamentary law are more important than the specifics. In most cases, insisting that people observe every itty-bitty technical rule is a misuse of the process and can grind a meeting to a halt. The rules of parliamentary law are based on the idea that the rules of procedure should assist a meeting, not inhibit it.

Effective officers know when to apply the rules strictly and when to take a more relaxed approach. Here are Robert's main rules:

1. **Majority-vote decisions.** A majority vote decides an issue. In any group, each member agrees to be governed by the vote of the majority.

2. **Equal rights and privileges.** All members have equal rights, privileges, and obligations. One of the chairperson's main responsibilities is to use the authority of the position to ensure that all people attending a meeting are treated equally—for example, not to permit a vocal few to dominate the debates.

Talk Soup

Parliamentary law is a series of rules created to facilitate the transaction of business in a fair and timely manner. It can also be seen as the art of using procedure legitimately to support or defeat a proposal.

3. **Equal obligations.** Just as all members have equal rights, they also have equal obligations. Here are some of the obligations that fall to members: attend meetings, be on time, stay for the entire meeting, be attentive and open-minded, participate actively, attack issues rather than individuals, help maintain dignity and decorum, know parliamentary procedure, and participate in committees.

4. **Protection of minority rights.** The rights of the minority must be protected at all times. Although the ultimate decision rests with a majority, all members have such basic rights as the right to be heard and the right to oppose. The rights of all members—both majority and minority—should be the concern of every member, for a person may be in a majority on one question, but in a minority on the next.

5. **Full and free discussion.** Every matter presented for decision should be discussed fully. The right of every member to speak on any issue is as important as each member's right to vote.

6. **Simple and direct procedure.** Believe it or not, parliamentary procedure is designed to guarantee that the simplest and most direct procedure will be used to accomplish a purpose.

7. **Order of motions.** All motions follow a specific order, arranged in order of importance. This keeps the meeting moving.

8. **Consideration of one question at a time.** A meeting can deal with only one matter at a time. The various kinds of motions have therefore been assigned an order of precedence.

9. **Voting.** Before members vote, they have the right to know the question before the assembly. This responsibility falls to the president or presiding officer. By extension, every member has the right to understand the meaning of any question presented to a meeting, and to know what effect a decision will have. A member always has the right to request information on any motion he or she does not thoroughly understand. Moreover, all meetings must be characterized by fairness and good faith.

10. **Maintaining impartiality.** The rules of parliamentary procedure must be administered without bias. Presiding officers serve best when they remain neutral. To help maintain this impartiality, presiding officers do not participate in debate.

The Least You Need to Know

➤ A formal debate pits one side against the other in order to discover the best side of a controversial issue.

➤ A formal debate begins with a proposition—an arguable statement that something should be considered or done.

➤ There are only two sides to a debate: the affirmative side (upholds the proposition) or the negative side (argues against the affirmative side).

➤ Unlike other public speaking situations, you can't have too much evidence when it comes to preparing for a debate.

➤ The three main debate formats are the standard format, the cross-examination format, and the Lincoln-Douglas format.

➤ Parliamentary law protects the right of the individual, the minority, the majority, and those absent from a meeting.

Part 5
Master of Your Domain

By this stage of the public speaking process, you're not only starting to hear yourself give your speech, but you're also starting to visualize yourself up on that podium. But perhaps what you see is a little scary—once again, you're facing the fear of the unknown.

Relax!

As I've said before, it's a matter of preparation. That's why you have this book. Think of me as your tour guide through Public Speaking Land. On your journey, I'll point out the important points and how to get the most from them. In this section, for example, you'll learn all about preparing visual aids, rehearsing, and dressing for success. So sit back and enjoy the journey as you prepare for the podium!

Chapter 25

A Thousand Words: Visual Aids

In This Chapter

➤ What are visual aids?

➤ How to use visual aids

➤ Emergency plans for using visual aids

The Short History of Medicine

2000 B.C.—Here, eat this root.

1000 A.D.—That root is irreligious. Here, say this prayer.

1850 A.D.—That prayer is superstition. Here, drink this potion.

1940 A.D.—That potion is snake oil. Here, swallow this pill.

1985 A.D.—That pill is ineffective. Here, take this antibiotic.

2000 A.D.—That antibiotic is artificial. Here, eat this root.

The more things change, the more they stay the same. Fads come and fads go, but visual aids are here to stay.

So far, I've discussed only the audible aspect of your speech. Equally important—and sometimes even more important—are the visible parts of your presentation: *visual aids*. The right image can convey your meaning with great effectiveness and might even linger in your audience's mind after your words have faded to make your speech truly memorable.

People process information through their eyes as well as their ears. Unfortunately, too many people don't use visual aids correctly when they deliver a speech. As a result, what was planned to help communication ends up harming it. Of course, that won't happen to you—not if I have anything to say about it!

In this chapter, you'll learn the basics of creating and using visual aids to enhance your speeches. The chapter opens with a detailed explanation of when and why you should use visual aids.

Then comes a list of dos and don'ts to give you a clear understanding of ways to make visual aids work for you. And since using visual aids is such a crucial aspect of successful speeches, the following chapter covers how to integrate each visual aid, step-by-step.

Show and Tell Time

Visual aids consist of charts, graphs, maps, handouts, models, objects, photographs, posters, slides, videotapes, movies, diagrams, audiotapes—in other words, any additional visual aspect of a speech presentation.

Why are visual aids so important to successful speeches? For starters, the right visual aid reinforces your main ideas and examples. It also helps to explain information that is difficult to visualize, such as the shape of an unfamiliar object. In fact, the right visual aid can introduce something your audience has never seen (such as a new invention), help you explain technical or unusual terms, and guide your listeners as they compare new as well as familiar information.

How do you decide when a visual aid is appropriate? First, decide which parts of your speech you want to support with visual aids. Then consider which visual aids will most help your audience understand your ideas. The following items can help you evaluate when and how to use visual aids.

Talk Soup

Visual aids are charts, graphs, maps, handouts, models, objects, photographs, posters, slides, videotapes, movies, diagrams, audiotapes—in other words, any additional visual aspect of a speech presentation.

1. **Relevancy.** First and most importantly, make sure that the visual aid is directly related to the content of your speech. No matter how attractive and beautifully designed a visual aid may be, it should be used *only* if it is relevant to your speech.

2. **Appropriateness.** A visual aid must suit your audience and occasion. For example, a talk on population trends to a group of scientists might be backed up by charts, graphs, and PowerPoint displays. Likewise, a birthday speech to relatives would be better enhanced by slides or poster-sized photographs of the honoree.

3. **Attractiveness.** Your visual aids must look professional, neat, and attractive. Keep charts, graphs, and diagrams simple and bold. A series of simple charts or graphs almost always works better than a single complex one: By the time the audience figures out a complex diagram, your speech will be over. Listeners can process a simple visual display much more easily.

4. **Visibility.** Your visual aids must be large enough to be seen by the person in the back row. If not everyone can see your visual aid, then the aid becomes a frustration rather than a help.

   If you need to preface your visual aid with "I know you can't read this, but…," then why include it at all? Your audience cannot be expected to pay full attention to what is being said while straining to read a visual.

5. **Variation.** In most instances, it's a good idea to use several different visual aids. This helps keep your listeners interested in what you have to say.

6. **Number.** Your speech should include enough visual aids to make your ideas clear and compelling.

Keep these simple do's and don'ts in mind to help you plan and use visuals.

Do...

1. Follow the "8H rule." If you can read an image from a distance of eight times its height, odds are your audience will be able to read it when projected. For example, let's say you have a flip chart that is 2 feet high. If you can read the chart from 16 feet away, that chart will probably be legible when converted to a slide or overhead transparency. For instance, 35-millimeter slides are about an inch in height. If you can read the slide from 8 inches away, the slide will be legible under most presentation conditions.

Class Act

Maintain personal control over all visual aids. For instance, if you're showing a video, press the on/off switch yourself. If you're showing slides, be the one to press the control button. Flip the pages of the flip chart; pass around the object you're displaying. This keeps you in control of the timing and sequence of events.

Speech of the Devil

The visual aid can't be so engaging that it distracts the audience from what you are saying. If the audience spends more time admiring your handiwork than listening to your speech, the visual aid will undercut your purpose. Your audience shouldn't be marveling—they should be listening.

2. Use a color printer. Traditionally, speakers prepared visual aids with conventional art tools, such as colored pencils and markers. While these are still useful tools, computers have added a new dimension to the preparation of posters, charts, graphs, and other visual aids. Today, it's relatively simple to use computer software to create polished diagrams and charts. Color printers make it a snap to print these documents in brilliant hues. Chapter 26, "Preparing and Using Visual Aids," examines the relationship between computers and visual aids more closely.

3. Consider computer clip art. This offers a great way to prepare impressive-looking visual aids easily and quickly. It's also easy on the pocketbook: Clip art comes packaged with most software programs.

4. Keep it simple. More images with fewer ideas on each are better than a few images that are complicated or difficult to understand. A single idea or set of facts per image, timed to the speaker's pace, will add punch and emphasis to each important idea, assuring maximum retention.

5. Remember that visuals *support* your speech. The operative word is *support*. Visuals are supposed to support or aid you in giving the presentation, not replace you. And you don't want to support your visual aids instead of the other way around: Make sure you have a solid speech written that would do well even without visual aids. (This also can be a lifesaver if something goes wrong.)

Class Act

Use bold, italic, underline, quotations, and/or color changes to emphasize key points or words in your visual aids.

Don't...

1. Keep an image on the screen longer than 7–10 seconds. Most people are easily bored, and it's generally accepted that if an image remains on the screen longer than this period, the speaker will begin to lose viewer attention.

2. Use "chartjunk." This refers to confusing elements that have no place on the image. Many presenters insist on having a glaring colored logo in the corner of every image, for example. While a common element can add continuity to a presentation, blazing logos and distracting objects can detract from the message.

3. Use "chartoons." These are overly cute attempts to make a presentation appear more polished by adding lots of distracting, tacky, aggravating symbols and such. Avoid them.

4. Go font crazy. Just because you have access to 35 fonts does not mean that you're required to use every single one of them. A single font throughout an entire presentation is usually quite sufficient to make your point effectively and powerfully.

5. Color your world. Keep colors to a minimum. A single background color throughout a presentation lends an air of continuity. You can separate broad sections of a presentation by changing background colors, but keep the changes to a minimum. Unless your purpose is to shock or grab serious attention, try to keep all background colors within the same color family.

6. Mix graphics. You wouldn't mix your metaphors when you speak, so don't mix graphics or colors without specific purpose. For example, you wouldn't use warm colors (yellow, orange) in a slide whose subject was ice hockey unless you wanted to emphasize the warm, comfortable temperature of the stadium. You'd go for a cool blue instead.

Speech of the Devil

It's very easy to make chartjunk and chartoons with clip art. Be strong, though: Resist the urge to clutter your visuals with too much clip art.

A Dollar Late and a Day Short

Say that your speech will take place in another city. The last thing you want to do is lug a slide projector with you. But how can you make sure that the meeting site will have the audiovisual equipment that you need?

The easiest way is to write a letter to the hotel meeting planner or seminar planner to arrange for the equipment you need ahead of time. I used the word "write" intentionally; this way, you can make sure that there's a written request on file. By the way, faxing and e-mailing also count as writing because all three methods provide a written record. Just remember to follow up with a telephone call a few days before your speech to make sure that everything is in place.

Dot the I's and Cross the T's

I'm a worrier. Maybe you are, too. Being a worrier is not such a bad thing when it comes to public speaking because it helps ensure that presentations go smoothly. I always call twice to double-check on all equipment I'll need. That way, I can be sure that I'll have the proper equipment, in working order, waiting for me. I even bring my own extension cord and three-prong adapter when I'm using a slide projector, computer, or any other device that will need to be plugged in.

Class Act

Always document phone calls regarding your speech. Be sure to get the name of the person you spoke with—this ensures that you'll have a real person to deal with if there's a problem.

Plan B

What happens if you're giving your speech in a hotel/conference center/auditorium/ church basement that doesn't have a slide projector, and you don't have one yourself? (Who *does* own a slide projector anymore, anyway?) Or, say you want to show a brief video and there's no video player available? What happens if you don't have the audiovisual machines you need? Rather than dropping the visual aid from your speech, you can rent the machinery you need. Consider these sources:

➤ **The public library.** Often, you can borrow audiovisual equipment free from your public library. For example, my library offers free rentals on slide projectors, VCRs, and tape recorders to county residents.

➤ **Video shops.** Nearly all video shops rent video equipment at a nominal fee.

➤ **Schools and colleges.** You might be able to borrow a machine from a local school for the day. In exchange, why not offer to give a brief speech for the public speaking class or a class in your subject area?

Use and Abuse

Be sure that you know how to operate any equipment that you need. Before your speech, check to be sure that you can easily turn on the overheard projector, computer, videotape recorder, or any other equipment you plan to use. Then double-check to make sure that everything is working correctly. I can't tell you how many speeches I have seen marred because the speaker did not know how to operate the audiovisual aids or because the machinery was not functioning properly.

As you practice your speech, be sure to include your visual aid, inserting it exactly where it would go in your speech. If your organization is weak and you display the visual too soon or too late in the speech, your visual aid will disrupt communication rather than enhance it.

Speech of the Devil

If you're planning to use a visual aid in your speech, always be ready to give your speech without it. Believe me, the number of technical and human errors possible is longer than this chapter. As a result, I advise you to be ready to carry on without any visual aids.

As you speak, point out each feature in the visual aid, but keep your eyes on your audience. This way, you can judge whether they understand what you're saying. In addition to making your delivery smoother and more professional, this will also help you make sure that you don't block the audience's view of the visual.

Use a pointer or one of those new laser pens with graphs, charts, and diagrams. This enables you to stand well away from the display, affording your audience the clearest possible view. Display the visual aid only when it is in use. Keep it covered until you're ready to use it, and remove it when you're finished. This helps prevent audience distraction.

The Least You Need to Know

➤ Use visual and audiovisual aids only if they enhance your speech. They're unnecessary if they don't add any new information, fail to help the audience understand your speech, or detract from your message.

➤ Suit the specific visual aid to your audience, purpose, and message.

➤ Check and double-check availability of equipment.

➤ Make sure you can use all visual aids correctly.

Chapter 26

Preparing and Using Visual Aids

In This Chapter

➤ Audiotapes

➤ Blackboards

➤ Charts, graphs, and computers

➤ Diagrams and films

➤ Flip charts and posters

➤ Handouts, maps, and models

➤ Overhead projectors, photographs, and slides

➤ Videotapes

This chapter zooms in on the specifics of integrating visuals into your speeches. You'll learn how to prepare and use audiotapes, the blackboard, and charts, and you'll also learn about graphs and computers. And let's not forget diagrams, films, flip charts, and posters. Other sections deal with handouts, maps, and models, and we also cover overhead projectors, photographs, and slides. The chapter concludes with a complete section on using videotapes to enhance your presentations. In other words, you'll find everything you need to know about using specific types of visual aids.

Audiotapes

Audiotapes are a superb way to present advertising slogans, short messages to focus groups, and music. What's more, they're easy to carry; even the recorder doesn't weigh much.

Here's how to best use audiotapes:

1. Use a high-quality recorder to prevent distortion.
2. Before your speech, be sure the tape is rewound and at its starting point.
3. If the recorder is portable, position it on a table that is level with the audience.
4. Before playing the tape, explain the purpose of the tape and identify the speaker.
5. Adjust the volume so everyone can hear.
6. Always carry a backup tape!

Blackboards

Blackboards are easy to use and easy to see. They also keep your hands busy, which can reduce nervousness. You can use a blackboard drawing as you would a chart, map, or other completed visual aid to point out relevant and salient features.

Class Act

If the tape recorder runs on batteries, be sure to carry spare batteries with you. If it gets plugged in, check ahead of time to make sure there's an electrical outlet close to the podium. And make sure that the outlet and recorder are both functioning correctly before it's time for you to give your speech.

Usually, it's a good idea to complete the drawing before you begin your speech. If the drawing is on the board beforehand, it frees you to concentrate on your words. Drawing while you are speaking carries the advantage of immediacy, but it can be distracting and difficult to concentrate on two tasks at once.

If you do decide to write on the blackboard during the speech, try not to turn your back on your audience as you write. Also, don't pull a Dan Quayle: Do you remember the hapless vice president who misspelled "potato" in front of a group of school kids? Be sure that you can correctly spell any word that you are going to write on the chalkboard.

If your handwriting is poor, don't be afraid to print. And if your printing is that bad, have an assistant or helper write on the board for you. This also frees you up to concentrate more fully on your speech.

Charts and Graphs

Charts and graphs offer a number of important advantages for public speakers. First, if well-prepared, they show the structure of something clearly. Next, they're easy to use and easy to transport. Finally, they're inexpensive.

You have several different types of charts at your disposal: Suit the type you use to both the specific kind of information that you're presenting in your speech and your audience's level of sophistication and knowledge. A general audience, for example, would expect a simple chart; an audience comprised of scientists would appreciate a more complex one. Try these suggestions for choosing, creating, and using charts effectively.

Class Act

Use soft chalk to lessen the chance of squeaking. If possible, use a green chalkboard and yellow chalk. It's easier on the eyes than white chalk on a dark blackboard. No matter what chalk and board you use, be sure that the chalk marks are bold enough so they can be read easily, even by the people in the back rows.

➤ Make charts communicate. Convey only one message per chart. (As discussed in the last chapter, it's much easier for an audience to grasp your message if you keep your visual aids simple.) This might mean that you have to pare down the ideas and simplify. While doing this, you might want to think about changing the chart form, perhaps switching from a line graph to a horizontal bar chart, for example, to communicate the message more effectively.

➤ Watch chart labels. Often, a speaker makes the mistake of putting a label such as "Sales 1990–1995," at the top of a chart. The chart's heading should always tell people what you want them to look for on a chart. Use an action statement, such as "Sales Reverse Downward Trend except in West."

➤ Check the verb. Once you have an action statement as a heading, look at the verbs in the statement to get an idea of the best chart to use to present your data. For example, if you want to show how college entrance test scores have changed over 30 years, you'll want to use a line chart. However, if you have fewer than five data points and you want to emphasize quantity at discrete times, use a column chart (vertical bars). People associate left-to-right with the movement of time, so vertical bars work better than horizontal bars for time series data.

➤ Compare items at one point in time. Use a horizontal bar chart if you want to show the highest profit, the lowest interest rate, or the most products sold, or if you want to rank variables from largest to smallest.

➤ Compare parts of a whole. A pie chart is best when you want to highlight one part of the whole. Key words such as "percentage," "portion," or "share" should let you know that a pie chart would work best. If you want

Talk Soup

A **chart** is a visual record of data, usually showing change.

to show the proportion of the state government budget spent on education, for example, use a pie chart.

➤ Compare data by geographic location. Look for key words such as "country" or "state." For instance, if you want to show sales by region, use a map. Distinguish among regions by using different colors, shadings, or symbols.

Use this handy-dandy Chart Checklist as you prepare your charts:

Class Act

Line charts are best when a variable has more than four or five data points and you want to emphasize continuity over several months or years. That's because the slope of the line tells viewers the direction of the trends at a glance.

Speech of the Devil

Never put too many statistics on a chart or graph; it will be too difficult for the audience to follow the visual. Also, don't use more than three curves per graph. After that, the graph starts to look like an Italian dinner special instead of a mathematical display. Use a bold line for your most important curve; use lighter lines for less important ones. Color works especially well to differentiate lines.

Chart Checklist

❏ Is the chart easy to read? For example, have I labeled the x and y axes, lines, bars, or pie wedges? Have I made the most important text largest and the most important data lines or sections darkest?

❏ Is the chart accurate? Did I start a numerical axis at zero? Did I compare only like variables?

❏ Have I eliminated all unnecessary details? Did I avoid grid lines, data points, boxes, and other devices unless they relate to the message?

❏ Did I use no more than four colors per visual?

❏ Did I avoid distracting fill patterns, such as contrasting lines, wave patterns, and crisscrosses?

❏ Did I focus attention on key points by using color, shading, or symbols such as arrows?

❏ Did I write in upper and lower case to avoid the difficulty of reading words written in all capitals letters?

❏ Did I use presentation software sensibly? When necessary, did I adjust the default mode to simplify a visual?

Computers

With the ever-improving software on the market, the possibilities for computer displays seem endless. You can prepare charts, graphs, illustrations, and more. Take a tour through a computer store to see what's available in your area for your computer. Then have some fun with it!

However, beware of the temptation to use computer-generated art and visuals just to show that you're in the know. There's no reason to flaunt your computer skills and flashy equipment. Remember: Include visuals only if they add something important to your speech.

Stay tuned: The use of computer visual aids (PowerPoint) is discussed more fully in Chapter 27, "Byte Me: Using PowerPoint."

Diagrams

Diagrams are great because they can be made in advance. This means that you can use them when you practice your speech. Diagrams are also inexpensive and easy to transport.

As with charts, you can use several different types of diagrams. The diagram can be as simple as an illustration of an object or process, or it can be as

Speech of the Devil

Be sure that any computer-generated graphics are large enough to be seen by the audience. You may wish to enlarge these documents through a computer or overhead projector to be sure that everyone can see them clearly.

sophisticated as a cutaway diagram of an object that shows its internal and external appearance. Three-dimensional diagrams also show an object completely. (These are especially helpful because they help an audience visualize an object most fully.) Flow charts or process diagrams trace the steps in a process.

Design and create the types of diagrams that best reinforce your topic. Sometimes the simple diagram will be most suitable; other times, a cut-away diagram, three-dimensional diagram, or flow chart will best reinforce your point.

The basic rule of thumb: Keep it simple. If you're compulsive, don't worry—just bring a bold-colored marker with you so that you can add more to the diagram as you speak. Do that only if you feel it's necessary, however—and keep in mind that it rarely will be.

Films

Popular and easy to use, films are well suited to presenting a slice of real life, which makes them a great way to work emotional appeal into a persuasive speech. Films show action, which few other visuals can do.

You can prepare your own films or use those already prepared. Stay away from making your own, however, unless you are accomplished in this art; homemade films can look cheesy and can spoil an otherwise polished speech presentation.

It's important to check all film equipment before the show, making sure that the volume is properly adjusted. And be sure to watch the film before you use it in your speech. This helps eliminate unpleasant surprises.

Flip Charts and Posters

Flip charts start with large pads of paper firmly mounted on an easel. To create a flip chart, draw one stage of the process on each sheet of paper. Flip charts are ideally suited to showing the steps of a process: As you deliver your speech, flip from page 1 to page 2, to page 3, and so on.

Many speakers take advantage of the fact that you can prepare the entire flip chart ahead of time. Or, you can prepare an outline of the flip chart on the paper, filling in the details with a bold-colored marker as you speak.

Class Act

Here's a side benefit to using a flip chart: It's a good alternative to handouts or speaker notes. For example, if you're going to make three points in your speech, you can write each point on a separate sheet of the flip chart.

Flip charts work best with small groups because they generally can't be read beyond the tenth row. Be sure that your writing is large enough to be seen clearly by all audience members. If you're right-handed, stand on the left side of the chart; if you're left-handed, stand on the right side. This will make it much easier for you to flip the pages and point out key features of the chart. And remember to avoid turning your back on the audience as you flip the pages.

Posters are inexpensive and easy to produce. Like charts and diagrams, however, you want to avoid certain pitfalls when making your poster. If your poster contains bulleted lists, for example, include only a few main points on each. For maximum visual appeal, keep the posters simple. Sharp colors have the greatest impact, but they can be hard on the eyes.

Display the posters as you would a flip chart or a photograph. The No. 1 rule: Make sure that everyone can see every part of the poster. Otherwise, it's useless.

Take a look at some additional tips for using flip charts and posters:

1. Before the presentation, check the height of the easel and make sure you have plenty of paper. You
   might want to use two easels, one that is already prepared and one for extemporaneous use.

2. During the presentation, title each page with a short topic or heading.

3. Make each letter 1-1/4 inches high, or larger if the room is deeper than 30 feet. Be sure your printing is neat and legible.

4. Prepare complex pages ahead of time in light pencil and then trace with a marker. If you travel with prepared pages, roll them up and carry them in a mailing tube.

5. Use different colors for page headings and primary points. Use red only for emphasis.

6. Do not use pastel colors. Black, blue, dark green, and brown work best.

7. Put the marker down when you are not using it.

8. Don't talk to the board while writing on it.

9. Don't write more than 10 lines on a page.

10. Don't fill the page to the bottom; people in the back will be unable to see.

11. Respond to and note input from participants.

12. Post important pages on the wall with masking tape or pins.

13. Don't write on the pages after posting them on the wall; the pen may bleed.

14. Highlight key points.

15. Allow time for reading, retention, and note-taking.

16. Use the "matador tear," a sharp tug at the corner, not straight down. This helps prevent tears across the page.

Handouts

Handouts offer a number of strong advantages. They're inexpensive. They can be prepared well in advance of the speech date; and the audience can refer to them later.

Distributing handouts is a tricky business. On one hand, distributing handouts during the speech supplies a concrete example of your topic that participants can refer to while you speak. This helps people follow the key points in your presentation.

On the other hand, handouts can be a distraction. Handing out papers takes up valuable time and distracts the audience. Furthermore, people will likely read the handouts rather than listen to you speak.

As a result, I recommend that you distribute any handout you might have after your speech. This way, participants will have the materials but still will be attentive during your speech. (Be sure to have extra handouts for unexpected participants.)

Maps

Maps can help you clarify the positions of countries, rivers, mountains, and other landforms and bodies of water. For ease of use and display, mount maps on stiff board. If you require a specialized map, you can always prepare your own maps. If you choose to do this, use bold colors and a standard map legend.

To be effective, maps must be large enough to be easily seen. You may wish to show a zoomed-in view of a map to ensure that there's enough detail.

Class Act

Prepare handouts on a computer, if possible. Resist the temptation to use many computer fonts; this can make a handout difficult to read. Make the design bold and easy to read.

Encores and Exits

The earliest maps were Babylonian clay tablet created around 2300 B.C. A clay disk about three inches by five inches, these maps show the world as a circle with two lines running down the center representing the Tigris and Euphrates rivers. More extensive regional maps, drawn on silk and dating from around the 2nd century B.C., have been found in China. The art of mapmaking was advanced in both the Mayan and Inca civilizations; as early as the 12th century A.D., the Inca made maps of the lands they conquered. The first map of the world is believed to have been made in the 6th century A.D. by the Greek philosopher Anaximander. His circular map showed the known lands grouped around the Aegean Sea.

Models

Models can be a great way to explain the structure, function, and design of an item. They're especially useful when the original is too big or small, too difficult, or—as in the case of a DNA molecule, for instance—simply impossible to pass around. Check to see that that the model is sturdy enough to withstand handling; if not, hold it up for display instead.

Speech of the Devil

If you point out something on a visual display, be sure that you're pointing where you want to point. Pointing to the wrong place on a display makes even the most accomplished speaker look foolish.

Props such as models and objects can be tricky to use. Try these suggestions:

➤ Be sure to display the object long enough for everyone to get a good look.

➤ Lift the object into the air, hold it steady for a few moments, and then move it slowly so that everyone in the audience has a chance to see it.

➤ Don't talk while people are looking at the object. This will ensure that people pay full attention to what you're saying. Also, your audience won't feel like they're missing something if they don't hear you because they're studying your model.

If the object isn't fragile or valuable, pass it around *after* your speech. This way, it won't distract from what you're saying. If you're going to pass the model around, be sure to clearly specify the direction in which you want it to be handed. For example, you can say, "Please pass this from the front to the back of the auditorium."

If your speech is informative, supplement the object with a diagram of it. You can display the diagram on an overhead projector or slide. If you show the diagram on a handout, remember that the same rules apply: Distribute the diagram *after* your speech, not during it.

Overhead Projectors

Overhead projectors are easily available, for the most part, and are easy to use. Prepare your visual displays carefully. Use bright colors for maximum appeal, but stick to a consistent color palette. You can also purchase prepared visuals to be used with an overhead projector. Good sources include scientific supply houses and school supply stores.

I'm a fan of the lowly overhead projector, but I also recognize that it's prone to be cranky. That's why I recommend that you bring a general audiovisual emergency kit: spare overhead projector light bulbs, masking tape, three-pronged adapters, scissors, screwdrivers, and a small flashlight. The cost and inconvenience are minimal and are well worth it.

Here are some additional guidelines for using overheard projectors:

1. Before your speech, make sure the plug reaches the socket. It's a good idea to bring your own extension cord, just in case.
2. Place the projector at a height that is comfortable for you.
3. Make sure the lens is dust-free.
4. Put the projector on a vibration-free base.
5. Arrange the electrical cord so that no one will trip over it.
6. Focus and center the picture on the screen before your speech.
7. Number your transparencies in accordance with your speech.
8. Never assume projectors will work. Have a backup strategy ready (see the previous advice about the audiovisual emergency kit).
9. During the speech, keep the screen above the participants' heads. Be sure it's in full view of the participants.
10. Make sure you're not blocking anyone's view when presenting.
11. Darken the room appropriately by blocking out sunshine and dimming nearby lights.
12. Turn off the screen between slides if you plan to talk for more than a couple minutes.
13. Keep in mind that no audience member should be farther from the screen than six times the width of the image.
14. Talk to the audience, not to the screen.
15. Use a pointer to emphasize points, but don't use it as a crutch or wave it wildly.

Photographs

Photographs can be visually stunning and can provide exquisite details and descriptions. As a bonus, they're also relatively inexpensive to produce.

Make sure that the pictures you use are of high quality. Consider cropping (removing) extraneous details that would distract from your point. Your photo-finisher can do this easily. Mount your pictures on sturdy boards to make them easier to display.

Be sure the photographs are large enough to be seen clearly from all parts of the auditorium. Display the photographs on an easel for maximum impact.

Slides

As with photographs, use only high-quality slides. If you're a skilled photographer, take the slides yourself. If you have any doubts, buy the slides you need or have someone skilled prepare the slides for you. It's worth the time and trouble: Amateurish slides look tacky and can harm your presentation.

Remember that slides require a darkened room. Be sure that you can adequately darken the room before you give your speech. Slide experts maintain that the room must be completely dark to achieve the maximum effect. Obviously, this makes it difficult—if not impossible—for people to take notes. It also moves the focus from the speaker to the slides, which is not your desired aim. I recommend that you merely dim the lights, which will work fine for your purposes.

Before the speech, run through your slide show to make sure the projector works and that the slides are in the proper order. Tape down the projector cord so no one trips over it. And be classy: Use a screen instead of the wall.

Videotapes

Videotapes provide dramatic, effective visual images and are very easy to use, which is why they're popular with audiences and speakers alike. As with films, though, stick with prepared videotapes unless you're skilled with a video camera.

Be sure to check the videotape before you use it to make sure that it's in good shape. Also be sure that the TV screen can be seen easily by all members of the audience—even those in the back rows.

Read over these additional guidelines for using videotapes:

1. Before the presentation, be sure the videotape is rewound and at the starting point.

2. Check to make sure that the playback machine and the monitor are playing properly. Check this before the session so that you may replace the machine if it is not working properly.

3. Check the audio level and contrast.

4. The lights should be dimmed but not off.

5. Explain the purpose of the tape before you play it. The exception to this rule: If you're opening your speech with a dramatic video, don't reveal the surprise. Show the video without introductory comment.

6. Show interest in the tape, and watch it with your audience. Summarize the main points after you have shown the tape.

The Least You Need to Know

➤ Audiotapes are a superb way to present advertising slogans, short messages to focus groups, and music.

➤ If you use a blackboard, try to complete the drawing before you begin your speech.

➤ Suit the type of chart and diagram to your topic and audience.

➤ Films are a great way to get emotional appeal into a persuasive speech.

➤ Flip charts work best with small groups.

➤ Distribute all handouts *after* your speech, not before or during it.

➤ Be certain that overhead projectors, slide projectors, and VCRs are working correctly.

➤ When it comes to audiovisuals, you can never be too prepared.

Chapter 27

Byte Me:
Using PowerPoint

In This Chapter

➤ What PowerPoint is

➤ How to run and use PowerPoint

➤ How to use toolbars, views, and text

➤ How to make the most of objects and colors

In today's media-savvy world, knowing how to produce and deliver professional, dynamic speeches to persuade, inform, or entertain is essential. Whether you're giving a simple speech using a few items on overhead transparencies or are pulling out all the stops with animation, sound, and photographic images, you can make your presentation easier and more polished by using PowerPoint. You'll learn how to do so in this chapter.

Power to the People

So what is PowerPoint, anyway? PowerPoint is a Microsoft software presentation package that can be used to produce presentations, slides, handouts, speaker's notes, and outlines. The software also comes with a gallery of sounds and images that you can work with, if you choose. After you create your presentation, PowerPoint can display it on a computer screen or projection system. You can also publish PowerPoint presentations on the Internet and establish links to Internet sites within your presentation. In addition, you can use PowerPoint to print notes and handouts for the speaker and audience.

Once you create a PowerPoint presentation, you can easily vary it for different audiences and purposes. Here's how it's done.

Run, PowerPoint, Run

Here comes the jargon: To *run* PowerPoint, you must have an 80386 or better IBM PC-compatible computer equipped with at least 4MB of RAM, and you must be using MS-DOS version 3.1 or later and Microsoft Windows 3.1 or later. If you're using PowerPoint on a Macintosh, your computer must be equipped with System 7.0 or later and a minimum of 4MB of RAM. Got that? Good.

Lock and Load

To *use* PowerPoint, you must first run Windows. After Windows has loaded, double-click the left mouse button on the PowerPoint icon to load the program. Every time PowerPoint starts on your computer, a "tip of the day" will appear. This dialog box displays a tip on how to better use a particular feature of PowerPoint. If you wish to disable the tip of the day, click the left mouse button on the Show Tips at the Startup check box.

Tool Time

To create your PowerPoint presentations, click your mouse on a series of *toolbars*—buttons that activate the commands. PowerPoint has several toolbars that appear by default when you open the program. (This means that they appear automatically.) You can customize the program to display, add, or delete other toolbars. Let's take a look at the four key toolbars.

Talk Soup

Toolbars are buttons that activate PowerPoint commands.

1. **Standard toolbar.** This toolbar, located at the top of the screen, lets you access many of the key Windows-based operations, such as opening a new or existing file, saving or printing a file, and rearranging text.

2. **Formatting toolbar.** This toolbar, located directly under the Standard toolbar, also contains common Windows functions, including font selection icons, bold, italics, underline, shadow, alignment, and bullets.

3. **Drawing toolbar.** This toolbar, located at the bottom of the screen, enables you to format and manipulate drawn objects, including shapes and clip art.

4. **Common Tasks toolbar.** This floating toolbar is aptly named. It can be moved around the screen or made into a stationary toolbar by clicking its title bar, dragging it to a toolbar area, and releasing it.

Views

PowerPoint has five *views* from which you can choose to create and edit your slides. Views let you isolate one element in your presentation so you can concentrate on it alone. The five views are Slide view, Outline view, Slide Sorter view, Notes Page view, and Slide Show view.

You can move the views around in two ways:

Class Act

In PowerPoint, the PC Ctrl key is equivalent to the ⌘ key on the Macintosh.

➤ Use the view icons at the bottom left of the screen. Click one of the five tools above the Drawing toolbar.

➤ Select the View menu and then one of the five commands to change views.

And now, more on views!

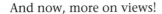

1. **View #1: Slide view.** In this view, you edit one slide at a time. A "slide" is the term for the image on the screen. Working with the current slide, you can add text, draw graphics, add clip art, and change the layout. The left side of the window contains a toolbar with all the necessary icons for supported editing functions.

2. **View #2: Outline view.** In this view, your presentation is displayed in an outline form. Only your headings and main text appear in the outline. This view is helpful when organizing your presentation.

3. **View #3: Slide Sorter view.** This view shows a miniature version of your slides. The slide number, transition, and display time are shown under each slide. All these attributes can be modified from this view. The toolbar right above the slide window contains the functions for setting the slide attributes.

4. **View #4: Notes Page view.** This view shows your slide in the upper half of the window and your notes in the bottom half. This is a useful view for correlating your notes with a particular slide. The notes you enter for each slide can then be used during your presentation.

5. **View #5: Slide Show view.** This view runs your presentation, filling the screen with your slides. With this view, you can perfect slide transitions and timing.

Wizards of Ahhs

PowerPoint *wizards* help you easily create slides by clicking on the desired options presented to you by the wizard and letting PowerPoint do all the formatting.

When you first start PowerPoint, a dialog box will open. It contains four options:

➤ **AutoContent Wizard.** This takes you step by step through a presentation. AutoContent Wizard is simple (and fun!) to use, so I recommend that you start here if you're new to PowerPoint.

➤ **Template.** This opens a second dialog box with built-in templates to use to build your presentation.

➤ **Blank Presentation.** This opens a blank screen, giving you the most flexibility to create your presentation.

➤ **Open an Existing Presentation.** This opens a browse dialog box that opens an existing PowerPoint file (one that you have already worked on).

Class Act

To avoid having to redo your formatting, save edited presentations under a different name. This way, if you don't like the new changes, you can reload the file and try another format. To save a presentation under a different name or in a different directory, select File | Save As from the menu. PowerPoint will then ask for a new name and directory for the presentation.

As in other Windows applications, pressing Control+S or selecting File | Save from the menu will save your current presentation. If this is the first time you've saved a specific presentation, PowerPoint will ask for a filename. If the presentation has been saved before, PowerPoint will save your presentation under the current filename.

Somewhere Over the Rainbow: Colors

Color enhances the message on your slides and makes them more effective. PowerPoint has hundreds of color schemes that you can use to make professional-looking presentations. To change the color scheme, choose the Format | Slide Color Scheme menu from the Standard toolbar.

This brings up a dialog box from which you can set colors for the background, text, lines, shadows, fills, and accents of your presentation.

In the lower corner of the dialog box, you'll see a sample slide that shows you how your color choices will look. If you decide you don't like the changes and want to go back to the color scheme used on the master slide, click the Follow Master button.

To make color coordination easier, click the Choose Scheme button. This displays another dialog box from which you can select a background color. After you've selected a background color, PowerPoint displays a list of good contrasting colors you can use for text and lines on your slides. You can also select the accent colors from the four squares that show sample slides with the different accent styles. After you've finished selecting the desired color scheme, click the OK button.

What's the Object?

PowerPoint makes it easy to add objects (such as clip art) to your slides. Select the object you wish to add by placing the mouse cursor over it and clicking the left mouse button. You can also group objects; cut, copy, paste, and duplicate objects; move, align, and stack objects; rotate and flip objects; and resize objects.

PowerPoint also lets you add shadows to objects to give them a three-dimensional look. To add a shadow, select the object, choose the Format | Shadow menu from the Standard toolbar, select the color you wish to use for the shadow, and click OK. You can remove a shadow by choosing No Shadow in the color drop-down box.

Picture This

PowerPoint comes with a large clip art collection. The Gallery has a box of categories and a box of clip art miniatures. You can maneuver within these boxes to find the clip art that suits your needs. Use the Find button to find a specific piece of clip art. If you don't find what you need, you can purchase many different clip-art software or download public domain clip art free from the Internet.

Charts

PowerPoint has a special application called Organization Chart that lets you easily design organizational charts for your slides. To start Organization Chart, choose the Insert | Object menu and then choose Microsoft Organization Chart from the object box. PowerPoint will then load Organization Chart so you can create your graph.

Movies and Sound Clips

PowerPoint also accepts movies and sound clips. With the use of Media Player for Windows or QuickTime for Macintosh, you can insert a movie image on your slide. Your computer must have Media Player or QuickTime installed to use PowerPoint's multimedia capabilities.

Text Time

PowerPoint helps you change the style and characteristics of your text. To change the text format, choose the Format | Font menu to display the font dialog box. From this dialog box, you can choose the font, point size, font style, and text color for the selected text. Don't use a lot of different fonts and effects because it's easy to overdo it. Take a look at some examples:

➤ The *Emboss* option places an embossing effect on your text.

➤ The *Superscript* option raises the text above the current text line.

➤ The *Subscript* option places the text below the current line.

Speech of the Devil

When you're creating a professional-looking presentation, spelling counts! To avoid spelling bloopers, take advantage of the PowerPoint spelling-checker. To check the spelling of your presentation, select the Tools | Spelling menu. PowerPoint will then search your slides for misspelled words.

PowerPoint also enables you to define formatting characteristics for paragraphs of text. The Format | Align menu command lets you select the alignment of the text within the paragraph. The Format | Line Spacing menu command is used to set the spacing between lines of a paragraph. Use the Before Paragraph and After Paragraph boxes to set the line spacing before and after each selected paragraph.

With WordArt, you can create special effects with text. These effects including shaping, rotating, and twisting text. To use WordArt, choose the Insert | Object menu and select Microsoft WordArt from the list of objects. PowerPoint will then load WordArt so you can create the desired text effect.

PowerPoint also lets you print handouts and upload your presentation to the Internet. The program will take you step by step through these simple applications, should you choose to do this.

Use this chapter to get started creating polished and professional multimedia presentations with PowerPoint. For additional information about more detailed features, try these sources:

➤ The online tutorial, accessed through Help

➤ The *Microsoft PowerPoint User's Guide*

➤ http://www.multimedia.com (formerly *Multimedia World Magazine,* now part of *PC World*)

➤ *Using Microsoft PowerPoint*

The Least You Need to Know

➤ PowerPoint is Microsoft software that creates presentations, slides, handouts, speaker's notes, and outlines. It includes sounds, pictures, and animation.

➤ To operate PowerPoint, start with toolbars—buttons that activate the commands.

➤ PowerPoint has five views from which you can choose to create and edit your slides.

➤ Wizards let you easily create slides by clicking on the desired options and letting PowerPoint do all the formatting.

Chapter 28

Smashing the Sound Barrier

In This Chapter

➤ Voice quality

➤ Clarity, articulation, rate, pitch, and inflection

➤ Pace and rhythm

➤ Those annoying speech "fillers"

➤ Speech volume

➤ The hearing impaired

Do you know this voice trivia?

➤ Cats have more than 100 vocal sounds, while dogs only have about 10.

➤ Giraffes have no vocal cords.

➤ The letter combination "ough" can be pronounced in nine different ways. The following sentence contains them all: "A rough-coated, dough-faced, thoughtful ploughman strode through the streets of Scarborough; after falling into a slough, he coughed and hiccoughed."

Now that you have the basics of speaking in public with confidence (and some useful trivia for your next cocktail party), it's time to focus on your voice, including its quality, clarity, articulation, rate, pitch, inflection, pace, and rhythm.

In this chapter, you'll also find a section on "fillers"—those annoying "uhs," "ehs," and "huhs" that distract your listeners. Then comes a section on the volume of your speech. The chapter concludes with hints for addressing hearing-impaired people. You'll discover how an effective voice helps speakers make their message more interesting and meaningful.

Read My Lips: Voice

I was shocked the first time I ever heard my voice on a tape recorder. "Do I really sound like that?" I wondered. After years of teaching, I've discovered that nearly everyone is disconcerted when they hear their voice for the first time. "That can't possibly be me!" they gasp. "I thought my voice was deeper, lower (louder, richer…)," they mutter. Doubts about voice can make even the most self-confident speaker a little squeamish.

Some of our most noted speakers and performers have less-than-thundering voices: Think of Dustin Hoffman's whine and Barbara Walter's "r" impediment. With extensive training, most people could learn to speak with the richness of Patrick Stewart or the late Sir Laurence Olivier. But you probably don't have time to invest in years of speech training. However, you can take a few minutes to help you smooth out some rough spots in your voice so you can make the best possible impression with your speeches.

How can you acquire a more effective voice? As with speech delivery, one of the secrets is practice. But the wrong kind of practice can do more harm than good because doing the same thing wrong over and over again just makes you better at making that mistake. To make your practice worthwhile, you should first learn something about the mechanics of voice. Let's start with the quality of your voice.

Voice Quality

What people first notice about your voice is its quality. Is it harsh? Nasal? Thin? Resonant? Although a pleasing vocal quality is basic to effective communication, it doesn't in itself create good speech. To communicate your ideas and feelings to other people, your voice must meet two requirements:

➤ It must be easy to understand.

➤ It must be flexible in pitch, force, and rate.

You can change your voice quality if it bothers you. If your voice shatters both your glass and your self-esteem, some time with a good speech therapist is a good idea. However, I don't recommend that you spend piles of money and heaps of time learning to talk like a television newscaster. Remember, communicating your ideas is what really matters.

Clarity and Articulation

Demosthenes, the ancient Athenian public speaker, is rumored to have practiced clear speaking by filling his mouth with pebbles. Fortunately, you don't have to resort to such extremes to achieve a clear speaking voice. You've got this book instead!

Are your words clear? Can everything you're saying be understood? Play back those rehearsal tapes again. Look carefully at problem places. Here are some examples of what you might find:

Talk Soup

Timbre, or **tone color,** is the quality of a person's voice.

➤ **Contractions.** Do you slur "wouldn't" as "wu'nt," "could've" as "cudda," and "should've" as "shudda"? If this is a persistent problem, drop the contractions completely and say both words.

➤ **Reversed sounds**. Do you switch sounds, such as "perscription" for "prescription"? If so, take the time to practice tricky words now so you have them letter-perfect for your speeches.

➤ **Omitted letters.** Many careless speakers leave out letters, such as the "t" sound in "lists." This makes it harder for listeners to understand what you're saying. Go over these words slowly and carefully.

➤ **Added letters.** Some speakers add letters to words, such as adding a "t" to "across," which ends up sounding like "acrost." Adding letters can be a regional habit. Think about the language patterns where you live. Do many people add extra letters to words? If so, take the time to comb your speech for errors.

Rate of Speech

How fast do you speak? Find out by timing yourself. Mark the beginning of a passage and read aloud for 1 minute. Then stop and count the number of words you said. Or, tape-record yourself speaking at a normal rate for 1 minute. Then play back the tape and count the number of words. You should be speaking at about 150 words per minute.

However, this rate is not uniform. In normal speech, the rate corresponds to the thought the speaker is transmitting. Speakers in command of their material vary the rate of their delivery to reflect the content of their speech. These speakers present main ideas and difficult points at a slower pace than when they summarize an argument or tell a joke. Follow these basic rules:

Idea	Rate of Speech
Complex	Slower
Serious	Slower
Humorous	Faster
Exciting	Faster

Pitch and Inflection

Everyone has a pitch at which their voice is most comfortable. It's usually a good idea to speak in your normal pitch range—otherwise, you might seriously strain your voice. However, few things improve the overall impact of your presentation as much as a varied pitch. Novice public speakers rarely take full advantage of their full pitch and inflection; instead, they tend to hit one level and stay there.

A speech that is easily understood can still be dull. More importantly, the speaker's voice may fail to communicate his thoughts. This often happens when the speaker's voice isn't flexible enough to express subtle shades of meaning upon which true communication often depends.

English is a multipurpose language: Often, the same expressions and words can have double meanings. This makes English a killer for non-native speakers to learn, but it gives the language an unparalleled richness. Let's look at the word *oh* as an example. We have about 10 different ways to say it. Try it yourself: Vary your pitch and inflection to match *oh* to each of the following expressions:

➤ Now I understand.

➤ I can't wait.

➤ I'm disappointed.

➤ You expect me to believe that?

➤ That's great!

➤ That's shrewd, but devious.

➤ Look out!

➤ That hurts!

➤ How disgusting!

➤ Poor little thing.

Class Act

Experienced public speakers mark key places in their text to help them make sure they pronounce each word correctly, emphasize key points, and slow down for emphasis. There's no magic code for marking; each speaker devises a code that suits his or her own speaking style. Create a simple code (the key word here is *simple*) that you can use to mark problem places in your script.

Now try the following exercise to further see the powerful effect of pitch and inflection. Repeat each sentence, changing the pitch and inflection of the bolded word to correspond to the prompt.

Sentence	Prompt
Did the company lose the new Campbell job?	It didn't!
Did the **company** lose the new Campbell job?	Or did the rep?
Did the company **lose** the new Campbell job?	Or just delay it?
Did the company lose the **new** Campbell job?	Or the old one?
Did the company lose the new **Campbell** job?	Or another one?
Did the company lose the new Campbell **job**?	Or the contract?

Pace and Rhythm

Pauses serve to punctuate thought. Just as commas and periods separate ideas in written communication, pauses of varying lengths separate spoken words into meaningful units. Using pauses in a careless manner therefore, confuses the reader and seriously undermines your message.

Make sure that you pause *between* units of thought, not in the middle of them. In addition, remember that written and spoken speech are different. Not every comma calls for a pause when speaking, nor does the absence of punctuation mean that there is no need to pause.

You can also use pauses for emphasis. For example, pausing after an important statement telegraphs to your audience that the statement is a key idea. In some cases, a dramatic pause can convey your meaning more effectively than words. And remember, a pause is rarely as long to an audience as it seems to the speaker. The ability to pause shows that the speaker is in control of the situation.

Encores and Exits

Many speakers are afraid to pause. Sometimes they think a pause will make them forget what they want to say; other times, they fear that pausing will make everyone look at them (which is what they should want, in any event). So instead of pausing, they ramble or fill the air with dead words, a string of "er-uh" sounds. Don't be afraid to pause; I have never heard of anyone ever being attacked by a pause.

Ditch the Fillers

A linguistics professor was lecturing to his class one day. "In English," he said, "a double negative forms a positive. In some languages, though, such as Russian, a double negative is still a negative. However, there is no language wherein a double positive can form a negative."

A voice from the back of the room piped up, "Yeah, right."

Go back to the tape recordings you made of your practice sessions. Play them back and listen to yourself carefully. Do you ruin the flow of your thoughts with annoying filler words such as "yeah" and "like"? If so, drop them now. They serve only to interrupt your thoughts and put off your audience.

Because these annoying fillers are unconscious, you'll have to work on getting rid of them. As you practice further, make new tape recordings. Listen to each succeeding tape and see how many fillers you've been able to eliminate. Keep working on this until they're all gone.

Loud, Louder, Loudest: Volume

Probably the single most important factor in making your speech understandable is the volume at which you speak. The *volume* is the loudness level at which you speak related to the distance between you and the listener and the amount of noise that surrounds the listener.

The farther away your listener is, the louder you must talk to be heard clearly. You make these loudness adjustments without thinking when you project your voice across wide distances, as when you call to a friend who is down the block.

What speakers often forget, however, is that the same principle applies over short distances. Your own voice will always seem louder to you than to your listeners because your ears are closer to your mouth than your listeners' ears are. Beginning speakers may also forget to consider the effect of background noise on their ability to be heard.

Talk Soup

The **volume** is the loudness level at which you speak related to the distance between you and the listener and the amount of noise that surrounds the listener.

How can you determine the proper strength of voice to use to compensate for the distance and background noise? Some mechanical devices work quite well, but you've got enough stuff to carry around as it is. Instead, judge your volume by the reactions of your listeners. As you speak, look at the people in the back row. Do they appear to be hearing you clearly? If you have any doubts, ask them.

In and Out

Normally, your lungs allow you to take about 18 breaths a minute, which provides you with the amount of air you need to breathe and speak. Protected by your ribcage, the lungs function as a bellows, pushing air in and out. At the base of your lungs is your *diaphragm*, a powerful band of muscle. You can use this knowledge to get more volume and voice projection.

As you inhale, your diaphragm lowers, creating a larger chest cavity and a partial vacuum. Air rushes in. When you exhale, the center of the diaphragm rises, forcing air through the trachea (the windpipe). Read on to find out why this is important for public speakers to know.

Class Act

If you're worried about speaking too softly, try putting the tape recorder across the room when you practice your speech. This will force you to speak louder.

Coming Up for Air

One of the most upsetting manifestations of stage fright is an extraordinary feeling of suffocation. Suddenly, you feel like you just can't get a breath. That's because you really *can't*. To make things worse, you need an extra large supply of air to produce a speech, especially when you address a large group. This mean that you have to concentrate on your breathing process to pump up the air pressure in your lungs. However, just being aware of how quickly and completely the diaphragm can fill your lungs with air can help you produce a forceful, impressive voice at a moment's notice.

Speech of the Devil

Remember: Public speaking isn't a competitive sport. The goal is to communicate, not to thrust as much information as possible onto your audience.

How can you get the air you need to deliver an effective speech? Try these volume-improving exercises :

➤ Place your right hand flat on your diaphragm, just below your ribs. Without lifting your shoulders, take a deep breath. Feel your diaphragm expanding? Now, hold your breath for a second and then shout, "Yes!" while exhaling. Notice how loud your voice is—and without strain.

➤ Fill your lungs with air again by expanding your diaphragm. Let the air out in little puffs, as though you were blowing out a candle.

➤ Inhale through your nose rather than through your mouth.

➤ Concentrate on using your diaphragm to fill your lungs. Think only about this process as you prepare to address an audience.

➤ As you speak, pace your exhalation so that you'll have enough air to speak and to complete longer thoughts without having to steal a breath at an ill-timed moment.

Cord Care

We pamper our cars, cats, and computers, but how many people take care of their vocal cords? Not many, I bet. However, from now on, you're going to be nice to your vocal cords. Here's how:

➤ Try not to yell, since this can strain your vocal cords and make it hard for you to produce sounds.

➤ If possible, avoid excessive coughing, since this can also damage your vocal cords.

➤ Ditto on excessively clearing your throat.

➤ Treat sore throats promptly. Don't let a sore throat go untended, especially if it's accompanied by a fever.

➤ Drink room temperature water, not cold water, before speaking. Your vocal cords don't like cold drinks.

Pump Up the Volume: Using a Microphone

A microphone or public address system can help you communicate much more easily with a large audience. Before you use a microphone, however, you should know the following:

➤ Remember that most microphone or amplification systems don't reproduce sound with high clarity. As a result, you must speak more slowly and clearly than usual to be understood.

➤ Microphones are pre-adjusted for a specific volume. Therefore, don't vary your speaking volume as much as you might if you weren't using a microphone. Louder sounds will very likely blast your audience; softer sounds won't be heard.

➤ Experiment before your speech until you find the best distance from your mouth to the microphone. Once you locate the distance that's best, stay there. And remember, if you turn your head away from the microphone, you'll be inaudible. In most cases, it's good to stand about 6 inches from a stand microphone.

➤ Just as a microphone will amplify your voice, it also will amplify any other sounds you make: shuffling papers, coughing, scratching, and so on.

➤ The microphone is your friend. Don't tap it, whack it, blow into it, or abuse it in any way.

➤ Be sure to test the microphone before the audience arrives. Ask a friend to stand in the back of the room and tell you if the level of your voice is appropriate and if you can be heard clearly.

➤ Repeat questions from the audience into the microphone. This helps everyone hear the question that was asked.

Speech of the Devil

Be especially careful about muttering under your breath if you're using a microphone. The audience might hear you.

If you're going to be moving around during your presentation, make sure that a clip-on (Lavalier) microphone is available. If you're using a Lavalier, be aware of where it's attached to your clothing. Also keep in mind where the cord and battery pack are located. This will help prevent you from disconnecting the microphone or yanking on the cord.

Attach the Lavalier to a jacket, lapel, collar, neckline, or tie above the mid-chest level, but not against the larynx—otherwise, your voice will become muffled.

Listen Up

About 14 million Americans have some kind of hearing impairment. About 2 million of these people are deaf, which means they can't hear or understand speech. Deaf people use several methods to understand what others are saying. It's especially important to be aware of these methods when you are making public speeches so you don't ostracize anyone in your audience.

Some people who are deaf use lip-reading to understand what others are saying. This means that you should be careful not to turn your head away from the audience. It's also important to move your lips clearly.

People with hearing impairments also use two kinds of manual communication. Sign language uses hand and arm gestures to represent words and ideas. The manual alphabet uses the fingers to represent each letter of the alphabet.

You can address these issues in several ways. Here are two effective methods to make sure you address *all* members of your audience:

➤ Use title slides and overheads to communicate the outline of the speech.

➤ Get an interpreter to sign as you speak. The interpreter should move his or her lips to reinforce your words. The interpreter should also use the manual alphabet to finger-spell unusual words or names.

The Least You Need to Know

➤ You can acquire a more effective voice through practice, but be sure to practice correctly so you don't reinforce bad habits.

➤ Make sure your voice is clear by using contractions correctly and not reversing sounds, omitting letters, or adding letters.

➤ Vary your rate of speech to correspond with the content of your speech. Present main ideas and difficult points at a slower pace.

➤ Get rid of annoying speech fillers, such as "uh," "ah," and "like."

➤ Speakers without a honeyed voice can make just as convincing a mark through the power of their volume, pitch, inflection, and pacing.

➤ Address the needs of the hearing impaired when speaking in public.

Chapter 29

An Ounce of Prevention: Rehearsing

In This Chapter

➤ Practice, practice, practice

➤ How to rehearse

➤ Preparing index cards and speech manuscripts

Two men waiting at the Pearly Gates strike up a conversation. "How'd you die?" the first man asks the second.

"I froze to death," says the second.

"That's awful," says the first man. "I had a heart attack," he adds. "I knew my wife was cheating on me, so one day I showed up at home unexpectedly. I ran up to the bedroom and found her alone, knitting. I ran down to the basement, but no one was hiding there, either. I ran up to the second floor, but no one was hiding there either. I ran as fast as I could to the attic, and just as I got there, I had a massive heart attack and died."

The second man shakes his head. "That's so ironic," he says.

"What do you mean?" asks the first man.

"If you had only stopped to look in the freezer, we'd both still be alive."

Now you see why it pays to be thorough? This chapter explains the reasons why preparation is crucial to a smooth and successful speech. In addition, you'll learn my tried-and-true method for making the most of your rehearsal time. Finally, the chapter discusses documents to use when rehearsing, whether index cards or an actual manuscript.

Why Rehearse?

Just as actors rehearse a play, public speakers also rehearse their speeches. Practice might not make you perfect, but it will definitely help make you a more confident and competent speaker.

Speech of the Devil

"You shouldn't worry about rehearsing," a friend once said to me. "You'll give a great speech. After all, you've certainly done it enough." This is flattering, but it's bad advice. Rehearsing is crucial to the success of your speech delivery, no matter how experienced at speech-making you are.

My analogy was chosen deliberately: In many ways, delivering a speech *is* like acting. In both cases, you're giving a performance. And repeated practice is the best way to discover which parts of your speech work and which ones don't. It's also the best way to maximize your chances for success. Read on to find out how to make the most of your rehearsal time.

How to Rehearse

Knowing your speech is not enough; you also have to know how you're going to deliver it. Your delivery includes your pauses and gestures. You have to know which words to stress and which ones not to. The following steps can help you get the most out of the time you spend rehearsing your speech:

1. **Practice the speech in front of a mirror.** Focus on correcting the parts of the speech that you noticed need work. Make sure that you're putting the stress on the right words and sentences. Make sure your gestures serve to emphasize your message. See if you're comfortable with what you see.

   While you practice, try to mimic the actual public speaking conditions as closely as possible. What do you do if you make a mistake while you're rehearsing? What would you do if you made a mistake in front of an audience? That's right, you'd just keep right on going. That's how you should rehearse. Don't allow yourself to go back and reread.

   By this time, you should have memorized the first 20 seconds and the last 20 seconds of your speech. These are the times when eye contact is most important. Having the opening and closing words of your speech down cold allows you to concentrate on other matters, such as settling your nerves, making eye contact, and using effective body language.

2. **Tape-record the speech.** Record the time it took you to read your speech, and see how close you are to your allotted time. Are you running short or long?

   Make any necessary adjustments by adding or subtracting text. If your speech is running long, don't speed up your speaking pace. Speaking faster won't fix the time problem—in fact, it will probably make things worse because your audience may not be able to understand you.

Then play back the recording and listen closely. Where do you need to pause for emphasis? Which words were hard to pronounce? Were there any words that were hard for your audience to understand? Which sentences were too long to say in one breath? Take careful notes to assess your performance.

Talk Soup

The word **rehearse** suggests the importance of continual practice: *re* means "to repeat."

3. **Videotape the speech.** Videotaping combines the benefits of tape recording and practicing in front of a mirror. You may be embarrassed watching yourself on tape, but you'll learn a great deal about your performance. It's the quickest way I know to get rock-solid improvement.

4. **Deliver the speech to a single person.** Choose a friend or family member to listen to your speech. The success of this depends largely on the friend and your relationship. You need someone who can be honest but not cruel, and forthright but not nasty. Loyal spouses or love-stricken suitors are rarely good choices because they are too biased; instead, go for someone who can realistically assess your performance.

   Try to match this rehearsal as closely as possible to the actual performance. Set up a stage, lectern, and chairs. Be especially sure to use all your visual aids, too. At this point, try to enjoy yourself—even just a little. Smile. Let your eyes twinkle a touch. If you pretend like you're having a good time, you may fool yourself into actually enjoying the experience.

5. **Rehearse the speech for a small group.** Gather together a group of friends, family members, neighbors, or coworkers. If at all possible, try to enlist the help of the types of people you will actually be addressing. They're more likely to be interested in your subject as well as your delivery. Once again, simulate the actual speaking conditions with a lectern, a table, and chairs.

   Use your audience; after all, you went to a lot of trouble to get them there. Pay careful attention to how they react to you. There's a reason why taped television shows are recorded in front of a "live studio audience." Performers need interaction with their viewers; the dead eye of the television monitor just won't do it. You want to be a pro, so use the tricks the pros use.

6. **Eliminate distracting mannerisms.** These include (but are not limited to) playing with jewelry, tucking your hair behind your ear, fiddling with your tie, and cracking your knuckles. These are actions you can easily avoid doing if you're aware of them.

7. **Practice at the site.** This is the hardest part of your rehearsal because it isn't always easy to get to the site ahead of time. If at all possible, visit the room where you'll be speaking. Stand at the lectern and rehearse your speech. You'll be

Speech of the Devil

Be sure that you rehearse the entire speech each time. If you don't, specific parts of the speech will be smooth; others will sound unprepared. For example, if you rehearse only the beginning, your body and conclusion will be weak. Or, if you concentrate on the introduction and the conclusion, the body just won't be as strong. Rehearse it all every time!

astonished at how much more relaxed you'll feel if you have practiced at the actual speaking site.

If this just isn't possible, be sure to arrive at the site a little early. Get the lay of the land; find out where the restroom is located and check all the audiovisual equipment you'll be needing.

8. **Practice the speech using all the visual aids.** This will help you judge how much time they will take up and how to incorporate them into your speech. You'll also find out if you've got a problem with a picture, prop, chart, or slide. Then you'll have the time to fix the problem well before the actual speech.

9. **Practice with background noise.** Turn on the TV or radio so you can practice your speech with distractions. After all, unless you lull your audience to sleep, they're going to be making noise during your speech—chewing gum, shuffling their feet, blowing their noses, and coughing. Get used to the distractions ahead of time.

10. **Practice your speech dressed as you plan to be for your actual presentation.** This will help you make sure your outfit is comfortable. If it isn't, you still have time to select a new one for the big day.

Rehearsing with Others

So far, I've been assuming that you're a solo act. As you have learned from previous chapters, however, this isn't always the case. What should you do if you are just part of the evening's entertainment? What about being part of a panel, for example?

The same rules explained earlier in this chapter still apply, except that you should try to rehearse with the other speakers. To ensure a smooth team effort, it's a good idea to see what everyone else is going to say—and how they plan to say it. If you're the chairperson of the event or the group organizer, you're very likely in a position to insist that everyone gather for one or more practice sessions. If not, it won't hurt to approach the chairperson with the idea of rehearsing in a group.

Group rehearsals allow you and all the other participants to see where each presentation should be cut or revised. For instance, one speaker may have a joke or story that strikes the other speakers as pointless or in bad taste. As gently as possible, the group should suggest alternatives. Group rehearsals have another important benefit: They allow each individual member even more quality feedback because the critics have a very real stake in the outcome.

Preparing Index Cards or a Speech Manuscript

When it comes to having your speech in front of you, you have two choices: index cards or an actual manuscript. The following sections talk about each in turn.

Note Cards

Good note cards meet these three requirements:

1. They contain enough material to help you remember the important points in your speech.

2. They are easy to use.

3. They don't distract the audience.

Class Act

If you're having a difficult time getting team or panel members to rehearse together, show them the audio- or videotapes you made of your own rehearsals. After they see the progress you've made, they will be more likely to set aside some time for a group rehearsal. You can also bribe them with food.

Many speakers write their notes on the smallest index cards: 3-by-5-inch. These cards have the advantage of being small enough to fit into your hand or pocket, so you can carry them to the podium without audience members being aware that you will be speaking from notes.

Other speakers prefer larger cards, 4-by-6-inch or 5-by-7-inch. These larger cards are easier to use if you have a lot of statistics to remember, if your handwriting is large, or if your vision is weak.

Unfortunately, you can't conceal these cards in your hand or pocket. But don't make secrecy your prime consideration when deciding on which size cards to use. Instead, select the cards that best serve your purpose.

Regardless of the size cards you use, be sure to fasten them securely with a rubber band or paper clip so they won't scatter if they happen to fall on the floor (God forbid!). Number the cards just in case this does happen.

What should you write on your note cards? Include key phrases to remind you of the major sections of your speech. Also write down any statistics or quotations.

Read the following passage from a speech about the history of comic books. Then see how the speaker made notes about this passage on an index card:

> "Meanwhile, over at Atlas (formerly Timely) Comics, the publisher, Martin Goodman, saw the success of his rivals and suggested to his young editor that they should start publishing super-hero comics as well. The editor, a long-time writer of comics for Timely/Atlas named Stan Lee, took a shot and created the Fantastic Four, Spider-Man, the Incredible Hulk, and X-Men."

Here's the speaker's card for the excerpt from the comics speech.

Atlas (Timely) Comics
Martin Goodman (publisher) suggests they publish super-hero
comics.
Stan Lee (editor) created the Fantastic four, Spider-Man,
Incredible Hulk, X-Men.

How many cards should you use? The answer depends on your speech and your comfort level. If you're giving a simple speech and know the material well, a few cards might be enough. But if you're delivering a long speech with a lot of detail, you might have to use at least 10 cards. But don't use *too* many note cards—they will distract both you and the audience.

Speech of the Devil

Too many note cards can make an unsightly lump in the smooth line of an elegant suit.

Full Text

It's a good idea to write out the full speech if at least four items from the following list apply.

➤ It's an important occasion.

➤ Every word of the speech counts.

➤ Time is strictly limited.

➤ Reporters might be quoting the speech.

➤ You have not had much public speaking experience.

➤ You are very nervous.

Follow these steps as you prepare your speech manuscript:

➤ Type or print on only one side of the paper.

➤ If you type your speech, use a large font, at least 12- to 14-point type.

➤ Use both uppercase and lowercase letters as you normally would. Do not use all capital letters.

➤ Double- or triple-space the text.

➤ Never hyphenate words at the end of lines. It's better to leave the line short.

➤ End each page with a complete sentence.

➤ Underline any words or phrases you want to stress.

➤ Number the pages clearly, preferably at the top-right corner.

➤ Type on only the top two-thirds of the page. This will prevent you from bending your face all the way to the bottom of the page, which muffles your voice.

Class Act

Always prepare an extra copy of your speech. Keep it in a separate place. That way, if you lose one copy, you'll have another.

➤ Leave margins of at least 2 inches on all four sides of the page.

➤ Never staple the pages of your speech together. Fasten them with a paper clip. That way, you can remove the clip when you're ready to speak.

➤ Keep the speech in a folder so it will stay clean and unwrinkled.

The Least You Need to Know

➤ Rehearsing your speech is a crucial step in a successful delivery.

➤ Consider tape-recording or videotaping your speech as you rehearse. Study the tape for ways to improve your performance.

➤ Prepare and read from index cards or the full text, depending on your audience and needs.

Chapter 30

Let Me Hear Your Body Talk: Body Language

In This Chapter

➤ Nonverbal communication

➤ First impressions

➤ Eye contact

➤ Gestures

➤ Nonverbal communication across cultures

You know you're nervous during a speech when…

➤ Your nervous twitching registers on the Richter scale.

➤ You don't need a hammer to pound in nails.

➤ People can test their batteries in your ears.

➤ You short out motion detectors in the lecture hall.

➤ Your audience gets dizzy just watching you.

Your body language can reveal a lot about your feelings, both good and bad. On one end of the scale, the way you hold your hands, arms, and torso can help you communicate your message in a polished and professional manner. On the other hand, inappropriate body language can kill any chance you have of bonding with the audience. And not understanding body language can make it much more difficult for you to enjoy your speech and get your message across.

In this chapter, you'll learn about nonverbal communication and the public speaking process. Upcoming sections deal with making eye contact, using body language to your advantage, and understanding nonverbal communication in other cultures. By the end of the chapter, you'll be well on your way to matching nonverbal and verbal communication to make your speeches dynamic and effective personal statements.

The Hidden Persuaders

People often think of a speech as merely a series of words spoken aloud. Not so! Actually, you communicate as much to an audience through nonverbal means as you do through words. Eye contact, platform movements, appearance, and the motions you make as you begin and end a speech can say a great deal about you and your message. As a result, *nonverbal communication*—communication that doesn't use words—is key to your success as a public speaker.

Dr. Ray Birdwhistell, one of the leading scholars in nonverbal communication, claims that words account for only 35 percent of what we communicate; the rest is largely accomplished by body language. Although that figure may be exaggerated, it does emphasize the importance of nonverbal communication for public speakers: You can communicate as much through what the audience *sees* as what they *hear*. Your nonverbal communication "says" a great deal about you and your message.

Talk Soup

Nonverbal communication refers to a series of gestures and body language that do not rely on words to convey meaning.

Most of the time, we're no more conscious of interpreting nonverbal signals than we're conscious of breathing. Yet nonverbal signals can be misinterpreted just as often as verbal symbols (words). And nonverbal misunderstandings can be harder to clear up because people may not be aware of the nonverbal cues that led them to misunderstandings in the first place.

It's Later Than You Think

When does your speech actually begin? Choose one of these answers:

➤ When you enter the room

➤ When you approach the podium

➤ When you start speaking

Answer: Your speech begins when you enter the room.

Your audience will form an opinion of you the minute they see you. It's no lie: First impressions do count, especially when it comes to public speakers. You may communicate leadership, poise, and self-confidence—or timidity, nervousness, and fear—just by the way you approach the platform.

Try these tips for making sure that your body language conveys authority:

➤ Walk to the platform energetically, but not hastily.

➤ Arrange your notes on the lectern.

➤ Hold your head high.

➤ Stand straight, with your shoulders back.

➤ Look at your audience.

➤ Pause for a few moments before beginning to speak.

The Eyes Have It

As you speak, establish eye contact with different members of your audience. This suggests to your listeners that you're speaking directly to them, just as you would if you were holding a one-on-one conversation. Giving someone your attention indicates respect, interest, and self-confidence. The greater the proportion of speaking time that you devote to eye contact, the deeper and more positive an impression you convey.

Encores and Exits

Ten eye blinks or fewer per minute indicates boredom, while 14 or more shows nervousness or stress.

To achieve successful audience contact, however, you can't just look at your audience: Your look must convey the feeling that you're really trying to communicate with them. Concentrate on each person you see, making it plain that you really want him or her to understand your message. Make each person feel that you're delivering the message to him or her alone.

Class Act

How long should you focus on each person? One whole sentence or one whole thought per individual audience member is about right.

Maintaining eye contact with your audience has another important benefit: It makes it possible for you to monitor feedback. *Feedback* is the total reaction you get from your audience. Feedback includes the following reactions:

➤ Yawning

➤ Booing

➤ Sleeping

➤ Smiling

➤ Hissing

➤ Giving questioning looks

➤ Clapping

➤ Fidgeting

Are people yawning, scratching their heads, or reading their newspapers? This suggests that your speech isn't engaging their attention. But if people are smiling at you, nodding their heads, and taking notes, you know that your speech is being well-received.

Here's how to make effective eye contact:

➤ As you speak, look at one member of the audience for about a minute. Pause long enough to finish a thought and make a connection.

➤ Turn your head slightly to look at someone else.

➤ Include people from all over the room, especially those at the side of the room near the front.

Class Act

Don't stand with your arms crossed or your hands in your pockets. This posture prevents you from gesturing and may even make your audience feel uncomfortable. If making eye contact frightens you, you can still follow my guidelines; instead, gaze slightly *above* people's eyes, at their foreheads. As you become more confident, shift your gaze downward into their eyes.

Remember that every public speaking event is a performance, and the most convincing performances acknowledge the audience. Even in a large audience, if the speaker looks at people's feet instead of their faces, it registers with the audience. Each person looking at you deserves a look back. Let your eyes show that you know the audience is out there and that you care.

But what if someone in the audience is scowling at you? Don't let their frown throw you—after all, it might just be a look of intense concentration.

Finger Play

Appropriate gestures are a key part of a successful speech. Communicating nonverbally through gestures is a natural part of human communication, but some public speakers freeze up when it comes to using their arms, hands, and body to communicate their message.

Not you! By the end of this section, you'll know what specific body language can enhance your speech—and what specific body language can undercut your words. With this knowledge, you'll be able to suit your nonverbal communication to your message.

How good are you at reading body language? Draw a line to match each gesture to its meaning.

1. Nodding your head	a. Calmness
2. Rubbing your neck	b. Desire to hide something
3. Playing with your hair	c. Impatience
4. Showing your palms out	d. Shows relaxation and interest
5. Clenching your fists	e. Arrogance
6. Clasping your hands behind your head	f. Uncertainty
7. Flexing your arm	g. Strength
8. Hiding your arms behind your back	h. Openness
9. Putting your hand on your hips	I. Stay away from me!
10. Tapping your foot	j. Stress

Answers

1. d
2. f
3. j
4. h
5. b
6. e
7. g
8. a
9. i
10. c

Gestures

Gestures can be classified into four categories: emphatic gestures, transitional gestures, descriptive gestures, and locative gestures. Let's explore each one in detail:

1. **Emphatic gestures** help the speaker stress his or her message. These gestures include making a fist, raising one hand with the palm up, and pointing at the audience.

2. **Transitional gestures** show that you are moving from one part of the speech to another. These gestures include using your fingers to tick off key points, placing both palms flat on the podium, and moving both hands, with palms facing, from one side to the other in front of you.

3. **Descriptive gestures** illustrate a point by drawing a picture in the air. These include using your hand to indicate the size of an object.

4. **Locative gestures** direct the audience's attention to a place, object, or person. You usually make these gestures with your index finger or your whole hand.

Break the Code

Following are some common gestures that public speakers make and the impression that each one conveys to most people. Body language isn't an exact science, so be sure to carefully evaluate each gesture against your personal style and audience before you decide to accept or reject it. Then select the gestures that convey the impression you wish to create.

Let's start with some gestures that convey a positive impression for public speakers:

Gesture	Impression conveyed
Taking long steps to the podium	Assured, forthright manner
Assuming an erect posture at the podium	Self-assured, honest, successful
Standing while others sit	Authoritative
Placing your hands on the podium	Receptive, open
Briefly lifting your eyebrows	Interested, lively, alert
Nodding your head	Agreement, interest
Placing your hand out, with palms up	Receptive
Placing your chin in your hand	Thoughtfulness

And here are some examples of nonverbal communication that carry negative overtones:

Gesture	Impression conveyed
Clamping the back of the neck	Anger
Fidgeting	Nervousness
Tugging your collar	Nervousness
Pulling your ear	Concealment
Rubbing your eye	Concealment
Drumming your fingers	Urge to leave
Scratching	Lying

Gesture	Impression conveyed
Lowering your eyes	Air of failure
Folding your arms over your chest	Resistance, fear
Staring for a prolonged time	Aggressive, threatening

Platform Movement

Platform movement refers to the way a speaker uses movements involving the entire body. Platform movement doesn't have to take place on a stage; this type of body language is also evident when a speaker is addressing a small group around a conference table or making a presentation for several colleagues, for example.

Class Act

When it comes to body language and public speaking, less is often more—the less attention you draw to your head, hands, and legs, the more powerful and intelligent you appear. Mother was right: Don't fidget!

As with gestures, platform movement should look and feel natural because it reinforces your message. Here are the two basic rules of platform movement:

➤ Move when there's a reason to move.

➤ Stand still when there's not a reason to move.

For instance, you'll want to move closer to the audience to show greater confidence or intimacy, to draw their attention to your words, or to signal a change in the topic.

Know When to Fold Them

We all feel comfortable with a specific series of gestures, just as we all feel comfortable with a specific level of language. Within day-to-day communication, we choose our gestures as unconsciously as we choose our words. But when it comes to making a speech, our gestures must fit the time, place, and subject, just as our words must suit our audience. Gestures should feel natural and appropriate to your audience, not forced or insulting. In other words, you might need to drop some of your body language if your speech requires it.

Talk Soup

Platform movement refers to nonverbal communication that involves the entire body.

One of my favorite techniques is to rise to my full height and then settle back comfortably. I also position my legs slightly apart for stability and power. And I tilt my head back just a little. This helps my voice project and conveys the attitude of ease and assurance.

Just as we improve on our language by studying books and listening to people speak, we also can improve the effect of our body language by studying ourselves and others. Here's how:

➤ Stand in front of a mirror, or video-tape yourself delivering your speech.

➤ Study your performance. Which gestures seem natural? Which ones are forced? Which ones help you transmit your message? Which ones hinder communication?

➤ Watch people on television and in person as they give speeches and perform on stage. Which gestures do they use?

➤ Which gestures feel comfortable and natural to you? Which ones suit your speaking style and best help you convey your message?

➤ Experiment with different nonverbal communication, suiting each gesture to the speech and audience.

➤ Make these gestures a part of your speech repertoire.

Speech of the Devil

Remember to vary your gestures. If you use the same gestures too often in a speech, the audience will be distracted.

Point the Way

Try these six traditional speech gestures to reinforce your point and to connect with your audience. No two people make the same gestures in exactly the same way, so use the following information as guidelines, not rules.

1. **Giving and taking.** Place your hand out with the palm turned upward to propose a new idea or ask for something. This gesture means, "This idea deserves your special attention," or "I appeal to you to help me with this." This is the most widely used gesture because it is forceful without being as blunt as the pointed finger.

2. **Raising a fist.** A raised fist shows strong feelings, such as anger or determination. This is an incendiary motion, so use it with care.

3. **Pointing.** Point your open hand to indicate position, to call attention to an object or idea, to show direction, or to make an accusation.

4. **Rejecting.** Show that you discard an idea by giving a sweeping gesture with your hand, palm downward. This gesture would be used with a statement such as, "That idea is not worth considering."

5. **Dividing.** When you wish to show that you are separating ideas into different parts, hold your palms in a vertical position and move your hands from side to side. This cutting and separating gesture parts ideas and allows new ones to form.

6. **Warning.** Place your hand straight out like a stop signal—palm out, heel of the hand down—to caution listeners. This gesture can also be used to calm an audience or to prepare listeners to accept another idea.

However, don't force it. Don't assume gestures and mannerisms that are alien to your personality. It will show, believe me.

Groove to the Beat

As stressed earlier, everyone varies the standard body gestures slightly, adapting them to individual speaking styles. Nonetheless, all successful body language has three qualities in common. Effective gestures have these characteristics:

➤ **Relaxed.** When you're under tension, your body cannot relax. Your body language will reflect this and will be tense, jerky, and uneven. To avoid being stiff and unnatural in front of an audience, it's important to relax before you begin your presentation. Refer to Chapter 2, "Stage Fright," for tips on doing this.

➤ **Definite.** Effective gestures are strong and accurate. The audience should be able to understand exactly what you mean. Vary the force and nature of your movements to suit your speech, but make every single movement count.

➤ **Appropriate.** The gesture must fall exactly where you want it, or it will be meaningless. Even worse, it could undermine your point. Practice making the right gestures until they become a natural part of your speech presentation.

Culture Clash

American public speakers sometimes assume that they can depend on gestures to communicate if language fails. But researchers have reported that no gesture or body motion has the same meaning in all cultures. Here are some examples:

➤ Bulgarians often nod their heads to signify "no" and shake their heads to show "yes." Americans have the exact opposite set of nonverbal signs.

Speech of the Devil

Badly timed and inappropriate body language is often a result of nervousness and inadequate planning.

➤ The thumbs-up sign, which Americans take to mean "good work" or "go ahead," is a vulgar insult in Greece.

➤ The circle formed with the thumb and first finger that means "OK" in America is obscene in Southern Italy and can mean "You're worth nothing" in France and Belgium.

➤ To many Americans, shaking your hands in front of your body as though you were shaking water off them is a sign of mental retardation; to many Puerto Ricans, it's a sign of intense excitement.

➤ Many North Americans see eye contact as a sign of honesty, but in other cultures, looking down is a sign of appropriate deference.

➤ In Muslim countries, men and women are not supposed to make eye contact.

➤ Americans smile much more often than people from other countries. The Japanese, for example, smile not only when they're amused but also to cover embarrassment, sadness, and even anger.

➤ People in southern and border states tend to smile more than those who live in northern states. As a result, Northerners have been known to doubt the sincerity of Southerners. This problem plagued Jimmy Carter during his presidency.

The moral of the story? Be especially careful of your body language when addressing a multicultural audience. Check with your hosts, people from the various cultures represented in your audience, or other knowledgeable people to make sure that you're communicating what you *think* you're communicating.

The Least You Need to Know

➤ You communicate as much to an audience through nonverbal means as through words.

➤ Mastering *nonverbal communication*—communication that doesn't use words— is key to your success as a public speaker.

➤ Your speech begins when you enter the room, before you say anything.

➤ Establish eye contact with your audience.

➤ Effective body language is relaxed, definite, and appropriate.

➤ Body language varies among cultures, so be careful when addressing a multicultural audience.

Chapter 31

Dress and Grooming

In This Chapter

➤ How appearance can affect performance

➤ Appropriate clothing

➤ Correct and complete grooming

➤ Preparing the night before

Take a look at some of these fun facts:

➤ American Airlines saved $40,000 in 1987 by eliminating one olive from each salad served in first class.

➤ Each day is 0.00000002 seconds longer than the one before it because the earth is gradually slowing down.

➤ In 1859, 24 rabbits were released in Australia. Within six years, the population grew to 2 million.

➤ Mosquitoes have killed more people than have all the world's wars combined.

See? Little things *do* matter—even when you're giving a speech!

In this chapter, you'll discover the subtle importance of appearance and grooming on your presentations. These may seem like insignificant issues in the grand scheme of speechmaking, but you'll learn that they matter very much indeed. I'll also teach you how to master the secrets of preparation to better maximize your chances for success. Let's start with some guidelines for your speech wardrobe.

Dress for Success

> Costly thy habit as thy purse can buy,
> But not expressed in fancy; rich, not gaudy,
> For the apparel oft proclaims the man.
>
> —*Hamlet*, Act I, scene iii

Shakespeare was right: Clothes do make the man—and the woman. Speakers are often judged as much by how they look as by what they have to say. Yes, we may be a shallow species overly concerned with appearance, but that's the truth of it. You've got to look the part to play the part.

When you deliver a speech, your overall appearance should suit each of these considerations:

➤ Personal style

➤ Purpose

➤ Audience

➤ The occasion at which you're speaking

Certain colors and styles of clothing are considered more professional and credible than other styles. Furthermore, your choice of clothing says a great deal about your attitude toward your listeners and how much importance you attach to the speech itself. Speakers who radically violate the audience's expectations concerning clothing are giving themselves a real handicap.

Put enough time into planning your clothing so that it reinforces the positive impression you wish to create. Follow these guidelines:

1. **Go standard: suits or their equivalent.** What kind of suit should you wear? If you've got good taste and a good eye for color (confirmed by people who are not direct blood relatives or owe you money), follow your instincts. If fashion is not your strong point, read John Molloy's *Dress for Success* (men's clothes) and *The Women's Dress for Success Book*. These books are based on research about how people in business perceive specific clothing styles.

2. **Start with the best.** First, visit quality, respected stores (meaning really expensive, classy ones) and note the details on the clothing—the exact shade of blue in a suit, the width of the lapels, the number of buttons on the sleeves. Then go to stores in your price range and buy a suit that has details found in more expensive garments.

3. **Stick to the basics.** When in doubt, err on the side of conformity. In traveling around the country, I've found that most people are still most comfortable with traditionally dressed speakers—especially when it comes to female speakers.

4. **Consider the occasion.** If you're speaking at a wedding, for example, don't wear something that will upstage the bride or the groom. This is their day, not yours.

5. **Consider the audience.** Orthodox Jewish people believe that women should dress modestly, with demure but elegant clothing. Hems are long, shoulders are covered, colors are subdued. As a result, I was shocked several years ago to see a female speaker at an Orthodox Jewish funeral wearing a tight, sexy, sleeveless black dress. The daughter of a rabbi, the speaker obviously knew that she was dressed inappropriately for the occasion, but she was clearly more concerned with making a personal statement than honoring the occasion. As a result, her words were totally obscured by her appearance. Don't let this happen to you: Always know your audience.

Speech of the Devil

It's often very hot on stage. Add your nervousness, and you're likely to perspire a lot. As a general rule, when you speak in public, wear lighter clothing than you would normally choose for the season.

6. **Watch the color of your clothing.** Studies have shown that black uniforms make football players appear—and act—meaner. Brown suits often convey an impression of weakness. Men, consider navy blue or gray suits if the occasion is formal, or conservative sport coats for more relaxed speaking engagements. Women should stay away from neon colors or other eye-popping shades and patterns—these are distracting to the audience.

7. **Choose comfortable shoes.** For years, my personal motto was: "If the shoe fits, don't buy it." I had a wardrobe of gorgeous but uncomfortable shoes. That was before I had three (yes, *three*) rounds of surgery to correct the years of damage I had done to my tootsies. Now I know better, and my shoes are *always* comfortable.

   Remember that you'll be on your feet delivering your speech and fielding questions. The last thing you want to deal with is sore, aching feet. Trust me: I speak from years of experience on this one.

8. **Take care of the details.** Here are some things to check:

   ➤ Check your heels to make sure that they aren't worn down.

   ➤ Make sure that your shoes are shined.

   ➤ See that your hem is securely sewed in place.

   ➤ Your shirt should have all its buttons; ditto for your blazer.

   ➤ No chipped nail polish, please. This is especially noticeable on long, dark nails.

   ➤ Check your clothes for last-minute stains and such. My down coat always sheds its feathers, for example. This is very noticeable on dark-colored outfits but is easily fixed.

➤ If you're wearing new clothing, be sure to cut off the tags. Several times I've seen speakers with price tags dangling from their armpits. It's not a good look.

Class Act

Say you get to your speech and discover that your hem is ripped. What to do? Staple it in place. It's not what Martha Stewart would do, but in a pinch, staples do the trick.

9. **Hair care counts.** Have your hair cut or styled conservatively; no mousse abuse. And go easy on the perfumed hair spray if you're speaking outdoors—bees just love it.

10. **Nix the gold.** Jewelry and makeup should be understated, unless you're addressing the annual Mary Kay convention.

11. **Never have a lot of change or keys in your pockets.** You don't want the sound of objects competing with your voice. And under no circumstances should you fiddle with anything in your pocket.

12. **Never wear a hat.** Unless it's part of your presentation, avoid hats—after all, the 1940's are long past.

I can't stress enough how important it is to dress appropriately when you give a presentation. It's better to make a credible first impression by looking as if you are interested in giving a good speech. The small details add up to a big impression: Make it a good one.

Speech of the Devil

Interviews with dozens of executives, both male and female, reveal that it still isn't acceptable to look too feminine or too sexy in a formal speech setting.

A Clean Machine

Personal hygiene is as important as clothing, and cleanliness and neatness are always necessary giving a speech or presentation. Being dirty or sloppy conveys the impression that you don't care about the audience. In effect, you're saying, "I'm not interested in giving this speech, so I didn't take much time getting ready to address you." Messy speakers come across as slobs—and inconsiderate ones, at that.

Here are some suggestions for being a clean speaking machine:

➤ Bathe that morning with deodorant soap.

➤ Wash your hair. Make sure to get rid of dandruff; it's distracting to your listeners.

➤ Clean and trim your nails.

➤ Use deodorant and antiperspirant—a lot.

➤ Brush your teeth and use a mouthwash.

➤ Wear clean clothes. Men should make sure that their tie isn't stained. Even if it's your favorite, lucky outfit, don't wear it unless it's squeaky clean.

➤ Make sure your fly is zipped.

➤ Ladies should make sure that stockings are new. (Runned stockings are very noticeable, especially if the stockings are dark-colored.)

➤ Clothes should fit correctly. Slips shouldn't show, and blouses or skirts shouldn't be transparent. Ties should reach the belt, and socks should meet the pants. No one wants to see those hairy ankles.

➤ Avoid cologne and perfumed aftershave lotions.

➤ If you smoke, use a breath mint before the speech, especially if you're addressing a small audience. And smoke outside so that your clothes don't reek of cigarette or cigar smoke.

➤ Never chew gum while you deliver a speech.

Night Moves

Remember how you prepared to take those terrifying standardized tests back in school? The same suggestions for how to treat yourself before the speech will serve you in good stead when you speak in public. Let's review the suggestions:

Class Act

I carry a disposable toothbrush, pre-loaded with toothpaste, to make sure that my pearly whites *are* pearly white.

1. **Get plenty of sleep.** According to recent studies, most of us are sleep-deprived—and seriously so. But I don't have to tell you that; you know it already. Nonetheless, for several nights before any important speaking event, get plenty of sleep. The night before isn't good enough—strive for at least two to three days of adequate sleep. You'll be amazed at how good you feel and how much better you perform when you're rested.

   Besides, fatigue can lower your self-confidence, your ability to concentrate, and your attention span. These are things that you need to be a good public speaker.

2. **Eat right.** Not only don't we sleep enough, but we also don't eat right. Be sure to eat nourishing meals—especially breakfast—on the day of the speech. Make a conscious effort to fill your stomach with whatever works best for it—and, no, that doesn't include a Greasy Glenn Burger Blast with a side of monster fries.

3. **Avoid caffeine.** Yes, I know you need your coffee. We all need a jump start from Mr. Coffee in the morning, but too much caffeine can make you nervous. And the last thing you want before a speech is a bad case of chemically induced nerves.

313

Don't forget that colas and teas also contain a great deal of caffeine. If you're a very heavy coffee drinker, however, don't go off the stuff cold turkey because you'll have a nasty case of caffeine withdrawal. Just don't pump yourself up with "a few" extra mugs of java.

4. **Avoid alcohol.** It's amazing how so many otherwise highly intelligent human beings think that a few drinks before a speech will make them more relaxed, witty, and funny. A few drinks actually might make you sound and act stupid. Commit this to memory: Alcohol *never* works for public speakers.

5. **Pack business cards.** Speaking in public is a great chance to network with interesting and important professionals. Odds are, after your speech, you'll get offers to address other events. You want to be prepared. Today, for example, I did a half-hour interview with the gracious Donna Hanover on WOR radio in New York City. After the interview, the next guest asked if I would address her group. She had heard my talk while she was waiting her turn to be interviewed. A physician, she runs a large organization that addresses women's lifestyle issues. She asked, "When are you available to speak to my organization? Do you have a card?" I whipped out my card, and we're in business.

After you give a speech, be ready with your business cards. Few things look as unprofessional as scrawling your name and phone number on a cocktail napkin.

7. **Pack an emergency bag.** Pack a small bag with items that you're likely to need. Here are some items to consider:

   ➤ An extra copy of your speech or notes.

   ➤ A bottle of water. This is usually provided, but you can never be sure.

   ➤ A small snack, such as a piece of fruit.

   ➤ Tissues.

   ➤ Breath mints.

   ➤ Pens.

   ➤ Business cards.

   ➤ Deodorant.

The Least You Need to Know

➤ Select attire that suits your personal style, purpose, audience, and the occasion at which you're speaking.

➤ As important as clothing is your personal hygiene. Be clean.

➤ Get plenty of sleep the night before your speech, eat right, and avoid caffeine and alcohol.

➤ Pack business cards and an emergency bag.

Part 6
The Moment of Truth

Five No-Fail Ways to Give a Terrible Speech: A Recipe for Disaster

1. *Don't prepare. Hey, we're all stressed for time. How can you be expected to find the time to write a speech? Besides, it's only a 5-minute speech. You can wing that, no sweat.*

2. *Talk to your concerns. Drop the assigned topic: You know what's really important. Talk about things that concern you and only you. After all, you have the stage.*

3. *Strive to impress. Use a lot of big words and difficult references. Your audience will think you're really smart, especially if they can't understand a word you're saying.*

4. *Avoid facts. Hey, who cares what the facts are? Anyway, facts are hard to find. Opinions are much better than facts any day.*

5. *Talk as long as you want. Make your point, then make it a few more times. Try your hardest to talk until the last person's head has dropped into the mashed potatoes.*

Chapter 32

Delivery

In This Chapter

➤ Delivering the speech

➤ The question of memorization

➤ The importance of attitude

➤ Coping with disaster

➤ The question-and-answer period

➤ Using humor

➤ Making a graceful exit

What, in your opinion, is the most reasonable explanation for the fact that Moses led the Israelites all over the place for forty years before they finally got to the Promised Land?

A. He was being tested.

B. He wanted them to really appreciate the Promised Land when they finally got there.

C. He refused to ask for directions.

The moral of the story? Be sure to get directions—nice clear ones—to the place where you'll be speaking. You can't win it if you're not in it. You'd be amazed at the number of speakers who have gotten lost on the way to the conference center, community hall, or Masonic lodge.

By the end of this chapter, you'll know how to cope with any speech emergency that might arise. I'll teach you how to snatch victory from the jaws of defeat. Let's start with the way you actually deliver your speech.

See and Say

As much as possible, you should sound like you're saying your speech, not reading it—even if you actually *are* reading it. Strive for a natural delivery by using the following techniques:

➤ Memorize the opening and closing of your speech. This will help you cope with stage fright; you'll feel more relaxed if you've got the beginning and end down pat.

➤ Don't jump right into the speech. It's perfectly all right—and even desirable—to give the audience a few seconds to look you over while you get your bearings.

➤ When you arrive on-stage, adjust the microphone, place your papers on the lectern, look around the room, smile, and take a deep breath.

➤ If you're holding your material, keep it near eye level. This shortens the distance between the words and your eye, and makes it easier for you to maintain eye contact with the audience as you speak.

➤ Don't flip or lift pages. Instead, smoothly slide one page or card under the next as you work your way through your speech. (That's why you should use a paper clip rather than staple your pages together.)

Speech of the Devil

Never stare downward at the podium as you read your speech. Your words will get muffled and you won't be able to make eye contact with the audience. Look down as you need to, but keep your head up to address the audience.

To Memorize or Not to Memorize?

Should you memorize your speech? In general, I don't advise novice speakers to memorize their entire speeches because I think it creates too much pressure to get the speech "absolutely perfect." Memorizing your speech can also result in a stilted, wooden delivery.

Professional speakers who repeatedly deliver the same speech often memorize it, yet with each delivery they adjust the speech to suit the occasion and audience. Only a very skillful speaker can do this. So unless you're a regular on the rubber chicken circuit, avoid memorizing the entire speech.

Put on a Happy Face

Your attitude makes a tremendous difference in the success of your speech. Show your enthusiasm from the very start. Let your audience know that you're pleased to have the chance to address them. True vivacity and excitement make your speech fresh and effective—even if you've given the same address before. Make each time you speak seem like the first time.

Along with enthusiasm comes audience rapport. Establish a link with the audience as soon as possible. Your audience has already formed an opinion about you from your appearance and the host's introduction, but you need to strike a chord with the audience that immediately sets up a bond. For example, President Kennedy once won over a French audience by announcing, "I'm the gentleman who accompanied Mrs. Kennedy to Paris."

I Should Have Stayed in Bed

An important aspect of staying in charge is dealing with problems without becoming rattled. Few speeches ever go exactly as planned, no matter how meticulous your preparation. Audiences tend to be sympathetic and receptive to speakers who deal with problems as they happen and keep on going. They lose patience with speakers who can't cope with problems. As a result, you have to know how to deal with problems, obstacles, and even emergencies.

Encores and Exits

Memory, the process of storing and retrieving information in the brain, has four distinct varieties: *recollection, recall, recognition,* and *relearning.* **Recollection** involves reconstructing events or facts by using cues. **Recall** is actively remembering something from the past. **Recognition** refers to the ability to correctly identify previously-encountered stimuli. **Relearning** shows the effect of memory, since familiar material is often easier to relearn than new information.

Because you'll know your speech material thoroughly, you'll have enough time to anticipate problems: rumbling subway trains, faulty video equipment, noisy latecomers, loud waiters, burned-out slide projector bulbs, and so on. Probably the most important thing to remember is to stay calm: Your grace under pressure will increase your chances of delivering a successful speech.

You Think You Have Problems?

You know how life works: Anything that *can* go wrong, *will* go wrong. But problems that arise during public speaking events can be especially disturbing because you're already pretty nervous about performing in front of a group. Here's how to handle some of the problems that arise most often:

1. *Problem*: The speaker before you preempts half your material.

   Solution: Don't repeat the material. Instead, shorten your speech. Refer to the previous speech. Say, "As so-and-so has just pointed out...."

2. *Problem*: The speaker before you takes up too much time. As a result, your speaking time is cut short.

   Solution: Go straight to your conclusion and "tell 'em what you told 'em."

3. *Problem*: Someone asks you a question that you can't answer.

   Solution: Honestly admit that you don't know the answer. Tell the individual that you'll get the answer and get back to him or her. Then do.

4. *Problem*: The hall is very noisy. There may be a major thunderstorm in progress, a wedding in the next room, or some workers outside trying to drill to China.

   Solution: See if the noise can be stopped or the sound system turned up. If not, acknowledge the distraction and soldier on. Your audience will admire your courage and determination.

5. *Problem*: You have a heavy accent.

   Solution: I was once privileged to hear the Nobel-laureate writer Isaac Bashevis Singer speak before a large crowd. Born in Poland in 1904, Singer had a very heavy accent. He opened his speech with these lines, "I speek many langwiches, English de best." The audience roared with laughter; Singer had won them firmly to his side.

So you have an accent? Check out these statistics:

Class Act

It's important not to get dehydrated during your speech. Make sure you have enough water during the talk.

➤ Nearly 1 in every 10 residents of the United States is foreign-born—this translates into about 26 million people. (This is a result of the highest level of immigration since the 1930s.)

➤ More than 32 million Americans speak English as a second language.

➤ About 17 million Americans speak Spanish at home; about 2 million speak French; and more than 1 million each speak German, Chinese, or Italian.

➤ About 140 different languages are spoken in America.

➤ More than 100 languages are spoken in the school systems of New York City, Chicago, Los Angeles, and Fairfax Country, Va.

If you have an accent, you have two choices: Acknowledge it as I. B. Singer did, or ignore it. Either choice is fine. As the previous statistics show, chances are very good that some members of your audience will share your accent—or have a different one of their own. This means they'll be on your side, so relax.

6. *Problem:* You have to revise your entire speech at the last minute.

   Solution: This can happen because of factors out of your control. For example, say you're giving a speech on politics or the stock market. A sudden shift in events might make your speech completely incorrect. If this happens, you'll be forced to shift gears. Here's what to do:

   ➤ Take a deep breath and whip together a new speech as fast as you can.

   ➤ If the previous subject was announced ahead of time or was printed in the conference proceedings, you'll have to announce the change. Keep the announcement short. Then deliver the new speech.

   ➤ If the topic of your speech wasn't announced ahead of time, don't explain the change. Never say, "Well, I had a much better speech prepared, but things changed at the last minute, so here's what you're getting instead." Just deliver the new speech as though it were the original.

7. *Problem:* You make a bad blunder while speaking.

   Solution: Never apologize if you make a mistake while giving a speech. Simply correct the mistake and move on. You never want to draw attention to an error—chances are most people will miss it anyway.

8. *Problem:* People in the audience are being rude.

   Solution: The world is full of jerks. Odds are, a few of them will be in some of the audiences you address. There are the everyday inconsiderate people: The ones who talk during your speech, paint their nails, or keep jumping up to check out the facilities. They're annoying, like gnats and mosquitoes, but they don't do any real damage.

Speech of the Devil

Never make faces when you make a mistake. It's the same as holding up a sign that says, "Wow! I goofed!"

Then there are the actively evil sorts: the hecklers who think they know more than you do and that it's their responsibility to point it out to everyone else. Hecklers can rattle you and make it hard for you to continue your speech. (It's especially difficult when they're drunk.)

Fortunately, hecklers aren't a frequent problem for most public speakers. You're far more likely to suffer through the gum-crackers and chattering children. But here's what to do just in case:

➤ Settle the issue with your host beforehand. Tell your host that if anyone in the audience is overtly rude, you'll pause to allow your host the time to remove him or her from the audience.

➤ Pause and wait a moment for the heckler to settle down. Chances are good that other audience members will try to hush him or her, since you've already won them over to your side with your opening remarks. And even if you haven't prearranged this, your host might use your pause to remove the offender.

➤ If all else fails, stop the speech and ask for the heckler to be removed. You deserve basic consideration.

Live and Learn

If you goof, don't be too hard on yourself. Everyone makes mistakes, especially in tense situations such as speaking in public. Chalk up your mistake to a learning experience and move on. Here are some things I've learned from my public speaking mistakes:

Speech of the Devil

When it comes to hecklers, turn-about isn't fair play. Never, never try to return an insult. You'll lose your audience support and will run the risk of embarrassing yourself.

➤ I've learned that you can get by on charm for about 15 minutes. After that, you'd better know something.

➤ I've learned that you shouldn't compare yourself to the best others can do. Instead, compare yourself to the best that *you* can do.

➤ I've learned that you can keep going long after you think you can't.

➤ I've learned that two people can look at the exact same thing and see something completely different.

I'm Glad You Asked Me That...

The question-and-answer period is a very important part of a speech. You can't be sure that you're getting your message across to your audience unless you get feedback from them.

Follow these guidelines when answering questions:

1. Be sure you understand a question before you attempt to answer it. If you aren't sure what the question means, ask for a clarification.

2. Unless you're speaking to a very small group, repeat each question before answering it.

3. If you're asked several questions by a single audience member, answer them one at a time. If your first answer is very long, ask your listener to repeat his or her other questions.

4. Answer directly.

Question-and-answer sessions are discussed further in Chapter 23, "Speaking Off-the-Cuff."

I'm Not Glad You Asked Me That...

Because it's very difficult to decipher the true motive underlying a question, I recommend that you answer every question at face value and treat it as a true request for additional information. Even if the question sounds negative, the questioner may just be expressing doubt or anxiety. The question may be the person's way of asking for reassurance. Deal with people politely and tactfully.

Be courteous. Never under any circumstances become defensive or nasty. Audiences appreciate good manners. If you stay cool, the audience will automatically reject the person who is making trouble for you and will be on your side.

Being polite doesn't mean that you have to be a chump, however. If the questioner is out of line, you can cut him or her off. You can always politely refuse to answer and then deflect the question back to an appropriate aspect of the discussion.

Class Act

Finish your speech early. Everyone will be happier. After all, how often have you heard, "That talk was great, I just wish they'd gone on for another 15 minutes"?

Humor

Resist the temptation to be witty or clever when you're answering questions. Audiences will think that you're not taking the matter seriously, and they'll identify and sympathize with the courageous soul who asked the question that you answered flippantly.

Remember that you're in control. The better your speech and the more direction you give the audience concerning questions, the more control you retain. Start by limiting the questions you'll take. Try this line: "I'll be happy to answer any questions that deal with [the subject you have explained]." Here are two other points to remember:

➤ Don't give a set time for questions; that way you can stay flexible.

➤ If you really run into trouble, you can always say, "I'm sorry—we seem to have run out of time."

Making a Graceful Exit

When you finish speaking, don't rush off; you're not finished yet. Just as your speech started before you opened your mouth, it also ends well after you stop talking. Give the audience a few minutes to absorb what you've said. Stay in front of the podium for a few seconds and look directly at the audience. Follow these steps:

1. Stay and take your applause. Don't rush off.
2. Gather your notes and walk away from the podium.
3. Walk with confidence; you're still in charge.
4. Take your seat.
5. Don't start talking to the people next to you; many people in the audience will still be looking at you.
6. Look attentive and confident.

The Least You Need to Know

➤ Strive for a natural delivery. Memorize the opening and closing, but not the entire speech.

➤ Show your enthusiasm.

➤ Deal with problems quickly and professionally—and don't beat yourself up about it later if you flub something.

➤ Respond to every question at face value, and treat it as a true request for additional information.

➤ Resist the temptation to be witty or clever when answering questions.

➤ When you finish speaking, don't rush off; give the audience a few minutes to absorb what you've said.

➤ Remember: You're in command.

Chapter 33

Last Licks

In This Chapter

➤ Speaker's bureaus

➤ Before your speech

➤ During your speech

➤ After your speech

➤ Summary of the speech process

You're almost at the end, troopers. My main purpose in writing this book has been to teach you that writing and delivering a powerful speech lies well within your abilities. You learned the basics of effective communication, what goals you should set for yourself when you give a public speech, and how to speak effectively in a wide variety of situations. You discovered that becoming an effective speaker requires a knowledge of audience, purpose, and task. Be proud of yourself—you earned it.

To sum up, this chapter covers speaker's bureaus. You'll learn how they may suit your professional speech needs. Then I'll summarize the entire public speaking process and provide you with a handy reference list for a quick overview and refresher. You'll be a speech star!

Speaker's Bureaus

How similar are the following situations to the problems you face on the job?

➤ You're the director of a manufacturing plant. People in the community are concerned that your plant is dumping industrial waste.

➤ You're an administrator at a hospital that has just opened a new clinic. You want to get the word out to the community about your services.

➤ You're employed by a telecommunications company. You want to convince people that they should switch their phone and fax service to your company.

➤ You're the manager of a supermarket and need to pursue customers more aggressively.

➤ You're a naturalist employed by the Environmental Protection Agency. As part of your job, you want to teach community members ways to conserve natural resources, such as water, soil, and air.

Many professionals in these and similar situations use a *speaker's bureau*. This is an organized effort to convey the company's message to specific groups. More firms are discovering that speaker's bureaus are cost-effective ways to reach people in business, social groups, schools, religious organizations, and community affairs.

First, the bureau needs to be set up, the materials developed, and the speakers trained. The public can then call and request a speech by a member of the bureau. Here are some guidelines for establishing a speaker's bureau:

Talk Soup

A **speaker's bureau** is an organization designed to convey the company's message to specific groups. The bureau is most often internally run and organized and is comprised of company members.

1. **Membership.** Decide who is eligible for membership in your speaker's bureau. For example, are all employees included, or only full-time people? Do you want both current and retired employees? Management and union? Entry-level and upper-management? Many speaker's bureaus include a cross-section of employees to meet the widest possible needs of the organization.

2. **Size.** Your speaker's bureau should be large enough to meet your needs but small enough to manage comfortably. It takes a great deal of time and effort to run a speaker's bureau efficiently. As a result, it's best to keep the operation small when you start—it can always be expanded later.

3. **Preparation.** To be effective, your speakers must be prepared. They must be kept informed of all company policies and relevant information, especially those matters that directly impact their speech and the company's image. Here are some factors to consider:

➤ Booking speaking engagements

➤ Matching speakers to audiences

➤ Preparing speakers to meet the needs of the company and the group they are addressing

➤ Checking audiovisual needs

➤ Preparing and copying handouts

➤ Arranging for publicity

➤ Setting up substitutes for speakers who cancel

4. **Publicity.** For a speaker's bureau to be effective, it must get the word out to the community. Publicity is a must.

Many companies publicize their speaker's bureau through brochures. The brochure should list the topics your speakers will discuss, the members, and their credentials. Include some jazzy graphics, snappy copy, and you're all set.

Class Act

Today, beautiful brochures can be prepared in-house on computers using widely available and affordable desktop publishing applications. They're cheap, too.

Distribute the brochure to all relevant organizations in the area. Target the groups who would be most interested in your speakers—and who can do your company the most good. Possibilities include the local Chamber of Commerce, parent-teacher organizations, service groups such as Rotary International, and religious groups. Be sure to mail copies of the brochure and a press release to the newspapers as well.

5. **Evaluation.** How can you tell if your speakers are effective? Consider using an evaluation form. Speakers can distribute these to the audience at the end of their presentations.

The evaluation forms should be easy to complete. Here's a model you can use: (see page 330)

6. **Audiences.** At first, you might find yourself sending your speakers to just about any forum, just to get some publicity. But as the word gets out, you'll be able to more closely match the needs of your organization to the needs of your prospective audiences. Consider these questions when matching speakers to audiences:

➤ Is the meeting the appropriate forum for your organization's goals?

➤ Do your speakers meet the profile of the speakers usually sent to this organization?

➤ Does the size of the audience justify the expense of sending the speaker?

➤ Who else will be on the agenda? Do you want your speaker grouped with others on this agenda?

Adapt this specific form to your company's own needs.

Speaker Evaluation

Speaker's name _____

Title of speech _____

Date _____

Circle one:

Presentation	excellent	good	fair	poor
Content	excellent	good	fair	poor
Audiovisual	excellent	good	fair	poor
Handouts	excellent	good	fair	poor

1. What was the most useful information you got from this speech?

   _____

   _____

2. What other topics would you like to hear in the future?

   _____

   _____

Optional: Name, company, address, and telephone number

   _____

   _____

---

7. **Payment**. In most cases, members of a company's speaker's bureau aren't paid for their speeches because there are too many possible areas for conflict. For example, should speakers be paid on the basis of their skill, the size of the audience, or the frequency with which they speak? Should speakers be paid more if the issue is sensitive and less if the speech is "easy"? Payment can also affect a speaker's credibility.

8. **Recognition**. Consider offering speakers other forms of recognition in place of money. Possibilities include letters of appreciation and comp time (such as two hours off as thanks for a one-hour speech). Speakers can also be given tickets to the theater, concerts, or sporting events. Appropriate gifts, such as attaché cases, are also appreciated.

Regardless of compensation, speakers should be reimbursed for any out-of-pocket expenses, such as travel costs, meals on the road, and necessary overnight accommodations.

Speech of the Devil

Keep all evaluation forms short if you want them filled out. Few people want to complete more than half a page.

Encores and Exits

The rewards of effective speaking go far beyond the lectern. As an effective public speaker, you'll be more at ease with people in all situations. The sense of accomplishment and achievement will enhance your feelings of confidence. Public speaking is empowering.

End Game

Now that you know some invaluable life lessons, let's review the high points of the public-speaking process.

Before...

➤ Settle on the purpose of your speech: to inform, to persuade, or to entertain.

➤ Analyze your audience.

➤ Research the information you need.

➤ Organize and outline your material.

➤ Write the introduction, body, and conclusion. (I suggest that you write the body first.)

➤ Revise and edit your speech.

➤ Make sure that you have used humor appropriately.

➤ Prepare visual aids, audiovisual aids, and props.

➤ Rehearse your speech.

➤ Practice appropriate body language.

➤ Memorize the opening and closing to your speech.

During...

➤ Make sure you're dressed properly.

➤ Make sure you've eaten properly.

➤ Be clean and well-groomed.

➤ Check and double-check all details.

➤ Use nonverbal communication to reinforce your message.

➤ Adopt the right attitude to suit the occasion.

➤ Deal with problems in a professional manner.

➤ Handle questions well.

➤ Don't beat yourself up if you make a mistake.

After...

➤ Don't rush off.

➤ Gather your notes and walk away from the podium.

➤ Take your seat.

➤ Don't talk to anyone.

➤ Look attentive and confident.

➤ Network, if appropriate.

The Least You Need to Know

➤ Speaker's bureaus may be a valuable addition to your company.

➤ The speechwriting process involves several clear steps.

➤ You've learned to speak in public with confidence.

➤ Go get 'em, tiger!

Word Power Glossary

Anecdote   A brief story, often used by speakers to illustrate their point.

Articulation   A way to form sounds. Effective articulation results in clear, crisp consonants and vowels that are easy to understand.

Audience   The people a speaker addresses; the listeners.

Body   The middle of the speech, the section that develops the main idea and supports it with suitable examples, details, and illustrations.

Body language   A series of purposeful gestures that reinforce or show what you want to say.

Chair   The person who runs a meeting.

Chronological order   A way to organize a speech. The information is arranged in the order of time, from the first to the last.

Cliché   A comparison or other phrase that has become stale through overuse.

Communication   The social process by which people in a specific situation construct meaning using symbolic behavior.

Conclusion   The last part of the speech, where the speaker's main points are summarized and reemphasized.

Connotation   A word's overtones; the special meanings that it carries within a culture.

Credibility   The speaker's believability.

Criteria   The standards by which something is evaluated.

Culture   Culture is generally passed down through the generations.

Deduction   A process of reasoning whereby a conclusion is derived from a general rule.

Denotation   A word's dictionary meaning; its definition.

Diaphragm   The muscle that separates the chest from the abdomen. Controlling the diaphragm results in good breath control.

Empathic listening   A type of listening that strives to provide the speaker with emotional support.

Eulogy   A speech given in praise of a person. Eulogies are often delivered at funerals, although they can also be given at testimonial dinners.

Evaluative listening   A type of listening that strives to assist in decision-making.

Evidence   Details, examples, facts, statistics, and other data that supports the speaker's thesis.

Eye contact   Making direct visual contact with members of the audience.

Feedback   The reaction that the audience gives to the speaker.

Figurative language   *See* Figures of speech.

Figures of speech   Language that is not meant to be taken in a literal sense. Figures of speech enrich ideas by making them more vivid and easier to visualize.

Goodwill   The audience's perception that the speaker shares their concerns and interests.

Identification   The audience's perception that the speaker is similar to them and can be trusted.

Impromptu speaking   Speaking at a gathering with very little preparation and without the use of notes.

Induction   A process of reasoning that arrives at a general conclusion from specific examples.

Inferring   Making generalizations; "reading between the lines."

Informational listening   Listening to gather information and facts.

Informative speeches   Clarifying a concept or process for your audience, defining terms and relationships, or in any way expanding the audience's knowledge. The object of your speech is to inform.

Introduction   In the introduction, the speaker gets the audience's attention, states the topic and purpose, and may preview the main ideas.

Narrative   A story or anecdote meant to inform or entertain.

Oral interpretation   The art of reading a selection aloud to communicate emotion or ideas.

Perception   The process we use to derive meaning from sensory data.

Persuasive speech   A type of speech that attempts to move the audience to action or belief.

Pitch   The highness or lowness of a sound. It is determined by the frequency of vocal waves.

Post hoc ergo hoc ("After this therefore because of this")   The mistaken belief that one thing was caused by another. It is a type of logical fallacy.

Prejudice   A preconceived judgment or opinion about a person or a group.

Public communication   Communication with a large group; one member talks while the rest of the group listens.

Rate   The speed of speech.

Reasoning backward   A logical fallacy whereby people assume that since members of a particular group share common qualities, anyone with those qualities must belong to the group.

Rehearsal   Practicing your speech.

Spatial organization   A pattern of speech organization that presents information in terms of its position.

Speaker's bureau   An organized effort to convey the company's message to specific groups.

Speech   Sending and receiving oral messages to create meaning.

Testimonial   Having a celebrity endorse a person, place, or thing.

Theme or Thesis   A speech's one main idea.

Timbre, Tone, or Color   The quality of a person's voice.

Topic   The subject of a speech.

Topical organization   A pattern of speech organization in which details are arranged according to subdivisions of the topic.

Transitions   Words that link ideas.

Visual aids   Charts, graphs, maps, handouts, models, objects, photographs, posters, slides, videotapes, movies, diagrams, audiotapes—any visual or audio aid to a speech presentation.

Volume   The loudness level at which you speak related to the distance between you and the listener and the amount of noise that surrounds the listener.

Sample Speeches

In this section of the book, you'll find three sample speeches: an informative speech, an entertaining speech, and a persuasive speech. Each illustrates a series of different speech techniques covered in this book. Study these examples to see how everything you learned fits together.

Sample Informative Speech

This speech was delivered before a group of community leaders and business people at a luncheon meeting of Rotary International. The purpose of the speech was to inform the audience about comic books; the speaker is Bob Rozakis, who has more than 25 years of experience in the industry. The speech took about 15 minutes to deliver, including the use of visual aids. It is presented here to illustrate a contemporary example of the type of informative speech you would be likely to deliver in similar situations.

The History of Comic Books

Good afternoon, ladies and gentlemen. I've been asked to give you a short history of the world of comic books. As some of you already know, I'm the executive director for production at DC Comics. I also wrote comic books for about 10 years. In my speech today, I'll hit the high points in the history of comic books and maybe have time for questions at the end.

The comic book industry began in the mid-1930s. A man named M. C. Gaines, known as "Max" to his friends, had the idea that compiling a collection of newspaper comic strips in a magazine form would work well as a premium giveaway. So, the first comic book was just that—reprints—and it was given away to people who bought Ivory soap. Other companies also saw the popularity of such magazines, and very soon all the usable strips were being reprinted.

In stepped Major Malcolm Wheeler-Nicholson, a man with a hefty paper supply and a solid printing contract. Nicholson started his company by printing New Comics and New Fun Comics, using all new material. And he hired Max Gaines to be in charge. In 1936, they started another new title, Detective Comics, the first comic book devoted to a single theme. It was this title that gave the company its name: DC Comics.

In 1938, looking for a lead feature to launch another new title, Gaines and his editors settled on a strip that had been created five years earlier. It had been unsuccessfully offered as a newspaper strip by two teenagers from Cleveland. The character could lift cars, leap over buildings, and bounce bullets off his chest. The young writer-artist duo were Jerry Seigel and Joe Shuster. The new magazine was named Action Comics. The character was called Superman.

Superman proved to be an overnight success. As quickly as they could, other publishers (and DC itself) sought to make economic lightning strike again and again. Costumed heroes arrived by the busload, including Batman, The Flash, Green Lantern, and Wonder Woman from DC; Captain America, the Human Torch, and Sub-Mariner from Timely; Captain Marvel and the Marvel Family from Fawcett; and Plastic Man and The Spirit from Quality. It was an age of heroes that lasted through the second World War and into the late '40s.

By the end of World War II, interest in the heroes was waning. Publishers started looking for new kinds of magazines that would sell. Crime comics, Western comics, war comics, and romance comics all started appearing. MLJ Publications, for example, started a back-up feature about "America's Typical Teenager": Archie! And at EC Publications—which Max Gaines had started after leaving DC and which was now being run by his son, Bill— there was the dawn of the horror comics.

With such titles as Tales from the Crypt and Weird Science, Bill Gaines and his crew sent the industry scrambling in a new direction, one that eventually spawned a parental uproar and a Congressional investigation. With each new rival publisher going for more and more gory material, it was an easy task for psychologist Fredric Wertham to gain notoriety and generate sales of his book Seduction of the Innocent, which blamed all the ills of society on comic books.

In an attempt to forestall Congressional action and public backlash, the larger comics publishers banded together and formed the Comics Magazine Association, with a Comics Code for appropriate comic book material. Virtually overnight, Gaines and his schlockmeister competitors were forced to abandon comics. Gaines continued on the fringe of the business, publishing a highly successful comic-book-turned-magazine: MAD.

Comics languished throughout the early- and mid-1950s until Julius Schwartz, an editor at DC, proposed bringing the superheroes back for another try. The year was 1956. He revised and revamped The Flash to an enthusiastic response, then followed with Green Lantern, Hawkman, The Atom, and the Justice League of America.

Meanwhile, over at Atlas (formerly Timely) Comics, publisher Martin Goodman saw the success of his rivals and suggested to his young editor that they should start publishing superhero comics as well. The editor, a longtime writer of comics for Timely/Atlas named Stan Lee, took a shot and created the Fantastic Four, Spider-Man, the Incredible Hulk, and the X-Men. It was not long before a new age of superheroes was upon us. The early '60s saw almost as many new characters as the '40s had, products of a frenzy fueled by the Batman TV series in 1966.

In the early '70s, the comic book industry became aware that its audience was changing. Instead of readers losing interest at age 14, they were staying on, looking for more diverse and challenging material. This was coupled with the utilization of new printing technologies and the growth of a direct market in which the publishers could supply books directly to comic book shops. As a result, the industry went through its largest expansion ever, with record numbers of titles being produced every month.

A new generation of horror comics, many produced by fans-turned-professionals from England, began to appear, aimed at an adult audience. Far more graphic than those of the '50s—but also with far more complex storylines—these books in particular have led former readers back into the comic book fold.

In leaps and bounds, led by DC Comics and its incredibly foresighted production director, the comic book industry dove into computerized color and art, bringing it up to techno-speed—and, in some cases, ahead of the curve. New printing techniques were utilized. Paper was reformulated to best show off the subtleties of the artwork.

Which brings us to the present, when it would cost more than $2,000 to buy a month's worth of titles. Superheroes still rule the day, but there is room for much, much more. There is something for every taste, for every reader.

Now, since I think we have a few moments left, are there any questions?

Entertaining Speech

The following entertaining speech is by Mark Twain (1835–1910), one of the most captivating writers and speakers to ever grace a podium. Mark Twain, the pen name of Samuel Langhorne Clemens, rocketed to fame with humorous local-color tales of the West; he became a media darling by transforming stories of his childhood into American myth. Twain was extraordinarily popular on the lecture circuit, a popular venue for public entertainment before movies, television, radio, and Ross Perot.

Mark Twain Reveals Stage Fright

My heart goes out in sympathy to anyone who is making his first appearance before an audience of human beings. By a direct process of memory, I go back 40 years, less one month—for I'm older than I look.

I recall the occasion of my first appearance. San Francisco knew me then only as a reporter, and I was to make my bow to San Francisco as a lecturer. I knew that nothing short of compulsion would get me to the theater. So I bound myself by a hard-and-fast contract so that I could not escape. I got to the theater 45 minutes before the hour set for the lecture. My knees were shaking so that I didn't know whether I could stand up. If there is an awful, horrible malady in the world, it is stage fright—and seasickness. They are a pair. I had stage fright then for the first and last time. I was only seasick once, too. I was on a little ship on which there were 200 other passengers. I—was—sick. I was so sick that there wasn't any left for those other 200 passengers.

It was dark and lonely behind the scenes in that theater, and I peeked through the little peek holes they have in theater curtains and looked into the big auditorium. That was dark and empty, too. By and by it lighted up, and the audience began to arrive.

I had a number of friends of mine, stalwart men, to sprinkle themselves throughout the audience armed with clubs. Every time I said anything they could possibly guess I intended to be funny, they were to pound those clubs on the floor. Then there was a kind lady in a box up there, also a good friend of mine, the wife of the governor. She was to watch me intently, and whenever I glanced toward her she was going to deliver a gubernatorial laugh that would lead the whole audience into applause.

At last I began. I had the manuscript tucked under a United States flag in front of me where I could get at in case of need. But I managed to get started without it. I walked up and down—I was young in those days and needed the exercise—and talked and talked.

Right in the middle of the speech I had placed a gem. I had put in a moving, pathetic part which was to get at the hearts and souls of my hearers. When I delivered it, they did just what I hoped and expected. They sat silent and awed. I had touched them. Then I happened to glance up at the box where the governor's wife was—you know what happened.

Well, after the first agonizing 5 minutes, my stage fright left me, never to return. I know if I was going to be hanged I could get up and make a good showing, and I intend to. But I shall never forget my feelings just before the agony left me, and I got up here to thank you for helping my daughter, by your kindness, to live through her first appearance. And I want to thank you for your appreciation of her singing, which is, by the way, hereditary.

Persuasive Speech

By May 14, 1940, the news from the front was uniformly bad. The Germans had broken through the French defenses at Sedan, and everywhere the French forces were reeling under a devastating barrage from land and air. "At almost all points where the armies had come in contact," Churchill later wrote, "the weight and fury of the German attack was overwhelming." Holland fell on May 15, and Churchill flew to Paris on the same day to confer with the French leaders. It was evident that the military situation was near to catastrophic and that the military commanders and political leaders were resigned to overwhelming defeat. Churchill agreed to send 10 fighter squadrons to France, thereby imperiling the situation in England, as a desperate attempt to restore the spirits of his ally. On May 19, the Cabinet was informed that Lord Gort was "examining a possible withdrawal towards Dunkirk." In these somber circumstances, Churchill made this, his first broadcast as Prime Minister to the British people.

"Be Ye Men of Valour"

I speak to you for the first time as Prime Minister in a solemn hour for the life of our country, of our empire, of our allies, and, above all, of the cause of Freedom. A tremendous battle is raging in France and Flanders. The Germans, by a remarkable combination of air bombing and heavily armored tanks, have broken through the French defenses north of the Maginot Line, and strong columns of their armored vehicles are ravaging the open country, which for the first day or two was without defenders. They have penetrated deeply and spread alarm and confusion in their track. Behind them there are now appearing infantry in lorries, and behind them, again, the large masses are moving forward. The re-groupment of the French armies to make head against, and also to strike at, this intruding wedge has been proceeding for several days, largely assisted by the magnificent efforts of the Royal Air Force.

We must not allow ourselves to be intimidated by the presence of these armored vehicles in unexpected places behind our lines. If they are behind our Front, the French are also at many points fighting actively behind theirs. Both sides are therefore in an extremely dangerous position. And if the French Army, and our own Army, are well handled, as I believe they will be; if the French retain that genius for recovery and counterattack for which they have so long been famous; and if the British Army shows the dogged endurance and solid fighting power of which there have been so many examples in the past—then a sudden transformation of the scene might spring into being.

It would be foolish, however, to disguise the gravity of the hour. It would be still more foolish to lose heart and courage or to suppose that well-trained, well-equipped armies numbering three or four millions of men can be overcome in the space of a few weeks, or even months, by a scoop or raid of mechanized vehicles, however formidable. We may look with confidence to the stabilization of the Front in France, and to the general engagement of the masses, which will enable the qualities of the French and British soldiers to be matched squarely against those of their adversaries. For myself, I have invincible confidence in the French Army and its leaders. Only a very small part of that splendid Army has yet been heavily engaged, and only a very small part of France has yet been invaded. There is a good evidence to show that practically the whole of the specialized and mechanized forces of the enemy have been already thrown into the battle; and we know that very heavy losses have been inflicted upon them. No officer or man, no brigade or division, which grapples at close quarters with the enemy, wherever encountered, can fail to make a worthy contribution to the general result. The Armies must cast away the idea of resisting behind concrete lines or natural obstacles, and must realize that mastery can only be regained by furious and unrelenting assault. And this spirit must not only animate the High Command, but must inspire every fighting man.

In the air—often at serious odds, often at odds hitherto thought overwhelming—we have been clawing down three or four to one of our enemies; and the relative balance of the British and German Air Forces is now considerably more favorable to us than at the beginning of the battle. In cutting down the German bombers, we are fighting our own battle as well as that of France. My confidence in our ability to fight it out to the finish with the German Air Force has been strengthened by the fierce encounters which have taken place and are taking place. At the same time, our heavy bombers are striking nightly at the tap-root of German mechanized power and have already inflicted serious damage upon the oil refineries on which the Nazi effort to dominate the world directly depends.

We must expect that as soon as stability is reached on the Western Front, the bulk of that hideous apparatus of aggression which gashed Holland into ruin and slavery in a few days will be turned upon us. I am sure I speak for all when I say we are ready to face it; to ensure it; and to retaliate against it—to any extent that the unwritten laws of war permit. There will be many men and many women in the Island who when the ordeal comes upon them, as come it will, will feel comfort, and even a pride, that they are sharing the perils of our lads at the Front—soldiers, sailors and airmen, God bless them—and are drawing away from them a part at least of the on-slaught they have to bear. Is not this the appointed time for all to make the utmost exertions in their power? If the battle is to be won, we must provide our men with ever-increasing quantities of the weapons and ammunition they need. We must have, and have quickly, more aeroplanes, more tanks, more shells, more guns. There is imperious need for these vital munitions. They increase our strength against the powerfully armed enemy. They replace the wastage of the obstinate struggle; and the knowledge that wastage will speedily be replaced enables us to draw more readily upon our reserves and throw them in now that everything counts so much.

Our task is not only to win the battle, but to win the war. After this battle in France abates its force, there will come the battle for our Island—for all that Britain is, and all the Britain means. That will be the struggle. In that supreme emergency we shall not hesitate to take every step, even the most drastic, to call forth from our people the last ounce and the last inch of effort of which they are capable. The interests of property, the hours of labor, are nothing compared with the struggle of life and honor, for right and freedom, to which we have vowed ourselves.

I have received from the Chiefs of the French Republic, and in particular from its indomitable Prime Minister, M. Reynaud, the most sacred pledges that whatever happens they will fight to the end, be it bitter or be it glori-ous. Nay, if we fight to the end, it can only be glorious.

Having received His Majesty's commission, I have formed an Administra-tion of men and women of every Party and of almost every point of view. We have differed and quarreled in the past; but now one bond unites us all—to wage war until victory is won, and never to surrender ourselves to servitude and shame, whatever the cost and the agony may be. This is one of the most awe-striking periods in the long history of France and Britain. It is also beyond doubt the most sublime. Side by side, unaided except by their kith and kin in the great Dominions and by the wide empires which rest beneath their shield—side by side, the British and French peoples have advanced to rescue not only Europe but mankind from the foulest and most soul-destroying tyranny which has ever darkened and stained the pages of history. Behind them—behind us—behind the Armies and Fleets of Britain and France—gather a group of shattered States and bludgeoned races: the Czechs, the Poles, the Norwegians, the Danes, the Dutch, the Belgians— upon all of whom the long night of barbarism will descend, unbroken even by a star of hope, unless we conquer, as conquer we must; as conquer we shall.

Today is Trinity Sunday. Centuries ago words were written to be a call and a spur to the faithful servants of Truth and Justice: "Arm yourselves, and be ye men of valour, and be in readiness for the conflict; for it is better for us to perish in battle than to look upon the outrage of our nation and our altar. As the Will of God is in Heaven, even so let it be."

Seven Speeches to Study and Remember (or: Only Crib from the Best)

1. George Washington's farewell address (1796). Washington stressed the importance of national unity as the "main pillar" of the nation's independence, peace, and prosperity.

2. Thomas Jefferson's first inaugural address (1801). Jefferson is revered as one of the finest prose stylists America has ever produced. This speech contains his famous reference to the United States as "the world's best hope" and his praise of "wise and frugal government which shall restrain men from injuring one another, [and] shall leave them otherwise free to regulate their own pursuits." At the time, the fact that Jefferson's election marked the first real change of the party control of the government made his promise to respect the rights of the Federalist minority seem the most important point in the address.

3. Daniel Webster's second reply to Hayne (1830). In this speech, the silver-tongued Webster called the American flag "the gorgeous ensign of the republic" and concluded the speech with this sentence: "Liberty and Union, now and forever, one and inseparable."

4. Abraham Lincoln's "House Divided" speech (1858). Lincoln delivered this speech on the occasion of his nomination as the Republican candidate for senator from Illinois. It was probably Lincoln's most radical statement about the implications of the slavery issue, the one he predicted that "this government cannot endure permanently half slave and half free."

5. William Jennings Bryan's "Cross of Gold" speech (1896). Bryan made the speech at the 1896 Democratic National Convention. Bryan, arguing for a plank in the

party platform calling for the free coinage of silver, ended his speech with this sentence: "You shall not press down upon the brow of labor this crown of thorns, you shall not crucify mankind upon a cross of gold." "You" were the Gold Democrats, the supporters of the incumbent President Grover Cleveland, who opposed the unlimited coinage of silver. The speech made Bryan a national figure and led to his nomination for the presidency.

6. Woodrow Wilson's call for declaration of war against Germany (1917). This speech contains the famous line: "The world must be made safe for democracy." The speech is also remarkable for Wilson's insistence that "we have no quarrel with the German people.... We fight without rancor and without selfish object." Such self-restraint and Wilson's promise that victory would result in "a universal dominion of right" helped win liberal support for the war effort.

7. Franklin Delano Roosevelt's first inaugural address (1933). This is remembered for its ringing line: "The only thing we have to fear is fear itself" and Roosevelt's promise to "put people to work." Although it was a very effective speech, it was also padded and full of doubtful advice. For example, Roosevelt felt compelled to point out that "happiness lies not in the mere possession of money."

Further Readings

Applewhite, Ashton, William R. Evans (contributor), Andrew Frothingham, and Tripp Evans. *And I Quote: The Definitive Collection of Quotes, Sayings, and Jokes for the Contemporary Speechmaker.* St. Martin's Press, 1992.

Brydon, Steven R. and Michael D. Scott. *Between One and Many: The Art and Science of Public Speaking.* Mayfield, 1997.

Capp, Carol C. and Glenn Richard Capp. *Basic Oral Communication.* Prentice Hall, 1990.

Desberg, Peter. *No More Butterflies: Overcoming Stagefright, Shyness, Interview Anxiety and Fear of Public Speaking.* New Harbinger, 1998.

Detz, Joan. *Can You Say a Few Words?* St. Martin's Press, 1991.

Gaukroger, Stephen and Nick Mercer. *A–Z Sparkling Illustrations: Stories, Anecdotes, and Humor for Speakers.* Baker Book House, 1997.

Glickstein, Lee. *Be Heard Now! How to Speak Naturally and Powerfully in Front of Any Audience.* Sounds True, 1998. Cassette.

Glickstein, Lee. *Be Heard Now! Tap into Your Inner Speaker and Communicate With Ease.* Broadway Books, 1998.

Hasling, John. *The Audience, the Message, the Speaker.* McGraw Hill, 1992.

Hodgin, Michael. *1001 Humorous Illustrations for Public Speaking.* Zondervan Publishing House, 1994.

Krannich, Caryl Rae. *101 Secrets of Highly Effective Speakers: Controlling Fear, Commanding Attention.* Impact, 1998.

Lieberman, Jerry. *3,500 Good Jokes for Speakers.* Doubleday, 1975.

Lucas, Stephen E. *The Art of Public Speaking.* McGraw Hill, 1997.

Maisel, Eric. *Fearless Presenting: A Self-Help Workbook for Anyone Who Speaks, Sells, or Performs in Public.* Watson-Guptill, 1997.

Orben, Robert. *2000 Sure Fire Jokes for Speakers and Writers: The Encyclopedia of One-Liner Comedy.* Doubleday, 1986.

Sarnoff, Dorothy and Gaylen Moore. *Never Be Nervous Again: The World-Renowned Speech Expert Reveals Her Time-Tested Method for Foolproof Control of Nervousness in Communicating Situations.* Ivy Books, 1990.

Stuart, Cristina. *Be an Effective Speaker.* Teach Yourself, 1998.

Verderber, Rudolph F. *The Challenge of Effective Speaking.* Wadsworth, 1996.

Wong, Thomas. *American Communication Training: A Practical Guide for Foreign-Born Professionals.* TransCore Strategies, 1996.

Index

A

ABI/Inform (database), 127
accepting awards, 222
adding elements to
  presentations, 279
addressing audiences
  hearing impaired, 289
  multicultural, 183-185
affirmative side (debate), 241
  evidence, gathering, 244
  see also negative side
age of audience, evaluating, 61
agendas, evaluating placement of
  speech, 64-65
alcohol, avoiding, 314
alphabetical order
  organization, 156
  themes, informative speeches,
  81
analogies, misleading, 96
anecdotes, 158-159
  as speech opener, 142-144
  point and proof speeches, 102
answering questions, 324-325
  impromptu questions,
  234, 235-236
  interview sessions, 198-199
appealing to audience
  for donations, 70
  in concluding remarks, 167
  to needs, 94
appearance, 14
  clothing, 310-312
  hygiene, 312-313
  of audience, evaluating, 62
appropriateness
  of humor, 175-176
  of propositions (debate), 240
  of source materials, verifying,
  91
  of visual aids, 256-257
  see also suitability
arguments
  emotional, 93-94
  logic, 92-93
    deductive reasoning, 92-93
    inductive reasoning, 92

researching, 88
  Internet, 89
  sources, verifying, 89-91
stance, developing, 92
  see also debate
articulation, voice, 283
asking questions as opener, 144-
  145
assessing
  audience, 154
  communication skills, 41-
  42, 45
assigned topics, 64
attacking status quo (debate), 241
attire, 310-312
audience
  asking questions, 145
  credibility, establishing, 94-95
  evaluating, 58-59, 60-61, 154
    age, 61
    appearance, 62
    knowledge, 63-64
    sex, 62-63
    size of group, 61
  experiences, sharing, 104
  eye contact, 301-302
  fear of, overcoming, 13-14
  feedback, monitoring, 301-302
  hearing-impaired, addressing,
  289
  motivating, 144-145
  multicultural, 183
    gestures, translating, 307-
    308
    idioms, translating, 189-190
  questions, answering, 324-325
  SPAM (public speaking model),
  53
audiotapes, 264
AutoContent Wizard
  (PowerPoint), 278
avoiding
  caffeine, 313
  clichés, 217-218
  digressions, 232-233
  jargon, 114-115
  public speaking, Top Ten
  excuses, 6-9
  sentence fragments, 233-234
  unnecessary words, 286

awards
  accepting, 221-222
  presenting, 69-70

B

backward reasoning, 97
bad speeches, fear of, 15
begging the question, 95
beginning, see openers
believing in yourself, 16
best man (weddings), speeches,
  224
bias
  loaded terms, 96
  source materials, verifying, 91
birthdays, entertaining
  speeches, 223
blackboards as visual aids, 264
blinking, stress indicator, 301
body language
  eye contact, 301-302
  gestures, 302-305
    interpreting, 304-305
    selecting, 305-307
  platform movement, 305
  qualities of, 307
bogus claims, 95-96
borrowing
  jokes, 176
  visual aids, equipment, 260
breathing techniques, 287
brevity, introductions, 216
briefs (debate), 242-244
buildings, dedicating, 70, 227
burden of proof, 241
business, 23
  databases, 127
  parliamentary procedure, 249
  sales presentations, 205-208
    checklist, 207-208
    direct approach, 206-207
    indirect approach, 207
  speaker's bureaus, 327-331

C

caffeine, avoiding, 313
campaign speeches, 74-75, 211-212
candidates, nominating, 73, 212
capital letters (outlines)
  concepts, separating, 135-136
  consistency, 134-135
  entries
    indenting, 137-138
    subordinating, 136-137
  parallel structure, 138
cardinal numbers (outlines)
  concepts, separating, 135-136
  consistency, 134-135
  entries
    indenting, 137-138
    subordinating, 136-137
  parallel structure, 138
cases (debate), 242
cause-and-effect
  themes, organizing, 81, 156
  subordinating, 127
celebration, birthdays, 223
central themes
  relevance to secondary themes, 79-81
  researching, 79-80, 82-84
  selecting, 78-79
  specificity, 78-79
  subpoints, subordinating, 126-129
ceremonies
  dedications, 70
  eulogies, 71
  installations, 71-72
chartoons (Power Point), 258
charts
  as visual aid, 264-266
  PowerPoint, adding to presentations, 279
checklists
  awards, presenting, 222
  charts, using as visual aid, 266
  impromptu speaking, 237
  introductions, 217
  sales presentations, 207-208
chronological order, organizing themes, 81, 124-125, 157
citing authorities from host countries, 184
clarity
  in diction, 111
  voice, 283
cleanliness, 312-313
clichés, 113, 217-218

Clinton, Bill, speech to American public, 52-53
clip art
  PowerPoint, adding to presentations, 279
  visual aids, preparing, 258
clip-on microphones, 289
closing remarks, 70
clothing, 310-312
  see also appearance
color scheme (PowerPoint), modifying, 278
comic lines, weddings, 226
commemorations, *see* dedications
commencement, graduation speeches, 218-220
comments, requesting from audience, 155
Common Tasks toolbar (PowerPoint), 276
communication, 32-34
  as problem-solving tool, 42-43
  assessment test, 41-42
  business climates, 23
  complexity of, 45-46
  context, 33
  creating meaning, 32-33
  debate, propositions, 240
  feedback processes, 35
    postspeech, 36
    presentation, 36
    prespeech, 35
  hearing-impaired, speaking to, 289
  intercultural, 182-183
    gestures, translating, 307-308
    guidelines, 184-185
    idioms, translating, 189-190
    translating, 185-189
  interpersonal, 34
  interpreting meaning of, 44
  intrapersonal, 34
  mass, 35
  necessity of, 42
  nonverbal, 40, 300
    eye contact, 301-302
    gestures, 302-305
    platform movement, 305
  public speaking, requirements, 25-30
  quantity vs. quality, 43-44
  signs and symbols, 33-34
  skills, assessing, 45
comparisons, 159
  see also similes
complexity of communication, 45-46
comprehension listening, 28

computer applications
  databases, business-related, 127
  PowerPoint, 275-276
    views, 277
    wizards, 277-278
  visual aids, preparing, 258, 266-267
concepts
  outlining, 135-136, 138
  proposing, gestures, 306
  subordinating (outlines), 136-137
  transitions, 161-162
conclusions, 166-170
  appeal techniques, 167
  illustrations, 168
  inducements, 168-169
  integrating into speech, 170
  quotations, 169
  summary method, 170
conducting
  interviews, 84, 198-199
  meetings, parliamentary procedure, 248-251
conferences
  agendas, evaluating placement of speech, 64-65
  location, evaluating, 65
conflicts, solving through communication, 42-43
connotation of words, 44, 96
conquering fear, 4-5
  causes of nervousness, 9
  stage fright, 11
    believing in yourself, 16
    fear of audience, 13-14
    fear of failure, 14-15
    releasing stress (exercises), 16-18
    symptoms, 12-13, 18
    test speeches, 19
consistency, outline entries, 134-135
constructive criticism, 200-201
contrasting information, 159
controlling voice
  volume, 286-288
  breathing exercises, 287
conventions, *see* guidelines
creating PowerPoint presentations, 276
credibility establishing with audience, 94-95, 142
critical listening, 28
criticism, 200-201
cross-cultural communication
  audiences, addressing, 183
  translating, 185-189

cross-examination format (debate), 246-247
current events as source of humor, 177
cutting information from speeches, 84-85

D

databases, business-related, 127
dates, as speech opener, 150
dating, rejection lines, 40
debate, 240
  affirmative side, 241
  briefs, 242-244
  cross-examination format, 246-247
  evidence cards, 242
  guidelines, 241-244
  importance of, 248
  Lincoln-Douglas format, 247
  need-plan wedge cases, 241
  negative side, 241
  partners, 244-245
  prima facie cases, 241
  propositions, 240
  rules, 247-248
  standard format, 246
dedications, 70, 227
deductive reasoning, 92-93
defining concepts, 201-202
delivery, 320-321
  enthusiasm, 320-321
  exiting, 326
  jokes, 178-179
  memorization, 320
  rate of speech, 283-284
  rhythm, 285
  unnecessary words, 286
  voice, 282-286
    articulation, 283
    breathing, 286-287
    clarity, 283
    inflection, 284-285
    pitch, 284-285
    quality, 282
    volume, 286-288
denotations of words, 44
descriptions as speech, 201
descriptive gestures, 304
developing central theme, entertaining speeches, 100-101
diagrams, 267
diaphragm muscle, 287
diction, 110-111
dictionaries, defining concepts, 201

diet, speech preparation, 313
digressions, avoiding, 232-233
direct approach, sales presentations, 206-207
dividing ideas, gesturing, 306
Douglas, Stephen A., Lincoln-Douglas debates, 248
Drawing toolbar (PowerPoint), 276
dress, *see* attire
drinks, avoiding alcohol, 314

E

editing
  introductions, 216-217
  written speech, 155
  see also revising
8H rule, 257
elections
  campaign speeches, 74-75, 211-212
  candidates, nominating, 212
  see also voting
Emboss option (PowerPoint), 279
emotional appeals
  arguments, 93-94
  entertaining speeches, 105
empathetic listening, 28
emphatic gestures, 303
employment, conducting interviews, 198-199
entertaining speeches, 69, 100
  awards, presenting, 221-222
  birthdays, 223
  central theme, developing, 100-101
  cross-cultural, preparing, 183-185
  emotional appeals, 105
  experiences, sharing, 104
  graduation speeches, 218-220
  introductions, 216-218
    checklist, 217
    clichés, avoiding, 217-218
    editing, 216-217
  keynote addresses, 222-223
  point and proof method, 102
  researching, 102-104
  ribbon-cutting ceremonies, 227
  roasts, 221
  samples, 340-341
  spoof point and proof method, 102
  toasts, 221

weddings, 224-227
  best man, 224
  father of the bride, 224
  groom, 224-225
  see also humor
enthusiasm, 27, 320-321
entries (outlines), *see* outlines
equipment
  microphones, 288-289
  overhead projectors, 271
  planning for use, 259-260
  renting, 260
  visual aids, 260
ERIC (Educational Resources Information Center), 127
errors (logical), *see* fallacies
establishing credibility with audience, 94-95, 142
etymologies, defining concepts, 201
eulogies, 71, 208-210
euphemisms, 113-114
evaluating
  audience, 58-61
    age of, 61
    appearance, 62
    knowledge, 63-64
    sex, 62-63
    size of group, 61
  location of speaking engagement, 65
  speaker's bureaus, 329
  written speech, 155
  see also criticism
evidence (debates), 242-244
examples, 159
  concepts, defining, 202
  subordinating, 127
excluding information from speeches, 84-85
excuses, avoiding public speaking, 6-9
exercises
  breathing, 287
  Public Speaking Inventory worksheet, 24-30
  releasing stress, 16-18
exiting, 326
experiences, sharing (entertaining speeches), 104
explaining processes, 196
expressions
  clichés, 113
  euphemisms, 113-114
  figurative language, 116-118

F

F&S Plus Text International
  (database), 127
factoids, 160
  as speech opener, 143-144
    locating, 144
    suitability, 143
  dates, 150
  statistics, 148-150
  see also facts
facts
  proving, 204
  subordinating, 127
failure, fear of, 14-15
fallacies (logical)
  backward reasoning, 97
  begging the question, 95
  bogus claims, 95-96
  false analogies, 96
  loaded terms, 96
  misrepresentation, 96-97
  oversimplification, 97
  post hoc ergo propter hoc, 97
false endings, 166
father of the bride, speeches, 224
fear
  causes of nervousness, 9
  conquering, 4-5
  excuses to avoid public
    speaking, 6-9
  stage fright, 11-13
federal guidelines, conducting
  interviews, 199
feedback, 35
  monitoring, 301-302
  postspeech, 36
  presentation, 36
  prespeech, 35
  requesting, 155
figurative language, 116-118
  hyperbole, 117-118
  images, 116-117
  metaphors, 117
  personification, 117-118
  similes, 117
films as visual aid, 267
finding
  quotations, 147-148
  translators, 189
flattery as opener, 145-146
flip charts, 267-269
food, prespeech diet, 313
formal speech
  debate, 240
    affirmative side, 241
    cross-examination format,
      246-247
    Lincoln-Douglas format,
      247
    negative side, 241
    propositions, 240
    rules, 241-244, 247-248
    standard format, 246
    teamwork, 244-245
  parliamentary procedure,
    248-251
    impartiality, 250
    rules, 249-250
Formatting toolbar
  (PowerPoint), 276
fragments (sentence), avoiding,
  233-234
full text manuscripts, preparing,
  296-297
full-text outlines, 132-133
funds, appealing for, 70
funerals, delivering eulogies,
  71, 208-210

G

gathering evidence, debates, 244
gender-neutral words, 115-116
gestures
  interpreting, 304-305
  selecting, 305-307
  see also nonverbal
    communication
Gettysburg Address, as model for
  speech, 50-51
Goldwyn, Samuel, 33
graduation speeches, 218-220
grammar, 118
graphs as visual aid, 264-266
groom, delivering wedding
  speeches, 224-225
group rehearsals, 294
guidelines
  debate, 241-244
  humor, 174-175
  intercultural communication,
    183-185
  interviews, 198-199
  public speaking (speaker's
    bureaus), 331-332
  quotations as openers, 146-147
  see also rules

H

handouts, 269
headings (outlines)
  concepts, separating, 135-136
  indentation, 137-138
  maintaining consistency,
    134-135
  parallel structure, 138
  subordinating entries, 136-137
hearing-impaired, speaking to,
  289
host country, citing authorities,
  184
humor, 174-175
  appropriateness, 174-176
  as opener, 150
  jokes
    borrowing, 176
    delivery, 178-179
  personal experience, 177
  rules of, 174-175
  targets of, selecting, 177
  topics to avoid, 179-180
  witticisms, 178
hygiene, 312-313
hyperbole, 117-118

I

Iacocca, Lee, 23
ideas
  gesturing, 306
  outlining, 135-136, 138
  subordinating (outlines),
    136-137
  transitions, 161-162
idioms, translating, 189-190
illustrations as concluding
  remarks, 168
images, 116-117
impartiality
  parliamentary procedure, 250
  sexist language, 115-116
impromptu speaking, 230-232
  checklist, 237
  digressions, avoiding, 232-233
  fragments (sentence), avoid-
    ing, 233-234
  organizing, 231-232
  practicing, 236-237
  questions, answering, 234-236
  researching, 231
  stage fright, 235-236
incident reports, 74
indenting outline entries, 137-138
index cards, preparing, 295-296
indirect approach (sales
  presentations), 207
inducements as concluding
  remarks, 168-169
inductive reasoning, 92
inflection (voice), 284-285

informative speeches, 68, 78-79
  concepts, defining, 201-202
  cross-cultural, preparing,
    183-185
  descriptions, 201
  excluding information, 84-85
  interviews, 73, 198-199
  job training sessions, 73
  nominations, 73
  organizing, 80-82
    alphabetical order, 81
    cause-and-effect, 81
    chronological order,
      81, 124-125
    numerical order, 81-82
    problem-solution order,
      125
    questions and answers, 82
    spatial order, 82
    topical order, 82, 125-126
  process analysis, 71-72
  processes, explaining, 196
  researching, 79-80, 82-84
    conducting interviews, 84
    supporting details, 84
  samples, 337-339
  testimonies, 199-200
  themes
    central themes, 79-81
    primary and secondary, 79
    selecting, 78-79
  training sessions, 73, 197
installation ceremonies, 71-72
integrating conclusions into
  speech, 170
integrity, public speaking
  requirements, 29
intercultural communication,
  182-183
  gesturing, 307-308
  guidelines, 184-185
  translating, 185-190
Internet, conducting research, 89
interpersonal communication, 34
interpreting
  gestures, 304-305
  meaning in verbal
    communication, 44
interviews, 73, 198-199
  conducting, 84
  federal guidelines, 199
intrapersonal communication, 34
introductions, 216-218
  checklist, 217
  clichés, avoiding, 217-218
  dates, 150
  editing, 216-217
  factoids, 143-144
    locating, 144
    suitability, 143

humor, 150
  praise, 145-146
  questions, 144-145
  quotations, 146-148
  statistics, 148-150
  stories, 142-144
  video clips, 150
  writing, 141-142
  see also self-introductions
invitations, reasons for, 58

J

jargon, 114-115
job-related communication, 73
jokes
  as opener, 150
  borrowing, 176
  delivery, 178-179
  from personal experience, 177
  topics to avoid, 179-180
  witticisms, 178
  Yiddish curses, 178
  see also humor

K

key word outlines, 133
keynote addresses, 222-223
knowledge
  of audience, evaluating, 63-64
  public speaking requirements,
    25

L

language, public speaking
  requirements, 25
laughter, cultural differences, 184
Lavalier microphones, 289
learning
  foreign languages, 184
  from mistakes, 324
limiting
  scope of speech, 155-158
  secondary themes, 122-123
  speaking time, 122-123
Lincoln, Abraham, 50-51
Lincoln-Douglas format
  (debate), 247
listening, public speaking
  requirements, 27-28
loaded terms, 96

locating
  quotations, 147-148
  translators, 189
  Web sites, 89
locative gestures, 304
logic
  arguments
    deductive reasoning, 92-93
    inductive reasoning, 92
    researching, 88-89
  fallacies
    backward reasoning, 97
    begging the question, 95
    bogus claims, 95-96
    false analogies, 96
    loaded terms, 96
    misrepresentation, 96-97
    oversimplification, 97
    post hoc ergo propter
      hoc, 97
loudness, *see* volume

M

maintaining consistency, outline
  entries, 134-135
manuscripts, preparing, 296-297
maps as visual aids, 269-270
mass communication, 35
meaning
  context, 33
  creating, 32-33
  signs and symbols, 33-34
media publicity, speaker's
  bureaus, 329
meetings, parliamentary procedure, 248-251
membership, speaker's
  bureaus, 328
memorization, delivery, 320-321
metaphors, 117
microphones, 288-289
Microsoft PowerPoint, *see*
  PowerPoint
minorities
  addressing, 183
  rights, protecting (parliamen-
    tary procedure), 250
mirrors, speech rehearsals, 292
mishaps, troubleshooting, 321-
  324
misrepresentation, 96-97
mistakes, learning from, 324
mistranslations, 185-189
models
  as visual aids, 270-271
  briefs, 242-244
  outlines, 138-139

public speaking, SPAM (situation, purpose, audience, method)
  audience, 53
  method, 54-56
  purpose, 51-53
  situation, 49-51
modifying presentations (PowerPoint), 278-280
money, appealing for, 70
monitoring feedback, 301-302
movies, adding to presentations, 279
multicultural audiences, 183
  gestures, translating, 307-308
  idioms, translating, 189-190
  speeches, preparing, 183-185
multimedia
  audiotapes, 264
  video clips as openers, 150
muscles, breathing, 286-287

N

narrowing topics, 78-79
neatness, 312-313
necessity of communication, 42
need-plan wedge cases, 241
negation, defining concepts, 202
negative side (debate), 241, 244
newsgroups, 89
nominating candidates, 73, 212
nonverbal communication, 40, 300
  eye contact, 301-302
  gestures, 302-305
    interpreting, 304-305
    selecting, 305-307
  platform movement, 305
  qualities of, 307
note cards
  outlines, 133
  preparing, 295-296
Notes Page view (PowerPoint), 277
numbers as opener, 150
  dates, 150
  statistics, 148-150
numerical order organization, 81-82, 157

O

obligations, parliamentary procedure, 250
off-the-cuff speeches, *see* impromptu speeches

openers, 141-142
  dates, 150
  factoids, 143-144
  humor, 150
  praise, 145-146
  questions, 144-145
  quotations, 146-148
  statistics, 148-150
  stories, 142-144
  video clips, 150
  see also introductions
operating visual aid equipment, 260
organization
  alphabetical order, 81, 156
  briefs, 242-244
  cause-and-effect, 81, 156
  chronological order, 81, 124-125, 157
  impromptu speeches, 231-232
  informative speeches, 80-82
  numerical order, 81-82, 157
  outlines, 132
    entries, consistency of, 134-135
    entries, separating concepts, 135-136
    entries, subordinating, 136-137
    full-text, 132-133
    guidelines, 133
    indenting, 137-138
    key word, 133
    models, 138-139
    note card, 133
    parallel structure, 138
  persuasive speeches
    emotional arguments, 93-94
    logical arguments, 92-93
  problem-solution order, 125, 157
  psychological needs, 158
  questions and answers, 82
  revisions, 128-129
  spatial order, 158
  three-part structure, 123-124
  time limits, 122-123
  topical order, 82, 125-126
organizations
  parliamentary procedure, 249
  speaker's bureaus, 327-331
  Toastmasters International, humor recommendations, 176-178
Outline view (PowerPoint), 277
outlines, 132
  briefs, 242-244
  full-text, 132-133
  key word, 133

  models of, 138-139
  note card, 133
  preparing, guidelines, 133
    concepts, separating, 135-136
    entries, consistency of, 134-135
    entries, subordinating, 136-137
    indentation, 137-138
    parallel structure, 138
overhead projectors, 271
  see also slides
oversimplification, 96-97

P

PA systems, 288-289
pacing, 285
parliamentary procedure, 248-251
  impartiality, 250
  rules, 249-250
partners (debate), 244-245
parts of a whole, subordinating, 127
pauses, speaking rhythm, 285
payment, speaker's bureaus, 330
personal experience
  anecdotal, 158-159
  as source of humor, 177
personal hygiene, 312-313
personification, 117-118
persuasive speech
persuasive speeches, 68-69, 203-205
  campaign speeches, 211-212
  credibility, establishing with audience, 94-95
  cross-cultural, preparing, 183-185
  debate, 240
    briefs, model, 242-244
    cross-examination format, 246-247
    guidelines, 241-242
    Lincoln-Douglas format, 247
    partners, 244-245
    propositions, 240
    researching, 88, 89
    rules, 247-248
    stance, developing, 92
    standard format, 246
  emotion, 93-94
  eulogies, 208-210
  fallacies (logical)
    backward reasoning, 97
    begging the question, 95

bogus claims, 95-96
false analogies, 96
loaded terms, 96
misrepresentation, 96-97
oversimplification, 97
post hoc ergo propter hoc, 97
logic, 92-93
deductive reasoning, 92-93
inductive reasoning, 92
nominating candidates, 73, 212
nonverbal communication, 300
eye contact, 301-302
gestures, 302-305
platform movement, 305
problem solving, 211
purpose, 204-205
sales presentations, 205-208
checklist, 207-208
direct approach, 206-207
indirect approach, 207
samples, 341-344
sources
appropriateness, 91
bias, 91
quality, verifying, 89-91
photographs
as visual aid, 272
see also slides
phrases, transitions, 162
physical needs, appealing to, 93
pictures, *see* photographs
pitch (voice), 284-285
planning speeches, visual aids, 259-260
point and proof method, entertaining speeches, 102
politics, campaign speeches, 211-212
post hoc ergo propter hoc, 97
posters, 267-269
postspeech feedback process, 36
PowerPoint
presentations
charts, adding, 279
clip art, adding, 279
color scheme, modifying, 278
creating, 276
movies, adding, 279
text, modifying, 279-280
running, requirements, 276
Tip of the Day dialog box, 276
toolbars, 276
views, 277
wizards, 277-278

practicing, 14
impromptu speaking, 236-237
rehearsals, 15
see also rehearsing
praise as opener, 145-146
predetermined topics, 64
preparing
cross-cultural speeches, 183-185
full text manuscripts, 296-297
index cards, 295-296
outlines, *see* outlines
visual aids, *see* visual aids
presentations, 73
awards ceremonies, 69-70, 221-222
PowerPoint
charts, adding, 279
clip art, adding, 279
color scheme, modifying, 278
creating, 276
movies, adding, 279
text, modifying, 279-280
rehearsing, 292, 292-294
group rehearsals, 294
index cards, preparing, 295-296
manuscripts, preparing, 296-297
techniques, 292-294
sales, 74-75, 205-208
checklist, 207-208
direct approach, 206-207
indirect approach, 207
visual aids, 256-259
see also visual aids
prespeech feedback process, 35
prima facie cases, 241
problem solving speeches, 211
problem-solution organization, 125, 157
process analysis speeches, 71-72, 196
professionals, speaker's bureaus, 327-331
projectors, *see* overhead projectors
proofreading written speech, 155
see also revising
propositions
debate
affirmative side, 241
appropriateness, 240
negative side, 241
gesturing, 306
props, *see* visual aids
proving facts, 204

psychological needs
appealing to, 94
speech, organizing, 158
public communication, 35
Public Speaking Inventory worksheet, 24-30
publicity, speaker's bureaus, 329
purpose, persuasive speeches, 204-205
purpose (SPAM), 51-53

Q

quality
of communication, versus quantity, 43-44
of sources, verifying, 90-91
voice, 282
question-and-answer periods, handling
questions, 324-325
as openers, 144-145
impromptu, answering, 234, 235-236
interviews, answering, 198-199
themes, organization, 82
quotations
as concluding remarks, 169
as opener, 146-148
cross-cultural, 184
locating, 147-148
witticisms, 178

R

rate of speech, 283-284
reasoning
backward, 97
deductive, 92-93
inductive, 92
recall, 321
receiving awards, 222
recollection, defined, 321
rehearsing speeches, 15, 292-294
feedback, 294
index cards, preparing, 295-296
manuscripts, preparing, 296-297
techniques, 292-294
rejected ideas, gesturing, 306
rejection lines (dating), 40
relearning, 321
releasing stress (exercises), 16-18
remuneration, speaker's bureaus, 330

renting visual aid equipment, 260
repetition, 55-56
requesting comments, 155
requirements, running
  PowerPoint, 276
researching
  arguments, 88-89
  impromptu speeches, 231
  informative speeches, 79-
   80, 82-84
    conducting interviews, 84
    supporting details, 84
restricting
  scope of speech, 155-158
  secondary themes, 122-123
  speaking time, 122-123
revising speeches, 128-129, 155
rhythm, speaking voice, 285
ribbon-cutting ceremonies, 227
roasts, 75, 221
Robert's Rules of Order, *see*
  parliamentary procedure
Roman numerals, *see* outlines
rules
  debate, 247-248
  humor, 174-175, 178-179
  interviews, 198-199
  parliamentary procedure,
   249-250
rules of outlining, 133
  entries
    consistency of, 134-135
    separating, 135-136
    subordinating, 136-137
   indentation, 137-138
   parallel structure, 138
running PowerPoint,
  requirements, 276
running-refutation negative
  case, 241

S

sales presentations, 74-75, 205-
  208
  checklist, 207-208
  direct approach, 206-207
  indirect approach, 207
sample speeches
  entertaining, 340-341
  informative, 337-339
  persuasive, 341-344
  speeches to remember, 344-
   345
search engines, locating
  Web sites, 89

secondary themes
  limiting, 122-123
  relevance to central theme,
   79-81
  revising, 128-129
selecting
  central theme, 78-79
  gestures, 305-307
  humor, targets of, 175, 177
  secondary themes, 79
  strategies, persuasive speeches,
   204-205
  words, 111
self-confidence, public speaking
  requirements, 27-28
self-introductions, 142
sentence fragments, avoiding,
  233-234
separating
  outline entries, 135-136
  public speaking from personal
   speaking, 24
serious lines, weddings, 225-226
sex
  gender-neutral language,
   115-116
  of audience, evaluating, 62-63
sharing experiences, entertaining
  speeches, 104
ships, dedicating, 70
signs and symbols, 33-34
similarities, comparing, 159
similes, 117
sincerity, public speaking
  requirements, 30
sites (Web), locating, 89
situation (SPAM), 49-51
size, speaker's bureaus, 328
skills (communication), assessing,
  41-42, 45
sleep, speech preparation, 313
Slide Show view (PowerPoint), 277
Slide Sorter view (PowerPoint),
  277
Slide view (PowerPoint), 277
slides as visual aid, 272
small group communication, 34
social clubs
  speaker's bureaus, 327-331
  Toastmasters International,
   176-178
social needs, appealing to, 94
software
  PowerPoint, 275-276
   running, 276
   Tip of the Day dialog box,
    276
   views, 277
   wizards, 277-278

visual aids, preparing, 258
  see also databases
solving
  common speaking problems,
   321-324
  conflicts through communication, 42-43
  problems with persuasive
   speeches, 211
sources (research), verifying, 89-91
SPAM (situation, purpose,
  audience, method)
  audience, 53
  method, 54-56
   repetition, 55-56
   worksheet, 54
  purpose, 51-53
  situation, 49-51
spatial order, organization, 82,
  158
speaker's bureaus, 327-331
  evaluating, 329
  membership, 328
  preparation, 328-329
  public speaking, guidelines,
   331-332
  publicity, 329
  remuneration, 330
  size, 328
speaking engagements, reasons for
  invitations, 58
special events
  agendas, evaluating placement
   of speech, 64-65
  audience, evaluating, 53
  location, evaluating, 65
  method, evaluating, 54-56
   repetition, 55-56
   worksheet, 54
  purpose, evaluating, 51-53
  situation, evaluating, 49-51
specificity
  in diction, 111
  of themes, 78-79
speeches
  as marketing tools, 22
  awards, presenting, 69-70
  business climates, 23
  closing remarks, 70
  concluding, 166-170
   appeal techniques, 167
   illustrations, 168
   inducements, 168-169
   integrating, 170
   quotations, 169
   summary method, 170
  court testimony, 71-72
  debate, *see* debate
  dedications, 70

delivery, 320-321
  attitude, 320-321
  exiting, 326
  voice, 282-286
  see also delivery
editing, 155
entertaining, *see* entertaining
  speeches
eulogies, 71
false endings, 166
funds, appealing for, 70
humor, 174-175
  appropriateness, 175-176
  guidelines, 174-175
  personal experience, 177
  selecting, 175
  targets of, selecting, 177
  topics to avoid, 179-180
impromptu, *see* impromptu
  speeches
incident reports, 74
informative, *see* informative
  speeches
installation ceremonies, 71-72
introductions, 72, 216-218
  checklist, 217
  clichés, avoiding, 217-218
  editing, 216-217
memorizing, 320
mishaps, troubleshooting,
  321-324
nominations, 73
nonverbal communication, *see*
  nonverbal communication
openers, *see* openers
organization, *see* organization
outlining, *see* outlines
persuasive, see persuasive
  speeches
preparing for, 313-315
process analysis, 71-72
proofreading, 155
question-and-answer periods,
  handling, 324-325
reasons for, 58
rehearsing, 292, 292-294
  full text manuscripts,
   296-297
  group rehearsals, 294
  index cards, 295-296
  techniques, 292-294
revising, 128-129, 155, 171
rhythm, 285
sales presentations, 74-75
samples
  entertaining, 340-341
  informative, 337-339
  persuasive, 341-344
  speeches to remember,
   344-345

scope of, limiting, 155-158
self-introductions, 142
supporting material, 126-
  129, 158-161
  anecdotes, 158-159
  comparisons, 159
  statistics, 160-161
  testimonies, 161
time limits, 122-123
titling, 171-172
toasts, 75
transitions, 161-162
typing, 162-163
visual aids, *see* visual aids
welcoming, 69
writing, 109-111, 154-155
spoof point and proof method,
  entertaining speeches, 102
stage fright, 11
  fear of audience, 13-14
  fear of failure, 14-15
  impromptu speaking, 235-236
  releasing stress, exercises, 16-
   18
  symptoms, 12-13, 18
  test speeches, 19
stance (arguments), developing,
  92
standard format (debate), 246
Standard toolbar (PowerPoint),
  276
Statistical Masterfile database, 127
statistics as opener, 148-150
status quo, debating, 241
stories as speech opener, 142-144
strategies, persuasive speeches,
  204-205
stress releasing exercises, 16-18
structure
  briefs, 242-244
  debates
   cross-examination format,
    246-247
   Lincoln-Douglas format,
    247
   standard format, 246
  outlining, 132
   concepts, separating,
    135-136
   entries, consistency of,
    134-135
   entries, subordinating,
    136-137
   full-text, 132-133
   guidelines, 133
   indentation, 137-138
   key word, 133
   models, 138-139
   note card, 133
   parallel ideas, 138
  see also three-part structure

subheadings (outlines)
  concepts, separating, 135-136
  entries, indenting, 137-138
  entries, subordinating, 136-137
  maintaining consistency,
   134-135
  parallel structure, 138
subordinate themes
  outline entries, 126-129,
   136-137
  transitions, 161-162
Subscript option (PowerPoint),
  279
success, visualizing, 15
suitability
  of humor, 174
  of quotations, 147
  of propositions (debate), 240
  of quotations, 147
  of visual aids, 256-257
summarizations, 166-170
  appeal technique, 167
  illustrations, 168
  inducements, 168-169
  quotations, 169
Superscript option
  (PowerPoint), 279
supporting material, 126-129,
  158-161
  anecdotes, 158-159
  comparisons, 159
  debates, 244
  entertaining speeches, 102-104
  examples, 159
  facts, 160
  humor, 174-175
  impromptu speeches, 231-232
  statistics, 160-161
  testimonies, 161
  visual aids, 256-259
symptoms of stage fright, 12-13,
  18

T

talking
  rate of speech, 283-284
  tone, 112-115
  vocal chords, caring for, 288
tape-recording speeches, 292
teaching sessions, 197
teamwork, debate, 244-245
techniques
  breathing, 287
  rehearsing speeches, 292-294
telling jokes, 178-179
terminology
  jargon, 114-115
  "loaded" terms, 96

testimonies, 161, 199-200
testing microphones, 289
text, modifying PowerPoint presentations, 279-280
themes
  central, developing, 100-101
  organizing, 80-82
    alphabetical order, 81
    cause-and-effect, 81
    chronological order, 81, 124-125
    numerical order, 81-82
    problem-solution order, 125
    questions and answers, 82
    revisions, 128-129
    spatial order, 82
    topical order, 82, 125-126
  researching, 79-80
  scope of, limiting, 155-158
  secondary
    limiting, 122-123
    relevance to central theme, 79-81
    subordinating subpoints, 126-129
  selecting, 78-79
  specificity, 78-79
three-part structure, 123-124
time limits, 122-123
  20-minute rule, 123
  scope of speech, limiting, 155-158
  three-part structure, 123-124
  see also chronological order
Tip of the Day dialog box (PowerPoint), 276
titling speeches, 171-172
Toastmasters International, humor recommendations, 176-178
toasts, 75, 221, 225-227
tone, 112-115
toolbars, PowerPoint, 276
topics
  assigned, 64
  entertaining, 69
  graduation speeches, 218
  humorous, avoiding, 179-180
  informative, 68
  narrowing, 78-79
  persuasive, 68-69
  researching, 82-84
    conducting interviews, 84
    supporting details, 84
  scope of, limiting, 155-158
  themes, organizing, 82, 125-126
training sessions, 73, 197
transitions, 161-162, 303

translating
  cross-cultural communication, 185-189
  idioms, 189-190
transparencies as visual aid, 271
trials (legal), testimonies, 199-200
tributes, eulogies, 208-210
trivia
  as speech opener, 143-144
  factoids, 160-161
troubleshooting common mishaps, 321-324
trust, establishing with audience, 94-95, 142
Twain, Mark, 25
typing speeches, 162-163
20-minute rule, 123-124

U-V

unnecessary words, avoiding, 286

vehicles, dedicating, 70
verifying research sources, 89-91
videotapes, 293
  as opener, 150
  as visual aid, 272-273
  see also films
views (PowerPoint), 277
visual aids, 256-259
  8H rule, 257
  blackboards, 264
  charts, 264-266
  clip art, 258
  computers, 266-267
  diagrams, 267
  equipment, 260
  films, 267
  flip charts, 267-269
  graphs, 264-266
  handouts, 269
  maps, 269-270
  models, 270-271
  photographs, 272
  planning for use, 259-260
  posters, 267-269
  slides, 272
  suitability of, 256-257
  transparencies, 271
  videotapes, 272-273
voice, 282-286
  articulation, 283
  breathing, 286-287
  clarity, 283
  inflection, 284-285
  pitch, 284-285
  quality, 282
  vocal chords, caring for, 288

volume, 286
  breathing techniques, 287
  microphones, using, 288-289
  voting, parliamentary procedure, *see* parliamentary procedure

W-X-Y-Z

WAIS (Wide Area Information Service), 89
warning gesture, 307
Web sites, locating, 89
wedding speeches, 224-227
welcoming speeches, 69
Wide Area Information Service, *see* WAIS
witnesses, incident reports, 74
witticisms, 178
wizards (PowerPoint), 277-278
word choice, 110-111
words
  clichés, 113
  denotation, 44
  etymologies, defining concepts, 201
  euphemisms, 113-114
  figurative language, 116-118
    hyperbole, 117-118
    images, 116-117
    metaphors, 117
    personification, 117-118
    similes, 117
  fillers, 286
  gender-neutral, 115-116
  grammar, 118
  jargon, 114-115
  rate of speech, 283-284
  selecting, 111
  tone, 112-115
  transitions, 162
  witticisms, 178
worksheets, speaking method, 54
writing speeches, 15, 109-110, 154-155
  grammar, 118
  conclusions, 166-170
  diction, 110-111
  editing, 155
  proofreading, 155
  revising, 155, 171
  titling, 171-172
  transitions, 161-162
  typing, 162-163
WWW (World Wide Web), conducting research, 89